ENOUGH

OF THIS BIBLE "CONFIDENCE GAME";

FINDING THE PRESERVED ORIGINAL

BIBLE JESUS PROMISED !

William Tyndale and so many others
gave their all that we might have God's preserved Word

Dr. Chris Sherburne
UCLA Systems Engineer's eye-opening evaluation of
the New King James (and most other modern English versions)–
a case for Scriptural and defensible inerrancy

COUP DE GRACE– all the subtle lies dead in a pool of blood!

What is a "Confidence Game"? A convincing but untrue demonstration which moves a victim to place his "confidence" (and money) in something that will be proven to be false—he has been "conned" out of somethng valuable. In the "Bible Confidence Game", people are moved by impressive-sounding verbal slight of hand of (often pseudo) "textual" scholars to place more "confidence" in over-simplified and unproven theories of "Textual Criticism" than in the Bible's promises of textual preservation (Matthew 5:18; Romans 16:17,18, etc).

Accepting bibles based on errant manuscripts, like the Critical Text, has historically been the first step down the slippery slope to where the spiritual compass, chart, and anchor have been lost by the Church. Without the Divinely Preserved Inspired Words of God we are adrift, unable to clearly see anything as heresy—or anyone as a heretic!

Henry M. Morris, Ph.D.,LL.D.,Litt.D., founder of the Institute for Creation Research (ICR):

"Thank you for your letter ... describing the work you have done on the New King James Bible. It certainly does sound like you have made a significant contribution and I commend you for what must have been a labor of love and some difficulty .... I do believe what you are doing is worthwhile and that the King James is better than any others, including the New King James."

Dr. Morris is the author of many breathtakingly Scriptural books – all written with the rigor of a good Engineer, which he was. He was also a member of the New King James North American Overview Committee. He said, "After trying to use it, and endorse it, I finally went back to the 'old' King James, convinced that it is still the best in terms of poetic majesty, spiritual power, and over-all clarity and reliability."

"I'm not 'King James Only', I'm Textus Receptus Only. If you're think-ing of throwing this book away, don't. It is worthwhile looking into. Did the Reformation come from the Bible in your hand or did it come from the Textus Receptus?"
                    John Higgins, Pastor, His Church (Calvary Chapel), Tempe AZ

© 2004 Chris Sherburne   (928) 927-5217
7th edition February 2021   e-mail: chris.sherburne@tbuworldwide.com
                             web: www.armoredsheep.com
                             ISBN 978-1-7371005-3-9
                             CONTACT DR. SHERBURNE FOR 2
                             OR MORE COPIES

INTRODUCTION

"If the foundations be destroyed, what can the righteous do?" Ps. 11:3
The **Divinely preserved** original Holy Bible is that foundation.

Is it a good thing or desperately bad that the NEW KING JAMES VERSION (and other modern versions) have virtually replaced the KING JAMES Bible in most fundamental churches? The answer given here to this actually quite strategic question may well affect your faith, and *"The just shall live by faith"* (Hab.2:4, ...) OR DIE!

The Lord Jesus Christ said, *"Heaven and earth shall pass away, but my words shall not pass away* (Matt. 24:35). This is one of the many promises that <u>every word</u> of God would be preserved from the original God-spoken "Scripture".

This book will solve the mystery of where this promised preserved original Bible is today. The Hebrew and Greek Textus Receptus (also called the "Traditional Text") is outstandingly intact, as promised, in the over 20,000 ancient Bible manuscripts found all over the world (and therefore impossible to be systematically corrupted). In stunning truth, 35,000 of the 40,000 words which differ between this Traditional Text and the modern "Critical Text" (mostly deletions) are found <u>only</u> in one "Vaticanus" manuscript discovered in the Vatican library in 1481 (and no one knows where it came from). This Critical Text is the text of virtually all modern Bible versions (and we shall see in Part I that it greatly influenced the NEW KING JAMES). **Is <u>your</u> spiritual foundation being destroyed by the bible in your hand?!**

The Gospel message and main Bible doctrines (except Inerrancy) are not missing entirely from the Critical Text, and we are not saying God hasn't used modern Bible versions in your life, but the Lord Jesus also said, *"**Man shall not live** ... but by* [each and] *every word that proceedeth out of the mouth of God."* (Matt. 4:4). As you begin to read this "ENOUGH", **please stop right now and pray** *"that the eyes of your understanding"* may be opened (Eph. 1:18).

1

TABLE OF CONTENTS

A SUGGESTED WAY TO STUDY THE FRUIT INSPECTION:
1. Read the King James verse(s), giving special attention to the **bolded** words. **2.** Read the New King James, comparing its **bolded** words to the KJ. **3.** Read the (fairly) impartial Greek or Hebrew witnesses as to what the words in **bold** mean. **4.** We highly recommend that you read in the Bible at least the paragraph context of the text for yourself before you read our comments. **5.** Read our comments under both verses. **6.** Note the clone-ish collusion usually (over 80% of the time) found between the NKJV and up to seven other major Critical Text versions. **7.** Make your own call as to which version is truest.

   Hundreds of verses have been compared in the Fruit Inspection— actually thousands when you realize that, in many cases, the verses cited are just a sample of many more with the same problem. (Please be patient with us. Don't allow an occasional questionable commentary to derail the overall analysis here, and do let us know so that these can be corrected or defended.)

Please turn to Appendix A (p.152,153) **to see a list of Abbreviations** used in this Book, and an Oath by the Lord Jesus Christ.

PART I: THE FRUIT INSPECTION

NEW TESTAMENT

King James	New King James
Matt.2:16 *Then Herod, when he saw that he was **mocked** of the wise men, was exceeding wroth, and sent forth, and slew all the **children** that were in Bethlehem, and in all the coasts thereof, from two years old and under, according to the time which he had **diligently inquired** of the wise men.*	*Then Herod, when he saw that he was **deceived** by the wise men, was exceedingly angry; and he sent forth and put to death all the **male children** who were in Bethlehem and in all its districts, from two years old and under, according to the time which he had **determined** from the wise men.*
mocked—SC (Strong's Concordance) 1702: to jeer at, i.e. deride, from: to sport or play **children**— SC 3816: a boy, a girl, a child, a servant **diligently inquired**— SC 198: [Matt.2:7also] exactly ascertain; superlative form	"**Deceived**" is a commentary, not a literal translation of SC 1702. It markedly changes the inspired Greek word picture by implying that the wise men were deceivers. Rather, in commanding the wise men to disregard Herod's deceitful request (Matt.2:8), God, the High King of Heaven, was indeed "mocking" this Teapot Tyrant.

Dean Burgon's denunciation of the 1881 ERV in Matt.2 applies: "*all the male children* as a translation of PANTAS TOUS PAIDAS is an unauthorized statement. There is no reason for supposing that the female infants of Bethlehem were spared in the general massacre, and the Greek certainly conveys no such information." (Dean of Chichester, Oxford. J.W. Burgon read 86,000 (almost all) of the early Church Fathers' existing ("extant") documents— word for word comparing (collating) their over 1,000,000 Scripture quotesl (by hand in the Greek, without a computer). This gave him a profound familiarity with the Bible read by the first through third century Church ("Patristic") leaders. They used the Textus Receptus—2:1 (3:1 on key passages). Doesn't this demonstrate that the KING JAMES Hebrew and Greek "Textus Receptus" (TR), also called the "Traditional Text" (TT), is the preserved original Bible (200 to 300 years older than the Vaticanus manuscript)?

The reader's already shocked mental picture of this ultimate child abuse is driven to disbelief by the implication that Herod's police did diaper checks of each child throughout the massacre, as would be required by the modern Bible versions. Doesn't this tend to make a macabre mockery of God's Word here? [continued next page]

NKJV "**determined**" lacks the "superlative" found in both the TR <u>and</u> the Critical Greek Text.

Please note carefully the "rat pack" of poor translation and "Scrollduggery" (Part II of this ENOUGH) as found in the NKJV, and
NASV "deceived ... male ... ascertained"; NIV "outwitted ... boys ... learned";
RSV " tricked ... male ... ascertained"; HCSV "outwitted ... male ... learned"
NRSV "tricked ... _____ ... learned"; ESV "tricked ... male ... ascertained"

Matt.4:10b ... **Get thee hence** *Satan*:	... ***Away with you,*** *Satan!*
get thee hence— SC 5217: to lead (oneself) <u>under</u>, <u>withdraw</u>, or <u>retire</u> as <u>sinking</u> out of sight; from SC5259 in compound, as here, implies inferior position or condition	An absolute order from the Lord Jesus Christ for Satan to stay away from Him, as here in the NKJV, and Satan would still be running; he would not have been around to engineer the crucifixion. This could be viewed as a serious mis-translation since it affects the Atonement.
Canine Corps in both the Army and the Police speak softly to their four-legged associates, as the Lord speaks to Satan here. The Lord Jesus Christ created Satan and "handles" him perfectly. We are not respecting God's promises and power when we overreact to the Devil!	The competent translator knows the correct punctuation from the context: there is no exclamation point here. See the KJ, and the following illustration. This poor translation damages the inspired thought picture here. NASV, RSV, NRSV, ESV, NIV, and HCSV all yell at Satan here.

Matthew 4:10b

4

King James	New King James
Matt.4:24 (See 17:15 also) *And his fame went throughout all Syria: and they brought unto him all sick people that were taken with divers diseases and torments, and those which were possessed with devils, and those which were* **lunatick**, *and those that had the palsy; and he healed them.*	*Then His fame went throughout all Syria; and they brought to Him all sick people who were afflicted with various diseases and torments, and those who were demon-possessed,* **epileptics**, *and paralytics; and He healed them.*

lunatick— SC 4583:
 moonstruck, i.e. crazy

The NKJV renders SC 4583 as "**epileptic**"; this is not a translation but a private interpretation; note that in Matt.17:14-18 "lunatick" refers to an extraordinary case of demon possession. The Greek word means "moon [or luna] struck". Now we don't think the Bible is indicating that the moon has anything to do with human "lunacy"; rather, this was what the Bible said people called this condition (and so we do today!)—and, in a literal translation, it therefore must be translated "lunatic". The modern versions certainly could give a reader the gist "no miracle here"—that is, that Jesus was just a healer (with herbs or advanced medical knowledge) treating cases of epilepsy. In fifteen of the thirty KJ mentions of "miracles" in the Bible, the NKJV translates them as "signs". All the new versions tend to be naturalistic, with the supernatural diminished in them. This is a KEY COMPARISON COMMENT.

Dr. James Price, senior O.T. editor of the NKJV (Ref.13), in reply to Pastor DK Madden (Ref.2), quotes Thayer's Lexicon as justification for changing "**lunatick**" here; but Thayer was an avowed Unitarian who therefore certainly had a bias to tend to attack any Scripture that attests to Jesus' Deity. Wouldn't this make his lexicon a poor support for the NKJV change here?

Then, we must always bear in mind the virtual quota of changes the NKJV had to meet in order to get their ROI (Return On Investment) "Derivative Copyright" as a "new version". NASV, RSV, NRSV, ESV, NIV, and HCSV agree with NKJV.

King James	New King James
Matt.6:6a *But thou, when thou prayest, enter into thy* **closet**, *and when thou hast shut thy door, pray....*	*But you, when you pray, go into your* **room**, *and when you have shut your door, pray....*
closet— SC 5009: a chamber on the ground floor of an oriental house for storage or privacy, a spot for retirement:– secret chamber, closet, storehouse **NOTE**: The words following the :- in the Strong's Concordance give an exhaustive list of how that word is translated in the KJ.	Isn't this a sad translation? Shutting the door to a general "**room**" would not guarantee privacy. The Lord's whole point here seems to be the need to shut oneself into a "**closet**", so that we are praying just with God and not to be seen by man religiously praying. RSV, NRSV, ESV agree with NKJV.

King James	New King James
Matt.6:19a *Lay not up for yourselves treasures upon earth, where moth and rust doth* **corrupt***,...*	*Do not lay up for yourselves treasures on earth, where moth and rust* **destroy***...*
corrupt— SC 853: (to return to dust,) <u>consume</u>, <u>disappear</u> Berry in KJ Interlinear, (Beka Book House, '98): "spoil"	Doesn't this NKJV translation "**destroy**" the picture of the gradual returning to dust, the way all earthly stuff wastes away before our eyes? Moths don't "**destroy**" (to nothing); they "spoil", "corrupt" by eating holes. Rust also "corrupts", not "**destroys**". NASV, NIV, and HCSV agree with NKJV.
Matt.6:**25a**, 27, 28, 31, 34 *Therefore I say unto you,* **Take no thought** *for your life,*	*Therefore I say to you,* **do not worry** *about your life,*
take thought— SC 3309: to <u>divide</u> or <u>share</u>, <u>disunite</u> the mind because of <u>distraction</u> No one ever spoke like Jesus did. He is hitting the nail square on the head. Don't even think about it; things are not to "distract" our minds. The entire focus (v.19 to the end of chapter 6) is about undivided attention on, confidence in, the King of the Kingdom of Heaven, during our TDY (Temporary Duty) down here. This is much more than just "don't worry".	Jesus didn't just say, "don't worry". "Worry" is a general term. The Lord is actually <u>diagnosing</u> the problem—that of being distracted or preoccupied by these basic matters for which we are to trust our Heavenly Father to care. Any doctor or mechanic will tell you that a good diagnosis is essential to a successful cure. NRSV, ESV, HCSV, and NIV say "worry"; NASV and RSV say "anxious".

King James	New King James
Matt.8:27b ... ***What manner of man is this***, *that even the winds and the sea obey him!*	***Who can this be,*** *that even the winds and the sea obey Him?*
what manner of— SC 4217: <u>what ever</u>, i.e. of <u>what possible</u> sort	"**Who can this be**" is flat, isn't it? Note the question mark in the NKJV and the exclamation point in the KJ. (Contrast NKJV Matt.4:10b, in this ENOUGH, where the exclamation point is used when it seems it shouldn't have been.) This seems, at best, poor translation. Punctuation is supplied from the context by the competent translator. Here we are comparing the competency of the KJ and the NKJV translators. RSV, NRSV, ESV, NASV question.
This narrative is a key introduction to our Lord Jesus, and therefore, all the more important to be translated with the full force of the Greek which seems very excited. Marveling men make exclamations.	
Matt.9:18 *While he spake these things unto them, behold there came a certain ruler, and worshiped him, saying, my daughter is **even now** dead: but come and lay thy hand upon her and she shall live.*	*While He spoke these things to them, behold, a ruler came and worshiped Him, saying, "my daughter has **just** died, but come and lay Your hand on her and she shall live."*
even now— SC 737: <u>suspended</u> [between]; from: "to weigh anchor" [the ship is at the point of sailing away, but for the instant couldn't have moved] Thayer's Lex: right at this moment	The NKJV parallel passages in other gospels say she was still alive: (NKJV) Mark 5:23 "*my daughter lies at the point of death*"; (NKJV) Luke 8:42 "*she was dying*".

We cannot inhale except God exhale — and He has exhaled His Word (II Tim. 3:16) in absolutely stunning freedom from confusion or internal contradiction as (1) inspired, (2) preserved and (3) literally translated. "Just died" as a translation of the Greek here is incorrect. Jairus <u>could not know</u> exactly when (or if) his daughter had died (because he had no cell phone!); messengers coming to tell him that she had died (Mark 5:35) shows that she was not dead when he left her bedside. The NKJV contradicts itself here—NKJV Matt. 9:18 with NKJV Mark 5:23 & Luke 8:42. This is a KEY COMPARISON COMMENT: Finding contradictions in the modern bibles lowers our respect for God's Word (for God)! NASV, HCSV, RSV, NRSV, ESV, NIV agree with the NKJV.

  This verse alone in the NKJV has three specific commentaries made on the text which aren't in <u>any</u> Greek text. NKJV capitalizes three personal pronouns the translators judge are referring to the Lord Jesus Christ.

We all should want to magnify the Lord, and the writers of this ENOUGH, do capitalize His pronouns in their writing (as we just did in this sentence), but do not do so when quoting Scripture since the Greek doesn't make that distinction. These capitalizations are commentary interpretations, not translation. The main rule of translation is to communicate all that is there into the next language—not adding, subtracting, or changing anything. The NKJV (and the NASV) has made these "Expansions of piety" commentaries of capitalizing these personal pronouns over 10,000 times in the New Testament alone, more than one commentary for every verse of the New Testament! Couldn't this be called linguistic hypocrisy for modern versions to make these thousands of "Expansions of piety" additions to Scripture while deleting or "footdoubting" thousands of words from the KJ manuscripts for unsubstantiated accusations of "Expansions of piety"? (See p.131, "B".)

Dr. James Price, senior O.T. NKJV Editor, in his review of Ref.2, said that since the translator is better able to judge the reference of the pronoun than is the "uninformed" reader, it helps the reader for the translator to capitalize or not capitalize for him; however, Price goes on to say that the reader should be instructed to "subject to careful evaluation" the work of the translator. Wait a minute. Price says we can't trust the reader to be able to accurately see the reference of a pronoun, but we should instruct him to critique the accuracy of the translation— which requires much more knowledge and experience of the reader! Besides, most Bible readers trust that what they read in the Bible are God's Words so they wouldn't critique the translator. No, Dr. Price, just translate what's there, plus or minus nothing!

Additionally, NKJV capitalizes many inanimate objects and concepts. This NKJV practice keeps bad company with the New Age pantheism in which god is all and all is god (a subtle way to actually deny the existence of God).

Matt.15:30b ... *having with them those that were lame, blind, dumb, maimed, and many others, and* **cast** *them down at Jesus' feet; and he healed them:* **cast**— SC 4496: (sudden motion) to fling (properly with a quick toss), deposit as a load Textus Receptus Greek says *"they flung them down"* . (INTERLINEAR GREEK-ENGLISH NEW TESTAMENT, 3rd Edition, by Jay P. Green, Sr.)	*... having with them the lame, blind, mute, maimed, and many others; and they* **laid** *them down at Jesus' feet, and He healed them.* "**Laid**" is very weak for the Greek. It loses the color of the original language, of the impassioned effort to carry these people up the mountain (v.29) to Jesus, and almost drop them in exhaustion. NASV, NRSV, ESV, and NIV agree with NKJV; RSV and HCSV say "put".

King James	New King James
Matt.20:20 *Then came to him the mother of Zebedee's children with her sons, **worshiping** him, and **desiring** a certain thing of him.*	*Then the mother of Zebedee's sons came to Him with her sons, **kneeling** down and **asking** something from Him.*
worshiping— SC 4352: to <u>kiss</u> (as a dog licking his master's hand) to do <u>reverence</u>, to <u>adore</u> **desiring**— SC 154/4441: strictly a <u>demand</u> of something due.	Ex.34:14;Deut.6:13;10:20;Is.42:8; Matt.4:10;Acts14:11-15;Rev.19:10 say that all worship shall be directed toward God alone. The truth that Jesus, <u>as God</u>, <u>accepted worship</u> is here obscured and His honor reduced by this NKJV rendering.

The NKJV not only poorly conveys the meaning of the Greek here, but is inconsistent with how the NKJV itself translates the same Greek word in Matt. 8:2; 9:18 and 15:25 ("worshiping").

"Kneeling" is called "genuflection" in the Catholic Church and is not what the Greek says here. Have the modern bibles been modified to agree with F.J. Hort's out of order deification of Mary? In LIFE OF HORT, Vol.2, page.50 Hort states, "I have been persuaded for many years that Mary worship and Jesus worship have very much in common in their cause and in their results." The NIV does this in Matt.8:2; 15:25; Mark 5:6. All eleven times this word occurs in the TR, KJ translates it "*worshipped*". KEY COMPARISON COMMENT: See also Matthew 26:45 and Luke 12:49, in this ENOUGH, where the incomparably compassionate Christ is converted into the angry Christ of Catholicism who can only be approached through Mary, as "Co-Redemptrix"! Hort is the key individual on the 1870-1880 modification of the KING JAMES BIBLE, who insisted on the some 35,000 word changes which basically re-created the Vaticanus manuscript—both Old (Septuagint) and New Testaments. Word for word comparison ("collation") of the Higher Critical text with the Received Text is the necessary foundation for scientific criticism and reveals these patterns of verse changes "catholicizing" the Bible—do see Appendix D, p.173. This NKJV (and the Critical Text it is from in so many place) is a veritable minefield of ancient and modern errors; read it at your own risk.

"**Desiring**" also is appropriately stronger than "**asking**" and seems a more accurate translation.

NASV says "bowing down"; HCSV says "knelt ... ask"; RSV, ESV agree with NKJV.

King James	New King James
Matt.26:15b ...*And they* **covenanted** *with him for thirty pieces of silver.* **covenanted**— SC 2476: to <u>stand</u> Lex: appoint, establish, set up The Word of God is not confused or self-contradictory.	*... And they* **counted out** *to him thirty pieces of silver.* (See the same account in NKJV Mark 14:11, in which the chief priests *"promised to give him money".*) "**Counted out**" is simply a wrong translation by which the NKJV contradicts itself in Mark 14:11. Besides, you never pay a crook in advance! RSV, NRSV, ESV, NASV, NIV, and HCSV agree with NKJV.
Matt.26:45b ... **Sleep on now, and take <u>your</u> rest**: Tender concern is shown for his disciples, even in this, His hardest hour. Had He abruptly awakened them in shame and guilt for sleeping instead of praying, their coming night of "scattering" could have destroyed some of them!	*... Are you still* **sleeping and resting**? The TR and the 26th Nestle Aland are identical here, but doesn't this seem wrongly translated—misses the Shepherd's heart. NASV, RSV, NRSV, ESV, NIV, and HCSV agree with NKJV.

King James	New King James
Mark 3:9 *And he spake to his disciples, that a small ship should **wait** on him because of the multitude, lest they should **throng** him.*	*So He told His disciples that a small boat should be **kept ready** for Him because of the multitude, lest they should **crush** Him.*

wait— SC 4342: <u>attend</u>
 continuously
throng— SC 2346: to <u>crowd</u>,
 from: to <u>rub</u>

The Lord Jesus Christ was not paranoid that he might be squashed by accident. Rather, He's in control of the crowd. Always get the context: the next verse explains further that the crowd wanted to "*touch*" Him. He used the boat to keep a physical separation; the boat wasn't just "***kept ready***" in case things got out of control as the NKJV says. The NKJV has paraphrased this verse into their own words—man's words rather than God's words, and they got it wrong. To change something that is perfect (the God-spoken Word), is to make something that is imperfect. At best, Dynamic equivalency will leave out part of the message; and, often, as here, it will get it wrong. The Lord Jesus Christ doesn't have to do anything "just in case"! He preempted the problem and <u>used</u> the boat—what a God/man!
RSV, NRSV, ESV and HCSV agree with NKJV; NASV and NIV have the boat on standby along with the NKJV, but they don't have a "crushing" problem.

Mark 3:9

King James	New King James
Mark 4:36a *And when they had* **sent away** *the multitude, they took him even as he was in the ship.* **sent away**— SC 863: to <u>send forth</u> Lex: 3rd person, plural— "they ... sent" The disciples clearly "*sent away ... took*" charge.	*Now when they had* **left** *the multitude, they took Him along in the boat as He was.* **"Left"** isn't right. It messes up the word picture of the disciples <u>taking charge</u> but soon realizing that only He should be in charge—He who alone can handle a <u>real</u> problem (v.37)! NASV, RSV, NRSV, ESV, NIV, and HCSV agree with NKJV.
Mark 6:8 *And commanded them that they should take nothing for* <u>*their*</u> *journey, save a staff only; no script, no bread, no* **money** *in* <u>*their*</u> **purse**: **money**— SC 5475: <u>copper</u> (implement, or coin) **purse**— SC 2223: a <u>belt</u>, by implication a <u>pocket</u>:—girdle, purse Jesus said, "no money", not no commodities.	*He commanded them to take nothing for the journey except a staff—no bag, no bread, no* **copper** *in* <u>*their*</u> **money belts** True, the Greek word for **money** is **"copper"**, as copper was worth a certain amount per ounce of metal (like silver has an intrinsic value per ounce); but isn't the better translation "*money*"? Their purse was wrapped up <u>in</u> their girdle (belt) with which they tied their robes. Doesn't "***money belts***" seem a chic paraphrase? NASV, RSV, NRSV, ESV, NIV, HCSV refer to "money", but they all put it into "belts".

King James	New King James
Mark 9:18a *And wheresoever he taketh him, he teareth him: and he foameth, and gnasheth with his teeth, and **pineth away***.	*And wherever it seizes him, it throws him down; he foams at the mouth, gnashes his teeth, and **becomes rigid**.*
pineth away— SC 3583: to desiccate, to shrivel Changing "foameth" to "he foams at the mouth" adds an entire prepositional phrase to the TR which isn't in the Greek of the TR or the CT. This is illegal Dynamic Equivalency translation, Apprendix F (p.183) which the NKJV said it didn't use. gives other examples of the over 2000 places where NKJV does this.	This is a mis-translation or (wrong) commentary perhaps even trying to explain away the deadly reality of demon possession by implying that the boy was just "epileptic" and having a seizure. (See Matthew 4:24 comments in this ENOUGH for more on what's wrong here.) RSV, NRSV, ESV, HCSV, and NIV agree with NKJV; NASV says "stiffens out".
Mark 9:49a *For everyone shall be **salted** with fire,*	*For everyone will be **seasoned** with fire,*
salted— SC 233: to salt	The word in the Word is "**salt**"! The NKJV is a paraphrase here, which is really changing God's Words into man's words. Maybe this is one of the quota of changes needed to get NKJV copyright.
Mark 11:4 *And they went their way, and found the colt tied by the door without in a place **where two ways met**; and they loose him.* **where two ways met**— SC 296: a fork in the road Berry, KJ Interlinear (Beka Book House, '98): "crossway"	*So they went their way, and found the colt tied by the door outside **on the street**, and they loosed it.* The Greek doesn't say anything about "**street**", and where's the "fork"? Vague directions could get a man hung as a horse thief— read verses 5 & 6 where they are challenged for loosing the colt! NASV, RSV, NRSV, ESV, NIV, and HCSV agree with NKJV.

13

King James	New King James
Mark 12:26a *And as touching the dead, that they rise: have ye not read in the book of Moses, how in the **bush** God spake unto him,*	*But concerning the dead, that they rise, have you not read in the book of Moses, in the **burning** bush **passage**, how God spoke to him,*
bush— SC 942: <u>brier</u>, shrub Turning "**bush**" into "**burning** bush **passage**" is definitely Dynamic Equivalency <u>adding</u> to Scripture, changing this text from the Words of God into the words of man. Kind of, sort of a children's Bible story book commentary.	"**Burning** ... **passage**" are supplied, and incorrect! God didn't speak to Moses in a passage of a book, but from a bush on a mountain. This is (incorrect) commentary—not permitted, in any case, in a literal translation. NASV, RSV, NRSV, ESV, NIV, and HCSV agree with NKJV.
Luke 6:33a *And if ye do good to them which do good to you, what **thank** have ye?* **thank**— SC 5485: charis = grace, <u>graciousness</u> especially the Divine influence on the life including <u>gratitude</u>	*And if you do good to those who do good to you, what **credit** is that to you?* "**Credit**" is a wrong word for "grace", even implying the balancing of a ledger, actually the <u>opposite</u> of the Lord's message here. NASV, RSV, NRSV, NIV, and HCSV agree with NKJV.

Luke 7:26 *But what went ye out for to see? A prophet? Yea, I say unto you, and **much more** than a prophet.*
 	
much more— SC 4055:
  more <u>super-abundant</u>, a compound word with 4053:-
  more abundant, over much
	*But what did you go out to see? A prophet? Yes, I say to you, and **more** than a prophet.*
	
	"**More**" is "**much**" too weak for the Greek here.
	
	NASV, RSV, NRSV, ESV, NIV agree with NKJV.

King James	New King James
Luke 11:53b ... *the scribes and the Pharisees began ...* **to provoke him to speak** *of many things:*	*... the Scribes and Pharisees began ...* **to cross examine Him** *about many things,*
provoke to speak— Lex: to endeavor to entrap into unguarded language They were apparently trying to get Him to say something "off-hand" that they could use to entrap Him.	"**Cross examine**" is cute but imprecise commentary. To "cross examine" is a modern courtroom art where one side questions a witness brought by the other side. NRSV and HCSV agree with NKJV.
Luke 12:49 *I am come to send fire on the earth*; *and* **what will I**, **if** *it be already kindled*?	*I came to send fire on the earth, and* **how I wish it were already kindled**!

This verse gives profound insight into the heart of the Savior: either it is as in the NKJV rendering which implies that He is vindictive, but powerless to judge whenever He chooses; or it is as in the KJ, which simply makes an observation that the fires of judgment have already begun (in automatic consequence to man's own sinfulness), and God's heart seems broken for this. The Greek, here translated *"what will I"* in the KJ, is in the subjunctive mood, which mood cannot always be rendered precisely in good English. The subjunctive mood, such as it exists in English, is usually the mood of wishing—which probably accounts for the NKJV "wish"; but isn't this schoolboy translation? The subjunctive mood in any language technically is the mood of contingency or possibility. Here the contingency is the will of the Son who *"is not slack ... but longsuffering ... not willing that any should perish"* (II Peter 3:9). But *"the Father hath committed all judgment to the Son"* (John 5:22,23) and is waiting for the Son to ask for the world (Ps.2:6-9). The Son's *"what will I"* was finally and truly answered in the garden of Gethsemane when He said, *"not my will, but thine be done"* Luke 22:42.

The KJ literally translates this phrase from the Greek and leaves it for the reader to seek out the meaning if sufficiently interested; but it's all there to be sought out!

Do we see here the Bible being changed into a Catholic catechism with its angry jesus who can only be approached by praying for Mary to intercede? See KEY COMPARISON COMMENT in Matthew 20:20.

The NKJV omits the Subjunctive Mood over 200 times in their translation in both the Old and New Testaments. Yes, the modern versions are sometimes easier to read than the KJ, because there's less there to understand. The KJ is a "Formal" translation, meaning that it conveys the grammar of the original Greek—the whole wonderful message. NASV, RSV, NRSV, ESV, HCSV and NIV agree with NKJV.

King James	New King James
Luke 22:31,32 *And the Lord said, Simon, Simon; behold, Satan hath desired <u>to have</u> **you**, that he may sift **you** as wheat: (32) But I have prayed for **thee**, that **thy** faith fail not: and when **thou** art converted, strengthen **thy** brethren.*	*And the Lord said, "Simon, Simon! Indeed, Satan has asked for **you**, that he may sift **you** as wheat, (32) but I have prayed for **you**, that **your** faith should not fail; and when **you** have returned to <u>Me</u>, strengthen **your** brethren."*
you— Lex: <u>plural</u> **thee**, **thy**, **thou**— Lex: <u>singular</u> Satan desired <u>all</u> the disciples. ("You" in v.31 is plural.) In verse 32, our High Priest, the Lord Jesus Christ, prayed specifically for Peter, so he could strengthen his "brethren" — the other disciples.	This is really a mis-translation here that obscures the blessed demonstration of how our High Priest (Heb. 3:1) prays for one of us as a channel for all of us to be strengthened. Dr. James Price, a NKJV Editor, says it's OK not to translate the plural/singular because modern English doesn't. Sorry, Doctor, but good translation conveys everything that is there.

These "thees and thous" are not archaic, they are accurate. God's precise thoughts are given in precise words—as inspired, preserved and literally translated. Not knowing whether a pronoun is singular or plural sometimes makes it impossible or guesswork to understand. The 10,000 "thees and thous" in the King James are <u>always</u> singular, and the 7000 "you, ye, your(s)" are <u>always</u> plural from the Hebrew and Greek. This amounts to 17,000 miss/messy translations of God's Holy Word in all the modern versions, as they translate both singular and plural pronouns as "you ... your(s)". **This is almost one error for every verse of the Bible!**

  Note the precision of the Word of God when properly translated. *"O thou of little faith"* (Matt.14:31), addressed specifically to Peter; and *"O ye of little faith"* (Matt.16:8) addressed to all the disciples. The NKJV has "you ... you" in both places. Actually 1611 English itself did not use "thee-ye", but the KING JAMES instituted a "Biblical English" here because it was the only way to translate the Bible correctly.

  This seems an appropriate place to mention THE KING JAMES 1611/2011 (KJ2011) which reads like the NKJV but translates "thee, thou, and thy" as "you^s", thus preserving the accurate original because the superscript "s" tells the reader that the pronoun is singular. See John 3:7 for another striking example of the information lost in all the modern Bible versions. *"Marvel not that I said unto thee [Nicodemus], ye [all men] must be born again."* The NJK Jesus was just saying Nicodemus had to be born again! (See inside back cover of this ENOUGH.)
NASV, RSV, NRSV, ESV, HCSV, NIV agree with NKJV—the same 17,000 translation errors in each version.

King James	New King James
John 4:29 *Come, see a man, which told me all things that ever I did: **is not** this the Christ?*	*"Come, see a Man who told me all things that I ever did. **Could** this be the Christ?*

NKJV has made a mistake in reading this Greek sentence. In this sentence there is a particle of negation, "not", prefixed to this interrogative clause, intimating either 1. If, and it is so as here, this is called "a first class condition", or 2. The woman is saying Jesus is <u>not</u> the Christ—which she clearly is not saying. NKJV translates this into a simple question which is not what the Greek says. She did imply the negative just a few minutes before (in John 4:12)—again with the "not" prefixed in the Greek, *"Art thou greater than our father Jacob?"* (At this point she obviously thought not.) The KJ has great Greek translation! NASV, RSV, NRSV, ESV, HCSV and NIV agree with NKJV.

King James	New King James
John 14:16a (John 14:26; 15:26; 16:7 also) *And I will pray the Father, and he shall give you another **Comforter**,* **Comforter**— SC 3875: 　"parakletos", an <u>intercessor</u>, <u>consoler</u>, to call near "Helpers" generally get paid minimum wage. "**Helper**" is one weak word for the <u>Divine Comforter</u> Who Jesus sent to be "another Comforter" to replace Jesus Himself Who was a great comforter to have physically with the Disciples (and Who we so need each day.)	*And I will pray the Father, and He will give you another **Helper**,* Doesn't this seem an unfortunate association in ideas with those who have problems with the reality of our triune God? There are those who rather prefer versions which demote God the Holy Spirit to a "**Helper**". See Eph.5:20 in this Fruit Inspection where the Holy Spirit is left out altogether in the NKJV. Is there a NKJV pattern here? (See Col.2:2;3:17 also.) Unitarians despise the Trinity. NASV agree with NKJV.; RSV, ESV, NIV, and HCSV say "counselor".

King James	New King James
John 18:26 *One of the servants of the high priest... **saith**...* **Saith**— Lex. present tense 　The Greek often speaks in the present, putting you into the action–live. 　We still use the present tense today—as, "The boss says to do it that way."	*One of the servants of the high priest...**said**,...* This is, at best, paraphrase; but literally it is mis-translated. This is done by all the modern versions hundreds of times especially in the four Gospels. Does a "translator" have such liberty to change tenses in the Word of God to fit the current idiom? Let the Bible determine the idiom! NASV, RSV, NRSV, HCSV and NIV. agree with NKJV

The new versions do properly translate, "Thus **saith** the Lord" as "Thus **says** the Lord", but when the KJ has "Jesus **saith**", they accommodate modern English by saying, "Jesus **said**".

King James	New King James
Acts 3:13 *The God of Abraham, and of Isaac, and of Jacob, the God of our fathers, hath glorified his **Son** Jesus; whom ye delivered up, and denied him in the presence of Pilate, when he was determined to let <u>him</u> go.*	*The God of Abraham, Isaac, and Jacob, the God of our fathers, glorified His **Servant** Jesus, whom you delivered up and denied in the presence of Pilate, who was determined to let <u>Him</u> go.*

Son— SC 3816: [God's] <u>boy</u>, a <u>servant</u>

"This Greek word can be translated "**servant**", but doesn't it seem wrong in this context where Moses ("*The servant of the LORD*" Deut. 34:5) is quoted, speaking of the Messiah (Acts 3:22,23) who was "*counted worthy of more glory than Moses ...*" Heb.3:3? What an unfortunate association here between the NKJV and many ancient and modern cults which vainly try to pull the "only begotten Son", the Lord Jesus Christ, down to Moses' level—that of just a servant, not God. NASV, RSV, NRSV, ESV, HCSV and NIV agree with NKJV.

King James	New King James
Acts 9:1,2 *And Saul, yet breathing out threatenings and slaughter against the disciples of the Lord, went unto the high priest, (2) And desired of him letters to Damascus to the Synagogues, that if he found any of **this way**, whether they were men or women, he might bring them bound unto Jerusalem.*	*Then Saul, still breathing out threats and murder against the disciples of the Lord, went to the high priest (2) and asked letters from him to the synagogues of Damascus, so that if he found any who were of **the Way**, whether men or women, he might bring them bound to Jerusalem.*

Here's another commentary capitalization by the NKJV. Luke did not use the definite article "the" or personalize "way" by capitalizing it as is done in Buddhism, Shintoism, Taoism, Islam, Hinduism, Gnosticism, NEW AGE BIBLE INTERPRETATION (The Book), Guru Da Free's IN THE WAY OF THE SHAMAN, ECK, The Way (cult), Rosicrucianism, etc. When those who are seeking the truth, but have been contaminated by the above false Ways, find these "Ways" in their Bible, trusting that they were written under Divine inspiration, they certainly could be misled back to error. Cults can quote this verse directly from these bible versions! NASV, RSV, NRSV, ESV, HCSV and NIV agree with NKJV.

King James	New King James
Acts 12:3b,4 *(Then were the days of unleavened bread.) (4) And when he had apprehended him, he put him in prison, and delivered him to four quaternions of solders to keep him; intending after **Easter** to bring him forth to the people.* **Easter—** SC 3957: paska= Passover—the meal, the day, the festival, or the special sacrifices connected with it	*Now it was during the Days of Unleavened Bread. (4) So when he had arrested him, he put him in prison, and delivered him to four squads of solders to keep him, intending to bring him before the people after* **Passover**.

"Easter" is not an "unfortunate translation" here. While the KJ does translate the Greek word "Paska" as "Passover" in the other 28 places it occurs in the New Testament, the forty-seven dedicated Christian first-rank scholars of 1611 agreed to make this obviously intentional choice of "**Easter**" here—some things that most modern scholars apparently have missed. Please consider:

1). Acts 12:3 tells us "then were the days of unleavened bread"—which follow the Day of Passover which is on the 14th of Nisan. So, Levitically, it was already "after Passover". Although Luke 22:1 says that the Jews called the two Feasts "Passover" (the day of Passover, followed immediately by the Feast of Unleavened Bread), the KJ was being translated for all the English-speaking world, who should be puzzled as to why Herod would be waiting for something that had already happened.

2). Should we expect heathen King Herod, who was doing the "intending" here, to appreciate these Jewish cultural details? If Herod celebrated anything at this time of year, it would be an ancient Babylonian observation named after Ishtar (Easter, with her "space egg").

Doesn't "Paska" translated "Passover" here misread the context? Herod intended to wait until all the festivities were over so the Jews could come to his execution of Peter.

RSV, NRSV, ESV, NASV, NIV, HCSV agree with NKJV.

King James	New King James
Acts 15:37-39a *And Barnabas **determined** to take with them John, whose surname was Mark. (38) But Paul **thought** not **good** to take him.... (39) And the contention was so sharp between them, that they departed asunder one from the other.* **determined**— SC 1011: to advise, deliberate, resolve **thought good**— SC 515: to deem entitled or fit The KJ sees no contention initially. Do we find what could be understood as another modern version attack on Paul's apostolic authority and character, and a scriptural justification for contentious church leaders? (See Colossians 4:10b, Acts 26:16, 1 Cor.6:4 in this Fruit Inspection and Appendix D, pattern 3, for what increasingly appears to be a pattern of putting down the Apostle Paul.)	*Now Barnabas **was determined** to take with them John called Mark. (38) But Paul **insisted** that they should not.... (39) Then the contention became so sharp that they parted from one another.* **"Was determined"** and **"insisted"** is commentary on the Greek and seems incorrect. Barnabas initially "advised" or "deliberated" about John Mark going with them. Paul simply responded that he felt John was not worthy or "fit" to accompany them. This was a difference of viewpoint, not a dispute. Then the "contention" arose; it wasn't already there and *"became so sharp".* Paul and Barnabas were not contentious old men insisting on their own way, as the NKJV implies—impossible people for God to lead in building His Church. Also, note that God actually used this situation to launch **two** missionary teams–with John Mark still aboard to finally write the Gospel of Mark. NASV, and NRSV agree with NKJV.
Acts 17:22 (25:19) *Then Paul stood in the midst of Mars' hill, and said, Ye men of Athens, I perceive that in all things ye are **too superstitious**.* **too superstitious**— Lex: Literally fear of the gods—of demons/devils	*Then Paul stood in the midst of the Areopagus and said, Men of Athens, I perceive that in all things you are **very religious**;*

Doesn't the NKJV turn the Apostle's rebuke into a hearty compliment by this poor translation? Behind all idols ("*superstitions*") are devils— Rev. 9:20; 18:2!
NASV, RSV, NRSV, ESV, and NIV agree with NKJV.

King James	New King James
Acts 20:23b [many other verses] ... *saying that **bonds** and afflictions abide me.* **bonds—** SC 1199: a <u>band</u>, <u>ligament</u> or <u>shackle</u> (of a prisoner) It just isn't accurate to say that in all these verses, all "bonds" were "chains".	... *saying that **chains** and tribulations await me.* Not specifically "**chains**" here; the passages refer to imprisonment, not to the way they would be bound; this is not a <u>literal translation</u>. Mankind has many ways to bind their fellow man! NASV, HCSV and NRSV agree with NKJV
Acts 24:22b ... *When Lysias the chief captain shall come down, I will **know the uttermost** of your matter.* **know the uttermost—** SC 1231: to <u>know thoroughly, ascertain exactly</u>	.. *when Lysias the commander comes down, I will **make a decision** on your case.* There is nothing about any **decision** (judicial sentence) being made here. NKJV is incorrect. Paul was being sent to Rome to be tried and sentenced. NASV, RSV, ESV, HCSV and NRSV agree with NKJV.
Acts 26:16b ... *and a witness both of these things which thou hast seen, and of those things in the which I will **appear** unto thee;* **appear—** SC 3700: to <u>gaze</u> (with wide open eyes as at something remarkable), by Hebrew: to <u>experience</u>, to <u>appear</u> <u>See Appendix D, Pattern 3, p.175 for</u> more on this modern version attack on Paul's authority.	... *and a witness both of the things which you have seen and of the things which I will yet **reveal** to you.* The Lord Jesus "appeared" to Paul (v.16a) and would "appear" again, not just "**reveal**" a message. This <u>personal communication</u> is a requirement for an Apostle. *"Am I not an Apostle ... have I not seen Jesus Christ?"* I Cor. 9:1 NKJV "**reveal**" undercuts Paul's apostolic authority by denying one of his Apostolic credentials. NIV says, "*and what I will show you.*"

King James	New King James
Rom.3:23-26 *For all have sinned, and come short of the glory of God; (24) Being justified freely by his grace through the redemption that is in Christ Jesus*: (25) *Whom God hath set forth to be a propitiation **through faith in his blood**, to declare his righteousness for the remission of sins that are past, through the forbearance of God; (26) To declare, I say, at this time his righteousness: that he might be just, and the justifier of him that believeth in Jesus.*	*for all have sinned and fall short of the glory of God*, (24) *being justified freely by His grace through the redemption that is in Christ Jesus*, (25) *whom God set forth <u>as</u> a propitiation **by His blood**, **through faith**, to demonstrate His righteousness, because in His forbearance God had passed over the sins that were previously committed,* (26) *to demonstrate at the present time His righteousness, that He might be just and the justifier of the one who has faith in Jesus.*

The KJ/TR Greek says, "***through faith in his blood***". ("DIA TES PISTOS EN TO AUTOU AIMATI"). "Redemption" (v. 24) means to buy (back) at a price, and the price of our redemption was the life blood of the Lord Jesus Christ. "*... ye were not redeemed with corruptible things, as silver and gold ... but with the precious blood of Christ ...*" (I Peter 1:18,19); Eph.1:7; Col.1:20; Rev.1:5.... Each person must personally put "***faith in his blood***". It is conceivable that He could have died without shedding His blood, but He died as a bloody sacrifice. The blood is the way our unrighteousness is washed away (v.25) AND how God's righteousness is satisfied ("propitiated", v.26). This is not just "faith in faith" (even in Jesus' teachings); this is "faith in His blood"—exactly as the sacrificial system throughout the entire Word of God says from Adam/Abel to Abraham, to Moses, to David, to the Lord Jesus Christ on Calvary. KEY COMPARISON COMMENT: This NKJV translation error could be mis-taken to strike at the heart of the Gospel (I Cor.15:1-4, "*Christ died for our sins according to the scriptures.*")

All the modern versions repeatedly take the "blood" out of the Bible. This really seems another example where the NKJV patches the obvious problem by not deleting the blood in these passages—yet here in Rom.3:25 the blood is deleted—as the focus of our faith for salvation. Since the NKJV clones the other modern versions in over 80% of the other changes, doesn't this patching of the glaring errors make the NKJV, in effect, even more subtly dangerous to the Remnant?

Note well how many of these differences between the KJ and the NKJV jackhammer the foundation, not just the periphery of our faith.

NASV, RSV, NRSV, AND ESV agree with NKJV.

King James	New King James
Rom.6:5a *For if we have been **planted together** in the likeness of his death,*	*For if we have been **united** together in the likeness of His death,*
planted together— SC 4854: <u>grown</u> along <u>with</u>	"**United**" is one weak word for a growing thing. See John 12:24.
The same word translated "nature" in Rom. 2:27, with the amplifying prefix "sum" added: "plants completely together" as a <u>rebirth</u>.	NASV, RSV, NRSV, ESV, NIV agree with NKJV; HCSV says "joined".

King James	New King James
Rom.11:30a, 31, 32 *For as ye in times past have* **not believed** *God, ...* (31) *even so have these also now* **not believed**, *that* **through your mercy** *they also may obtain mercy.* (32) *For God hath concluded them all in* **unbelief**, *that he might have mercy upon all.*	*For as you were once* **dis-obedient** *to God, ...* (31) *even so these also have now been* **disobedient**, *that* **through the mercy shown** *you they also may obtain mercy.* (32) *For God has committed them all to* **disobedience**, *that he might have mercy on all.*
not believed and unbelief— SC 543: <u>disbelief</u> (obstinate and rebellious), from: 545 <u>unpersuadable</u>	Confused? Choose your translators carefully! The Old KJ is tried and true.

What is going on here? The difference between "**unbelief**" and "**disobedience**" can be the difference between going to Heaven or Hell! While both KJ and NKJV translate SC 543-545 as "**unbelief**" and "**disobedience**" in different places in the Bible, the context determines how the word must be translated. See the context of Rom.11:20-29, specifically v.26, "*so all Israel shall be saved.*" We are talking about salvation here, which is about belief not works. "*For by grace are ye saved through faith ... not of works* [obedience]." The word must be translated "**unbelief**", not "**disobedience**" in Rom.11:30-32 "*...because of unbelief* (in both KJ and NKJV) *they were broken off, and thou standest by faith... .*" Rom.11:20 is a comparison of "**unbelief**" and "**faith**". The conclusion of the argument in verse 32 refers to **unbelief** also: "*For God hath concluded them all in* **unbelief** ...*" NOT **disobedience**. Obedience was both the keynote and the death knell of the Old Covenant. All the modern versions confuse this key passage. Moses "*took the book of the covenant ... and they said, all that the LORD hath said will we do, and be obedient*" (Ex.24:7,8). But they didn't–they couldn't; they needed the Messiah. These Jewish people would not believe, <u>would not be "persuaded"</u>, about the Lord Jesus Christ. Translating "a + peitho" ("not + persuaded") as "disobedience" here in Rom.11:30-32 causes confusion in understanding the conclusion to this strategic text (Romans chapters 9-11)! This is very serious indeed as it affects understanding the atonement and the "*depth of the riches ...*" (Rom.11:33-36).

The issue here seems to be that a man can be obedient to religion, even to God's laws; but because no man but Jesus could <u>perfectly</u> obey, he would still be lost. "*For Christ is the end of the law* [He perfectly obeyed and thereby fulfilled it] *for righteousness to every one that believeth*" [is "persuaded"] (Rom.10:4). If we reject Jesus, that is, if we will not be "persuaded" that He is our Creator/God/Savior (proven by His fulfillment of all the first advent Messianic prophecies), we cannot be saved—our pride has stumbled at the law's stumbling stone (Rom.9:31-33) in thinking we can measure up to the perfect standard of the Law. The law, without sacrifice for man's utter inability to keep it, never worked and wasn't expected to. So the issue is (and always was, before the Law came to Israel, as in Genesis 15:6) faith, not obedience. And now, in this "Church/Grace" age, it again is "*... no more of works: otherwise grace is no more grace*" (Rom.11:6).

"*That through your mercy they also may obtain mercy*" (Rom.11:31b) is a wonderful charge to the Church. Rom.11:31b, in the NKJV, confuses this charge by talking about some "*mercy shown*" us. (There is no "shown" in the Greek, and yet it is not indicated as "supplied".) Rather, isn't the Bible saying that God would be merciful to the Jewish people through us? Isn't verse 31 confusion in the NKJV? A real Christian's mercy is shown in sharing God's compassion and burden for the lost sheep of the house of Israel (and "*to the Jew first*" Rom.1:16) thereby helping to "persuade" them to "believe" by our demonstration of His love.

Just how is one "*committed ... to disobedience*" (NKJV Rom.11:32)? "*Concluded in unbelief*" is the proper translation in this whole context of grace versus works.

KEY COMPARISON COMMENT: To mix "obedience" and "belief" (works and grace) is a diabolical word game. These passages are deep ("*O the depth of the riches...*"Rom.11:33). Isn't the KJ clearer and truer than the NKJV here, (and in Hebrews 3)?

NASV, RSV, ESV, NIV, and HCSV agree with NKJV.

I Cor.6:4b ... **set them** to judge who are least esteemed in the Church.	... do you **appoint those** who are least esteemed by the church to judge?
set them— Lex: second person, plural, present imperative The "present imperative" is a command, not a question—a command from the Apostle Paul! Changing this command into a question could be viewed as another attack on Paul's apostolic authority. (See Acts 15:37 in this Fruit Inspection and Appendix D, pattern 3, p.175.)	Making this verse a question, in the teeth of the Greek command here, reverses the whole message of the verse and therefore seems a mis-translation. NASV, RSV, NRSV, ESV, and HCSV agree with NKJV.
I Cor.16:22 *If any man love not the Lord Jesus Christ, let him be Anathema* **Maranatha**.	*If anyone does not love the Lord Jesus Christ, let him be accursed.* **O Lord**, **Come**!
Maranatha— SC 3134: (of Chaldean—Aramaic—origin) meaning "Our Lord has come" Lex. perfect [past] tense	This is mistranslated.

THE THEOLOGICAL DICTIONARY OF THE NEW TESTAMENT, vol. 4, p. 469, says, "To the best of my knowledge, there is not a single instance in all Aramaic ... to construct the perfect [as in I Cor.16:22, which is completed action] ... as our Lord comes, in the future tense...."

Also, the early church Fathers took "Maranatha" as "Our Lord has come"—referring to His finished work—and if we love not the Lord Jesus, referring to our pending judgment, absolutely as good as finished, as sure as His finished first coming.

RSV, NRSV, ESV. and NIV agree with NKJV.

24

King James	New King James
II Cor.1:23a *Moreover I call God for a record **upon** my soul,* **upon**— SC 1909: "epi" <u>over</u>, <u>on</u>, <u>upon</u>...	*Moreover I call God as witness **against** my soul,* This is not a good translation of "epi" here. Besides, under grace, God is not prosecuting "**against**" his servants. RSV, NRSV, ESV, and HCSV agree with NKJV
II Cor.2:15 (I Cor.1:18 also) *For we are unto God a sweet savour of Christ, in them that **are saved**, and in them that perish:* **are saved**— Lex: present passive; <u>saved</u>, ransom	*For we are to God the fragrance of Christ among those who **are being saved** and among those who are perishing.* See NKJV I Cor. 1:18 for another instance of this.

J.W. Burgon, "the dean of New Testament Greek" (who analyzed and assembled into one reference work over 1,000,000 Scripture texts from almost 90,000 early Church Father witnesses to the Greek N.T.) says, "in evaluating these two translations, translating this 'present' here as 'are being saved', the school boy method of translation is thereby exhibited."

There is more than just poor Greek here however; "**are being saved**" seems to deny the finished work of Christ in a believer's heart. We do need to choose our holy men (and translators) carefully; and in translating the New Testament, they must be humbly great in their Greek. The Tyndale, Great, Geneva, Bishops Bibles; the Peshitta etc. render this "**are saved**". The 1881 English RV was <u>first</u> to say "**are being saved** " due to Winer's (Unitarian) grammar, says their own RV Chairman Bishop Ellicott. Doesn't "**are being saved**" sound like the Roman Catholic <u>process</u> of salvation controlled by their hierarchy and leading through purgatory?

NKJV editor, James Price, defends this rendering by arguing that "clearly Paul must have had the ongoing aspect of salvation in mind ...". A nice subjective Higher Critical comment to justify following the English 1881 Unitarian translation in the teeth of all other ancient readings to the contrary.
NASV, RSV, NRSV, ESV, HCSV and NIV agree with NKJV.

King James	New King James
II Cor.10:13,15 *But we will not boast of things without our measure, but according to the measure of the **rule** which God hath distributed to us, a measure to reach even unto you ... when your faith is increased, that we shall be enlarged by you according to our **rule** abundantly.*	*We, however, will not boast beyond measure, but within the limits of the **sphere** which God appointed us—a sphere which especially includes you ... as your faith is increased, we shall be greatly enlarged by you in our **sphere**.*
rule— SC 2583: "Kanon", (a straight <u>reed</u> or <u>rod</u>) a standard of faith and practice kanon=Canon, as in "The Canon of Scripture"—the God-inspired (spoken), supernaturally assembled ("Canonized"), and preserved Holy Bible. Note the contrast between how the false apostles brought the Corinthians into bondage, devoured them, took from them, exalted themselves, struck them on the face (II Cor.11:20) whereas Paul's "rule" over them was simply the Canon of Scripture—the "thus says the Lord". Praise God!!	KEY COMPARISON COMMENT: Here, in II Cor.10-12 in which Paul gives his inspired defense of his apostleship, we have his rule busted in rank in the NKJV. This is the issue here being attacked. For, Paul's apostolic command authority now abides in the Canon of Scripture. If he didn't have it, neither does the Bible. RSV, NRSV, ESV, NASV, NIV, and HCSV agree with NKJV.

King James	New King James
II Cor.11:12 *But what I do, that I will do, that I may cut off occasion from them which desire occasion;* **that wherein they glory, they may be found even as we**.	*But what I do, I will continue to do, that I may cut off the opportunity from those who desire an opportunity* **to be regarded just as we are in the things of which they boast**.

glory— SC2744 to <u>boast</u>, to <u>brag</u> about   (See II Cor. 10:17)

The last thing these people, who are looking for occasion/opportunity, want is "to *be regarded as*" Paul was—who 1) preached without pay or "Nicolaitan" power over the people (II Cor.11:29, Rev. 2:6,15) and 2) was so routinely mis-treated (II Cor.11:22-28). What Paul apparently said was, *"... that I may cut off occasion from them that desire occasion"* <u>to fleece the flock</u>. The immediate context (11:7-11,20) seems to say this. It's as simple as that; *"the love of money is the root of all evil"* (I Tim.6:10 in the KJ; not "**a** root"). Remove the financial incentive and you eliminate those whose primary motive is money.

However, there really is something even more profound here; look at the next verses: *"For such are false apostles, deceitful workers...* [as] *Satan himself....*(II Cor.11:13-15). This is as serious as it gets. WHO ARE THESE PEOPLE? Yes, they love money—other people's money. We've all sinned over money at some time, and Paul effectively dealt with this issue there in Corinth by simply not using their expensive money—like Abraham wouldn't take any reward from the King of Sodom. (Gen. 14:21-23) However, why is the Apostle so strong here with these greedy critics? Is it not because in criticizing Paul here in II Cor.10-12, they are challenging the authority of the book(s) written by Paul under Divine inspiration—EXACTLY as the NKJV and the other Critical Text bible versions have this pattern of challenging Paul. This is a KEY COMPARISON COMMENT (See Acts 15:37 and Appendix D, pattern 3.) The Critical Text bibles are challenging the Preservation/ Authority of Scripture. Accept them and accept the **loss** of the Word of God.

The key phrase in **bold** here, which is so subtly wrong in the modern versions, is "**that wherein they glory**". Paul's Apostolic pen touches <u>the very heart of the matter</u>, the heart condition of those who attack the authority of God-spoken Scripture. In II Cor.10-12, the same Greek word translated, "**glory**" and "**boast**" is found twenty (20) times—the keynote of the entire passage. Read John 7:17 for what the Lord Jesus Christ has to say about that in which one glories: "*He that speaketh of himself seeketh his own glory.*" When a Bible teacher or Bible translator uses Hebrew and Greek texts or translations which he knows have been subjectively critically edited, he is not speaking from Scripture but is speaking *"of himself"*, seeking *"his own glory"*. Isn't he trying to counsel God (Rom.11:34) who has magnified His Word above all His name (Ps.138:2)? Westcott and Hort, and all who knowingly use the subjective "Critical Text" (please do see "The Naked Truth", p.114 in this ENOUGH) are "false apostles...(Satan's) ministers"—II Cor.11:13-15! And now, dear reader, don't we know ENOUGH to resolve the bible/Bible battle? Those who don't trust the preservation of the Word of God are challenging the authority of the Bible and are "his (Satan's) ministers!! (II Cor. 11:15) Could some church leaders refuse to resolve, or even consider, the issue of the inerrantly preserved Bible, because **they want to be the authority**? Don't they thereby rob God's **glory** for themselves? And rob their people, who without the so sharp *"sword of the Spirit which is the Word of God"* (Eph.6:17b) are ill-equipped to participate in the Great Commission to *"go...teach all nations..."*. (Matt.28:19-20)?

NASV, RSV, NRSV, ESV, HCSV, and NIV agree with NKJV.

Gal.2:6 *But of these who seemed to be somewhat, (whatsoever they were, it maketh no matter to me: God **accepteth no man's person**:) for they who seemed to be somewhat **in conference added** nothing to me:*	*But from those who seemed to be something—whatever they were, it makes no difference to me; God shows **personal favoritism to no man**—for those who seemed to be something **added** nothing to me.*
accepteth— SC 2983: to take, (in very many applications) **In conference added**— SC 4323: a compound word to add by consulting	"**Personal favoritism**" is paraphrase, not literal translation. There is no human glory or position next to God's. "**Added**" is just half of this strategic message. The whole message is that God's leaders over us will have a message from God which gives additional direction from God for us. NASV, RSV, NRSV, ESV, NIV, and HCSV agree with NKJV.

KEY COMPARISON COMMENT: This is perhaps the clearest instruction in the Word about how to know which leaders we should follow: those to whom God gives guidance for us. This is pretty well lost in all the modern versions. Paul did not submit his ministry under Peter and James because God didn't choose to give him guidance through them.

King James	New King James
*Gal.2:20 I am crucified with Christ: nevertheless I live; yet not I, but Christ liveth in me: and the life which I now live in the flesh I live by the faith **of** the Son of God, who loved me, and gave himself for me.*	*I have been crucified with Christ; it is no longer I who live, but Christ lives in me; and the <u>life</u> which I now live in the flesh I live by faith **in** the Son of God, who loved me and gave Himself for me.*
of— Lex: "Tov", genitive (=possessive) singular, "<u>of</u>" Gal.2:20 is a foundation block of the Christian life, a KEY COMPARISON issue. "*Christ liveth in me ... by the faith **of** the Son of God,*" not by our faith "in" the Son. His faith keeps us "in Christ." The Christian's position "in Christ," does not hang on our "faith **in**" Christ, but on the finished work (and intercessory ministry) **of** the Son of God, our great High Priest. "In Christ" is elaborated approximately 14 (fourteen!) times in Eph.1. This is a precious instance of a doctrine that has been aptly called "Positional Truth".	In this immediate context (a strong proof), see Gal.2:16 (twice) and 3:22—three more strikes by the NKJV. That's an "out" for the modern bibles just on this error. You ask just how do we live by someone else's faith? Isn't it that by His faith He paid our sin debt? Now, we don't have to try to pay but just accept His finished work.

Note that NKJV *"it is no longer I who live"* is in <u>flat contradiction</u> to the statement in the KJ, *"I...live"*. Clearly the NKJV is an obliterated bible here (John 10:35), blowing away this Divine revelation of the majestic mystery of how Christ lives in His people—not as in the NKJV here which says that we no longer live yet we must hang on to Him by the fingertips of our "faith in" Him! ENOUGH of this rough draft bible. NASV, RSV, NRSV, ESV, NIV and HCSV agree with the NKJV.

King James	New King James
*Gal.4:13 Ye know how **through** infirmity of the flesh I preached the gospel unto you at the first.*	*You know that **because** of physical infirmity I preached the gospel to you at the first.*
through— SC 1223: a primary preposition denoting the channel of an act; <u>through</u>	"**Because**" doesn't even make sense here; Paul didn't preach **because** of his infirmity but in spite of and **through** it. NASV, RSV, NRSV, ESV, NIV agree with NKJV.

King James	New King James
Gal.5:4a *Christ is become **of no effect** unto you,*	*You have become **estranged** from Christ,*
of no effect— SC 2673: to <u>be</u> (render) entirely idle (<u>useless</u>)	This is cute but inaccurate paraphrase, not literal translation.

Confidence in our works—even in keeping the law—will not so much "**estrange**" us from Christ as render His saving Grace seemingly useless, unnecessary to us (Christ becomes "**of no effect**" to us). Also, which is more readable to the average reader, "**estranged**" or "**of no effect**"?

  NKJV is supposed to be "unveiling the KJ antiquities" (quoted from a NKJV preface); yet the Flesch–Kincaid Research Company's "Grade Level Indicator" ranks the KJ <u>easier to read</u> than the NKJV, NASV, and NIV in 23 of 26 categories (Ref.8, p.208). In the following list of words, a control group of 2nd graders could define all of the KJ words, and none of the NKJV:

NKJV	KJ		NKJV	KJ	
elderly	old	Deut.28:50	captivity	stranger	Obad.1:12
descendants	children	Josh.22:24	hades	hell	entire N.T.
clans	thousands	I Sam.10:19	shrewdly	wisely	Luke 16:8
keva	house of rolls	I Kings 10:2	denarii	pennyworth	John 6:7
residence	throne	Neh.3:7	praetorium	judgment hall	John 18:28
vindicate	judge	Ps.43:1	were not persuaded	believeth not	Acts 17:5
anxieties	thoughts	Ps.139:23	Areopagus	Mars Hill	Acts 17:22
gratify	give	Eccl.12:3	SyrtisSands	quicksands	Acts 27:17
skillful	right	Eccl.4:4	resolve	judge	Rom.14:13
walk prudently	keep thy foot	Eccl.5:1	habitation	house	II Cor.5:2
mortal	man	Isa.13:12	eminent	chiefest	II Cor.11:5
verdant	fat	Isa.28:1,4	Symbol of authority	power	I Cor.11:5
overflowing	fat	Isa.34:6	estranged	of no effect	Gal.5:4
catastrophe	evil	Jer.19:3	the former	The one	Phil.1:16
waif	fatherless	Lam.5:3	the latter	the other	Phil.1:17
rivulets	little rivers	Eze.31:4	mortal man	man that dies	Heb.7:8
elders	old men	Joel 1:2	distinction	difference	Jude 22
savor	smell	Amos 5:21			

WHY does the NKJV use harder words than the KJ? The Derivative Copyright Law insists that: "To be copyrightable, a derivative work must be different enough from the original to be regarded as a 'new work' or must contain a substantial amount of new material. Making minor changes or additions of little substance to a pre-existing work will not qualify the work as a new version for copyright purposes." Therefore all new Bible versions must change those simple one or two syllable Anglo-Saxon words to complex Latinized words. Consequently the KJ reads at the 5th grade level and the NKJV reads at the 6th grade level. Because of this copyright law, there will never be an easier to read Bible than the KJ.

NEW KING JAMES

* omits the word "JEHOVAH" entirely.
* omits the word "new testament" entirely.
* omits the word "damnation" entirely.
* omits the word "devils" entirely.
* ignored the KJ *Textus Receptus* over 2000 times.
* replaced the KJ Hebrew *(ben Chayyim)* with the corrupt Stuttgart edition *(ben Asher)* Old Testament, which has more questions about what the Masoretic Text is than there are verses in the Old Testament.

[The body count: NKJV makes over 100,000 changes from the KJ.]

Gal.5:22 *But the fruit of the Spirit is, ... **faith**,*	*But the fruit of the Spirit is ...* ***faithfulness**,*
faith— SC 4102: <u>confidence</u>, <u>trust</u> (in what God has said in His Word)	Isn't this at best a very poor translation? "Faith" is the key, for *"the just shall llive by faith"* Hab.2:4, Gal.3;11, Heb.10:38.

"**Faithfulness**" is not the same as "**faith**". **Faithfulness** is a work which is a result of saving **faith** ("*by grace are ye saved through faith ... unto good works*" Eph 2:8-10). See Appendix D, p.173 to understand the pattern in all these, at best, poor translations.
NASV, RSV, NRSV, ESV, and NIV agree with NKJV.

King James	New King James
Eph.4:22a *That ye put off concerning the former conversation the old man, which **is** corrupt ...*	*that you put off, concerning your former conduct, the old man which **grows** corrupt ...*

The old man **is** corrupt; "**grows**" is neither in the Greek, nor is it an accurate description of our totally depraved enemy, our old sin nature. NASV, NIV agree with NKJV.

King James	New King James
Eph.5:20 *Giving thanks always for all things **unto God and the Father** in the name of our Lord Jesus Christ;*	*giving thanks always for all things **to God the Father** in the name of our Lord Jesus Christ,*
Καί Patri "and Father" NKJV leaves out "**and**" .	The Greek says to give *"thanks always ... unto God"* (the Father, the Son, and the Holy Spirit), **and** specifically to *"the Father, in the name of our Lord Jesus Christ"*.

THIS IS REALLY IMPORTANT—Aaron lost two sons for offering "**strange fire**" (Lev. 10:1) before our Holy God. They knew better because God had told them. He has revealed much more of His triune character to us. By the choice of translation words in Eph.5:20, the Holy Scriptures are distinguishing between the triune God and the individual Persons that make up the Godhead. To leave out the Holy Spirit, as NKJV does here, is "strange" and keeps sad company with the Gnostic Jehovah Witnesses who do not believe in God the Holy Spirit.

There is one other difference between these two verses: the NKJV says "**to**", the KJ says "**unto**". The NKJV New Testament has 6000 "to"s. The KJ has approximately 3000 "to"s and 3000 "unto"s. A brief survey of these 6000 places indicates that the KJ uses "to" in marking the following verb as an infinitive or generally for prepositions (and adverbs) of motion or action. The KJ uses "unto" with phrases of "being": "*But **to** Israel he saith, All day long I have stretched forth my hands **unto** a disobedient and a gainsaying people*" Rom.10:21. In this verse both "**to**" and "**unto**" are translations of the same preposition "pros". The NKJV handles this very talented "pros" without these differentiations—across the board of the entire New Testament. The KJ "**unto**"s seem to represent 3000 little flags to the English reader to look a little more abstractly, deeply. This would be a very interesting word study which would be impossible to do with the NKJV.

RSV, NRSV, ESV, HCSV and NIV agree with NKJV.

King James	New King James
Eph.5:33b ... *and let the wife <u>see</u> that she* **reverence** <u>*her*</u> *husband.* **reverence**— SC 5399: to <u>frighten</u>, to <u>be alarmed</u>, to <u>be in awe</u>	*... and let the wife see that she* **respects** *her husband.*
"**Respects**" is more than too weak; it misses the Lord's awesome insight into what marriage is designed to be—an adventure in which the man so dynamically leads that his wife holds onto her seat in awe; meanwhile the wife models for her man how he must be towards his Lord in lovely feminine suppliance (as the Bride of Christ will be! Rev.19:7) by her attitude towards him. RSV, NRSV, ESV, NASV, NIV, and HCSV agree with NKJV.	
Eph.6:5 *Servants, be obedient to them that are <u>your</u> masters according to the flesh, with fear and trembling, in* **singleness** *of your heart, as unto Christ;* **singleness**— SC 572: <u>singleness</u>: figuratively <u>clear</u>, subjectively <u>sincerity</u> (<u>without self seeking</u>) Lex: <u>single</u>, hence <u>simple</u>, <u>uncompounded</u>, <u>sound</u>, <u>perfect</u>	*Bond servants, be obedient to those who are your masters according to the flesh, with fear and trembling, in* **sincerity** *of heart, as to Christ;* "**Sincerity**" loses the profound truth that a servant cannot have <u>two</u> masters ("*Ye cannot serve God and mammon* Matt.6:24). See NKJV Colossians 3:22 for another "**singleness**" translated as "**sincerity**". NASV, HCSV and NIV agree with NKJV.

King James	New King James
Phil.2:6 *Who, being in the form of God, thought it not* **robbery** *to be equal with God*:	*Who being in the form of God, did not consider equality with God something to be* **grasped**,

robbery— SC 725: <u>plunder</u>,
  to <u>seize</u>

We have here perhaps the most powerful picture in all of Scripture of the all-conquering Christ, the true and only Master of the Universe. To Him are added the rights of conquest on top of His rights of ownership of His Universe. He became *"sin for us"* (II Cor.5:21) to win our freedom from sin's slavemarket and to win our hearts in gratitude and awestruck admiration and love!

   "**Robbery**": the power/right by conquest of a conquering army throughout history in all times and places. The losing country in war, if the reserve forces failed in enabling some sort of retreat of their military forces, are without any defense against being totally overrun, raped and pillaged— "plundered" ("robbery"). (Do read Luke 11:17-23.) The Lord Jesus Christ is this Almighty conquering Christ who with His finger routs Satan's whole system (Luke 11:20).

This is the "Arian Heresy" (started by Arius)—that there was a time that the Lord Jesus was not God (and so Satan was equal to Jesus). Arius based this lie on Origen's translation of John 1:18, as found in the Critical Text. This NKJV translation can definitely be misunderstood to imply that there was such a time when He was not equal with God.

TO TWIST <u>THIS</u> VERSE TO TEACH <u>THAT</u> IS A SATANIC MASTERPIECE !

The later 1990 NKJV does a patch job correction, barring Arius, but still butchering the entire passage. In Phil.2:1-7 the KJ Bible says "... *be like minded ... let this mind be in you, which was also in Christ Jesus: who ... thought....*" Compare this with the <u>new</u> NKJV which says the opposite: "*who ... did not consider it....*" That is, the KJ tells us what He thought (and what mind we should let be in us), and the new NKJV tells us what He did not think.

Notice that the NKJV isn't finished yet—and virtually every correction is back to the original KJ. Please also note that when the Church accepted the Arian Heresy, under Emperor Constantine, it was transformed from the persecuted Church into the persecutor of the Church—the Arian Heresy is deadly! James White, (Ref. 10) wondered why the King James brothers take such exception to this new version verse. White calls this KJ verse "awkward". We stand <u>in awe</u> of the Lord Jesus Christ who chose to go from the very Top to become worse than all heinous criminals when He died for all the crimes

of all us criminals on that cross. (Incidentally, Paul had a micro-parallel experience when he, a <u>Roman citizen</u>, received "many stripes" and did time "in the inner prison" in Philippi! Acts 16). Therefore "*let nothing be done through strife or vain glory ... let each esteem other better than themselves ... let this mind be in you, which was also in Christ Jesus*". <u>That</u> unity of mind resolves all differences!
NASV, RSV, NRSV, ESV, and NIV agree with (the first edition) NKJV.

Col.2:14 *Blotting out the handwriting of* **ordinances** *that was against us, which was contrary to us, and took it out of the way, nailing it to his cross;*	*having wiped out the handwriting of* **requirements** *that was against us, which was contrary to us. And He has taken it out of the way, having nailed it to the cross.*
ordinances— SC 1378: <u>law</u>, (civil, ceremonial, ecclesiastical), from: the Greek for "dogma"	Isn't "**requirements**" a poor synonym for the "dogma" he nailed to His cross?
Col.2:15a <u>*And*</u> *having* **spoiled** *principalities and powers,*	*Having* **disarmed** *principalities and powers,*
spoiled— SC 554: to <u>despoil</u>, to <u>wholly divest</u> [Dict: "divest" = strip off property, authority, rights]	There are no "arms" in the Greek. The word has the prefix "apo", which intensifies—<u>totally</u> stripped of everything including "arms". NASV, RSV, NRSV, ESV, NIV and HCSV agree with NKJV.
Col.3:5 *Mortify therefore your members which are upon the earth;* ... ***inordinate affection*** ...	*Therefore put to death your members which are on the earth:* ... ***passion****....*
inordinate affection— SC 3806: <u>suffering</u> (as in lust) "Affection" that is wrong = twisted passion = lust.	**Passion** does not equal "lust". Holy passion is a rare beauty in this earthly travail—in a spirit-led family and for our God. NASV, RSV, NRSV, and ESV agree with NKJV.

King James	New King James
Col.4:10b ... *and Marcus, sister's son to Barnabas, (touching whom ye received* **commandments**: *if he come unto you,* **receive** *him*;)	*... with Mark the cousin of Barnabas (about whom you received* **instruction**: *if he come to you,* **welcome** *him*),
commandments— SC 1785: injunction, authoritative prescription; from: to enjoin **receive**—SC 2983 rather passive KEY COMPARISON COMMENT: Is not the effect of these translation decisions in these modern versions to diminish or even challenge Paul's Apostolic "**command**" authority (and the authority of the Bible books God inspired through Paul)? See more of this possible pattern in Col.4:10b, in I Cor.6:4b (in this ENOUGH), and in II Cor. 10:13,14 where "rule" was translated by NKJV as "sphere".	"**Instruction**" is a poor, weak word for SC1785, an Apostolic order regarding a very sensitive and crucially important matter. Paul had judged Mark "unfit" in Acts 15:38! Therefore, a "**command**", not just "**instruction**", was necessary for the GOSPEL OF MARK (inspired through the pen of this same John-Mark) to be accepted as Scripture! Where did this **welcome** come from? With Paul's command was a word which seems to imply submission to Mark. NASV, RSV, NRSV, ESV, NIV, and HCSV agree with NKJV.
I Thess.2:4 *But as we were* **allowed** *of God to be put in trust with the gospel, even so we speak; not as pleasing men, but God, which trieth our hearts.*	*But as we have been* **approved** *by God to be entrusted with the gospel, even so we speak, not as pleasing men, but God who tests our hearts.*
allowed— SC 1382: tested, trustiness	**Approved** is a permitted translation, but there is a fine point here:

Doesn't "**approved**" imply self-merit within us? Rather, the concept contained in the Greek here seems of trustiness, permitted to preach based on His grace which has been refined into our lives by the fires we have been willing to go through with Him. Humbly think on this: does the Father **approve** of anything in us but Christ in us?
NASV, RSV, NRSV, ESV, HCSV, and NIV agree with NKJV.

King James	New King James
I Thess.2:6 *Nor of men sought we glory, neither of you, nor yet of others, when we might have been* **burdensome**, *as the apostles of Christ.* **burdensome**— SC 1722: and 922 <u>going</u> down, a <u>weight</u> or <u>load</u>, <u>authority</u>	*Nor did we seek glory from men, either from you or from others, when we might have made* **demands** *as apostles of Christ.* "**Demands**" isn't wrong, but poor; there are many ways of being **burdensome** besides making **demands**—like not paying their own expenses. See immediate context in the next comparison verse, I Thess.2:9, in which "burden", (taken out of I Thess.2:6, where it belongs) is put back in 2:9, where it is not a literal translation. RSV, NRSV, and ESV agree with NKJV.
I Thess.2:9 *For ye remember, brethren, our labor and* **travail**: *for laboring night and day, because we would not be* **chargeable** *to any of you, we preached unto you the gospel of God.* **travail**— SC 3449: <u>sadness</u>; from: <u>with difficulty</u> **chargeable**— SC 1912 to <u>be expensive</u> to	*For you remember, brethren, our labor and* **toil**; *for laboring night and day, that we might not be a* **burden** *to any of you, we preached to you the gospel of God.* "**Travail**" is a much heavier word than "**toil**". Again, "toil" isn't wrong, but it blurs the inspired picture. Labor is toil! The NKJV is redundant here while losing the truth of "travail", which implies sadness, painfulness which is a part of the true pastor's experience.

There really seems to be a "quality control" problem in NKJV translation of Thessalonians (and Timothy)—notice how many problems are found even in this brief comparison; so many poor translations. KEY COMPARISON COMMENT: By the "Derivative Copyright Law", in order to be able to copyright the NKJV Bible (necessary in order to have exclusive <u>sales</u> right), they had to change <u>significant</u> KJ words in most verses of the Bible. But since the KJ is literally translated from the inspired Greek, this required NKJV to make non-literal translations—like these poor words we've been finding here in Thessalonians. This is more than just making the NKJV actually harder to read, it is also less accurate. (Also, is there a reason why these texts dealing with fleecing the sheep instead of caring for them seem to enter into a fog bank? See II Cor.11:12. This could be another KEY COMPARISON COMMENT.)

NASV, RSV, NRSV, ESV, and HCSV agree with NKJV.

King James	New King James
I Thess.4:11a *And that ye* **study to be quiet**, *and to* **do** *your own business,*	*that you also* **aspire to lead a quiet life**, *to* **mind** *your own business,*
study— SC 5389: and Lex: eager, ambitious **to be quiet**— SC 2270: refrain from meddlesome speech, still (undisturbed, undisturbing) **do**— SC 4238: practice, execute, accomplish	This seems shallow and "off the paper target" paraphrase. The text isn't speaking so much about being a busybody or meddling in another's "business"—"**mind your own business**" is a modern idiom for being a busybody. Working with your hands...walk honestly... having lack of nothing is the context here.
God's servants don't duck the fight as passive spectators; but executing their *"own business"*, they live an absolutely adventurous life as His *"ambassadors"* (II Cor. 5:20) and, *"having done all, to stand"* (Eph.6:13).	NASV, RSV, NRSV, ESV, NIV and HCSV agree with NKJV.

King James	New King James
II Thess..2:7 *For the mystery of iniquity doth already work: only he who now **letteth** will let, until he be taken out of the way.*	*For the mystery of lawlessness is already at work; only He who now **restrains** will do so until He is taken out of the way.*
letteth— SC 2192: to hold + 2592 down fast Lex: have in full and secure possession	(See preceding verse, 6, for same poor translation.) If the word "**restrain**" were a true translation, the implications would be frightening, as if God has a hard time restraining Satan. NO! The Greek says there's no contest!

To "hold down fast" is so much stronger than to **restrain**. In order to be able to simply **let** something happen you must be in total control of it. A hungry cat that has caught a mouse only **lets** the mouse seem to get free, to tenderize the meat. Isn't the literal message here that the Holy Spirit (through the church!) only **lets** Satan do God's will? The Church is in charge of this age as the reigning Christ's Ambassadors (Matt.28:18; 1 Cor.15:25, Col.2:15)—if we will just attack the gates of hell (Matt.16:18)! The accurate translation here in the KJ empowers the Church; the inaccurate translation has the Church on the defensive trying to hold Satan back rather than holding him "down fast".
NASV, RSV, NRSV, ESV, HCSV, and NIV agree with NKJV.

King James	New King James
II Thess.3:5 *And the Lord direct your hearts into the love of God, and into the **patient waiting for** Christ.*	*Now may the Lord direct your hearts into the love of God and into the **patience of** Christ.*
patient waiting for— SC 5278: to stay under, persevere Lex: patient awaiting	Gutted!
This verse is about the Blessed Hope, which is the main context of this letter. (Especially see II Thess.1:7; 2:1.)	NASV, RSV, NRSV, ESV, NIV and HCSV agree with NKJV.

King James	New King James
I Tim.6:5a *Perverse disputings of men of corrupt minds, and destitute of the truth, supposing that **gain is godliness**:*	*Useless wranglings of men of corrupt minds and destitute of the truth, who suppose that **godliness is a means of gain**.*

These are quite different in meaning. NKJV needs to supply "**means of**" (without indicating as supplied) to make the verse say that these people were trying to use godliness for making money—which doesn't make much cents (sense); ask the true "godly" man who spends his money on ministry and seems poor. The literal Greek can be stated "holding gain to be godliness"—that is, the false idea that having lots of money is evidence that you have God's blessing (when in reality, having and holding on to wealth could actually be evidence against a person for misappropriation and false stewardship of God's money).
NASV, RSV, NRSV, ESV, HCSV, ERV and NIV agree with NKJV.

King James	New King James
I Tim.6:10 *For the love of money is **the root** of **all** evil: which while some coveted after, they have erred from the faith, and pierced themselves through with many sorrows.*	*For the love of money is **a root** of **all** **kinds of** evil, for which some have strayed from the faith in their greediness, and pierced themselves through with many sorrows.*

Isn't it interesting how the roaches run when the light is turned on—here in trying to blunt this precision revelation of the self motivation of "*all evil*" doers.

It is true that I Tim. 6:10 has no "the" (definite article) either, but if we leave out both the NKJV-supplied "a" and the KJ-supplied "the", the KJ Translation is preserved: "*For the love of money is root of all evil*". Also note the NKJV must also supply "*kinds of*" in trying to make their translation fly although it certainly doesn't seem to be required to translate the Greek.

Now, no one but the Lord Jesus Christ was ever totally right in his attitude towards the things of this world so let's each be brutally honest right now: consider that this "fondness of silver" syndrome (SC 5366 for "love" in I Tim. 6:10) even causes some to print bad bibles if there's a good profit in it.

Do look back at ENOUGH I Tim. 6:5 where there seems to be a similar scurrying to cover up the light by seven of the modern versions.
NASV, NRSV, ESV, HCSV, ERV and NIV agree with NKJV.

King James	New King James
I Tim.6:20b ... *vain babblings, and **oppositions** of **science** falsely so called*:	...*idle babblings and **contradictions** of what is falsely called **knowledge***

opposition— SC 477:
  antithesis, conflict of theories
science— SC 1108:
  knowledge used in a great
  variety of applications
Lex: knowledge of a special kind
and relatively high character
	"**Knowledge**" is an allowed translation here; but the context dictates that the best translation is **"science"** since we are talking about "antitheses", "conflict of theories" and "special", high character knowledge.

Webster says, "Science: knowledge covering general truths of the operation of general (verified) laws especially as obtained and tested through the Scientific Method". "Science" is *falsely so called* when theories are generated which have not been so arrived at and tested. "Science" (= "gnosis" in the Greek) was being abused by the "Gnostics" of the first century, whose theories would not stand up to the "Scientific Method" or "general laws". Their "babblings" were therefore an example of *science falsely so called*. Many types of "Gnostics" are with us today so this warning is still needed; and it is much more clearly given in the KJ than NKJV. NASV, RSV, NRSV, ESV, HCSV, and NIV agree with NKJV.	
II Tim.2:26b ... who are taken captive by him at his will.	... *having been taken captive by him to **do** his will.*
The "**do**" needed to be supplied for the NKJV reading; or, is it as in the KJ "taken captive" whenever Satan wills? The difference is very important practically; the KJ indicates that Satan has many (of us) on a leash— seemingly free—until Satan wills, and always at the worst possible time. NASV, NRSV, ESV, HCSV, and NIV agree with NKJV.	
II Tim.3:3a ***Without natural affection**,* SC 794: hard hearted towards kindred	*unloving,* So poor; general; un-literal translation. If your mother (kindred) doesn't love you, you are forlorn. NASV, HCSV, and NIV agree with NKJV.

King James	New King James
Heb.2:16 *For verily he took not on him the nature of angels; but he took on him the seed of Abraham.*	*For indeed He does not give aid to angels, but He does give aid to the seed of Abraham.*
The differences are totally in the translators' theology, not in the Greek text. To quote D. K. Madden, (see Ref.2), "It is sad that NKJV, ... has adopted the theologically inferior reading at Hebrews 2:16, which was first advocated by the Socinians [Unitarians], and continues to be so by their present day representatives, the Jehovah's Witnesses—see their "New World Translation". There were two, possibly three Unitarians on the 1870 committee with Westcott and Hort in the conversion of the TR into the Vatican Vaticanus. Unitarians are very vocal, like Jehovah Witnesses, in demanding their perversions.	This NKJV verse doesn't make sense. These non-sense verses (as we shall see) break the intricate chain of reasoning in the book of Hebrews, and thereby prevent understanding and being able to participate in God's purposes in *"the new testament in my blood"* (I Cor.11:25) which made the Mosaic covenant "old" (Heb.8:13) and opens the door to the Throne of Grace for whosoever truly wants to live with God.
NKJV editor Price says it is "ridiculous" to challenge the NKJV [ridiculous] translation here. The NKJV completely misses the dramatic and contextual statement of the hypostatic union—God and man in Christ	Without a good grasp of the Book of Hebrews, we just cannot participate in God's priority plans *"to the Jew first."*
What actually is being said here is that our God became a man—Abe's promised Son. *"Now to Abraham and his seed were the promises made...."* Gal.3:16	NASV, NRSV, ESV, HCSV, ERV and NIV agree with NKJV.

King James	New King James
Heb.3:8,15 *Harden not your hearts, as in the* **provocation**, *in the day of temptation in the wilderness*:	*Do not harden your hearts as in the* **rebellion**, *in the day of trial in the wilderness*,
provocation— SC 3894: <u>irritation</u>, from: <u>embitter alongside</u>, to <u>exasperate</u> These people were <u>tired</u> of serving God. (See conclusion of this argument in next comparison verse, Heb. 3:18,19.) They wanted to party and would even rather make bricks for Pharaoh "*in the land of Egypt, when we sat by the flesh pots*" (Ex.16:3). See Psalms 106.	"**Rebellion**" is the wrong word. It derails the entire analysis being made in the book of Hebrews. The word is to become "embittered", provoked at God in the heart (like an unthankful child gets so he will accept no discipline). This is hardening of heart towards God. RSV, NRSV, ESV, HCSV, NIV agree with NKJV.
Heb.3:18,19 *And to whom swear he that they should not enter into his rest, but to them that* **believed not**? (19) *So we see that they could not enter in because of unbelief.*	*And to whom did He swear that they would not enter His rest, but to those who did* **not obey**? (19) *So we see that they could not enter in because of unbelief.*
believed not— SC 544: <u>not convinced</u>; not <u>persuaded</u>	(Also see the KJ/NKJV comparison of Rom.11:30-32.)

The word should not be translated "**not obey**" here in v. 18, as shown by the conclusion in v.19 that the problem was "unbelief". After having failed to trust God in ten tests (Num.14:22)—what a personal insult or "provocation" (Heb.3:8,15) to God!—all the adults of Israel over twenty were guilty of <u>contempt</u> of God; their hearts had become un-persuadable (that is, they seemed fed up with the disciplines and rigors of being His people on this earth). Therefore they would not, and did not, enter into the Promised Land. Translating SC 544 in v. 18 "**not obey**" makes this strategic text unintelligible.

    Obedience is a work; faith (belief, persuasion) is our response to the grace of God, and to the God of grace, for salvation (Eph.2:8) and for entering into the victorious "living sacrifice" (Rom.12:1) Christian life as Jesus loves through us, calling out a people for His name and sabotaging Satan's system.

    See Heb.4:11-14 for the same fuzzy translation of "disobedience" for "unbelief". Dear Reader, do you want to cease from your own works

(your "obedience") and enter into the finished work of the Lord Jesus Christ? This isn't a textual problem here, it's, at best, poor translation in the NKJV preventing a grasp of the faith/rest life. KEY COMPARISON COMMENT: Here is why inerrancy of the Bible is under such attack! Read Heb.4:11-14 carefully. The "*word of God...is a discerner....Neither is there any creature that is not manifest in his sight...[our] great high priest...Jesus the Son of God.*" Do you see the union between the word of God and the Word, the Lord Jesus Christ? To attack the preservation of the Bible by these Dynamic Equivalent "corrections" is an attack on the perfection of the Lord Jesus Christ who promised to preserve His Word. Now who would want to do that? Would you?
NASV, RSV, NRSV, ESV, HCSV, and NIV agree with NKJV.

Heb.4:8a *For if **Jesus** had given them rest,*	*For if **Joshua** had given them rest,*
Jesus— SC 2424: Jesus (a word of Hebrew origin, Jeshoshua or "Joshua") "**Jesus**" is the Greek name for "Joshua".	A literal translation, not a paraphrase or Dynamic Equivalent commentary, must transliterate this Greek proper name "**Jesus**". This also points out that Jesus' name is indeed in the Old Testament many times – "**Joshua**" – which is a great surprise to many Jewish people who tend not to see the Jewishness of Jesus. See Acts 7:45 also. NASV, RSV, NRSV, ESV, NIV, ERV, and HCSV agree with NKJV.

King James	New King James
Heb.7:21b ... *The Lord swear and will not* **repent**, *Thou* <u>art</u> *a priest forever ...*	*... The* L<small>ORD</small> *has sworn and will not* **relent**, *You are a priest forever ...*
repent— SC 3338: to <u>care afterwards</u>, to <u>regret</u> Lex: to change one's judgment ...	"**Relent**" is a poor or even wrong word. It mainly implies "to slacken" or "become less severe". It does not mean "to change one's judgment".
Heb.10:35, (11**:**26) *Cast not away therefore your confidence, which hath great* **recompense of reward**.	*Therefore do not cast away your confidence, which has great reward.*

recompense of reward —
  SC 3405: from 3409 promise+
  SC591 reward: so, "recompense
  of reward" is working for an
  agreed upon wage
 	
In Heb. 11:26, we see how Moses simply walked away from everything the world was offering him (and he could have had it all) just on God's promise of the coming <u>wedding day</u> with Messiah. What a trust in God's Word—and we have the whole Word of God compared to Scripture Moses had!!
  Isn't this just as an engaged couple focuses everything on the wedding day, more than on the life which is to follow?
	This only translates half the word and leaves off the promise referring to "the marriage supper of the Lamb"! This is the primary and righteous motivation of those who actually produce for God! It's half-deleted from the modern bibles. There is a real cost to serving God rather than ourselves—and a real reward! These half-translations are the new translators' doing since both the TR and the Nestle-Aland have the same compound words which are fully translated in the KJ.
	
	NASV, RSV, NRSV, ESV, NIV, and HCSV agree with NKJV.

45

King James	New King James
Heb.12:13 *And make straight paths for your feet, lest that which is lame be **turned out of the way**, but let it rather be healed.*	*and make straight paths for your feet, so that what is lame may not be **dislocated**, but rather be healed.*
turned out of the way— SC 1624: to <u>deflect</u>, <u>turn away</u>	"Lame" is already **dislocated.** This translation doesn't hold water.

In this passage the Lord seems to be admonishing Christians not to stray from the path lest they mislead or fail to make a way for weaker ("lame") brothers following behind them. "**Dislocated**" is not a translation for "***turned out of the way.***" Doesn't NKJV drop the ball on this so needed admonition? Also, note that "dislocated" is supplied by the translators, by which they acknowledge that it is not literally in the Greek. A supplied word substituted in the place of the key word in the text! How often NKJV must supply words for translations which don't agree with the literally translated Greek or the context.
NASV, RSV, NRSV, ESV, HCSV, ERV and NIV basically agree with NKJV.

Hebrews 12:13

46

King James	New King James
James 1:6a *But let him ask in faith, nothing* **wavering**. *For he that* **wavereth** *is like a wave of the sea ...*	*But let him ask in faith, with no* **doubting**, *for he who* **doubts** *is like a wave of the sea ...*
wavering— SC 1252: to <u>separate</u> <u>thoroughly</u>,... <u>discriminate</u>, <u>hesitate</u>	

Isn't "**Doubt**" too general a word for SC1252? This is sad, for "he who hesitates is lost" the saying goes. This verse, in the KJ, is warning us that if we just keep on analyzing a problem, going over and over— "hesitating" to trust the "wisdom" that God will give us if we ask, as He promises in the preceding verse, then we can't rest on a decision; or we won't even take the action needed. (By the way, God's "wisdom", referred to in v.5, usually isn't a pat answer—it is His perspective! Selah)

Many trust Bible versions which accept doubts in the reliability of the Bible manuscripts from which they are translated, and then, having accepted human reason as a higher authority than God's promises of a preserved Bible, they feel free to go with liberties in translation. This whole mess makes total confidence in God impossible. It <u>causes</u> **wavering**, spiritual sterility: *"Let not that man think that he shall receive any thing of the Lord"* (James 1:7). Obviously!
NASV, RSV, NRSV, ESV, NIV, ERV and HCSV agree with NKJV.

King James	New King James
I Peter 1:7a That the **trial** of your faith,	*that the* **genuineness** *of your faith,*
trial— SC 1383: "<u>testing</u>", <u>current</u> [negotiable] money after <u>assayal</u> (by fire)	**(G)enuineness** seems a poor word for SC 1383.
In the old days, a random sample of gold was actually melted down to liquid to verify its purity—base metals would separate out from the gold. It was called "burnt money"; and you were credited only for	The word is "**trial**", to check the **genuineness**, and to prove (and refine) the faith by the trial.
the percentage of gold found in the sample.	RSV, NRSV, ESV, HCSV, ERV and NIV agree with NKJV.

47

King James	New King James
II Peter 3:5a *For this they **willingly are ignorant of**, that by the word of God the heavens were of old,*	*For this they **willfully forget**: that by the word of God the heavens were of old,*
willingly— SC 2309: to <u>choose</u>, prefer **Ignorant**— SC 2990: to <u>lie</u> hid, <u>unwitting</u>	They haven't forgotten. (The Greek word for "**forget**" isn't in this verse.) They refused to learn from Gen.1, refused to observe the "creation" scientifically and impartially to learn the truth.

His-story, Archeology, Geology, Biology, and other hard sciences (vs. scientism) confirm the "Scripture of truth" (Dan.10:21) because the Bible, while not a science textbook, is free of contradictions with our world full of data. Many scientists <u>choose</u> not to know this—look at the theories, like evilution, full of unexplained data and speculation. Please review I Tim.6:20 for help in understanding real science.
NIV, RSV, ESV, ERV agree with NKJV.

IN THE BEGINNING GOD CREATED

II Peter 3:5

King James	New King James
Jude 22 *And of some have compassion, making a **difference***: **difference**— SC 1252: to <u>separate</u> <u>thoroughly</u>, <u>hesitate</u>, <u>withdraw</u>, <u>decide</u> Cause them to hesitate and reconsider, on their way to hell!	*And on some have compassion, making a **distinction***; "**Distinction**" doesn't even make sense in this verse, does it? (HCSV has no "difference" or "distinction", but comes up with a doubtful "have mercy on some who doubt"? RSV, NRSV, ESV, NASV, NIV agree with NKJV.
Rev.1:15a *And his feet like unto fine brass, as if they **burned** in a furnace*; **burned**— SC 4448: to <u>kindle</u>, <u>glow</u>	*His feet <u>were</u> like fine brass, as if **refined** in a furnace*, The "glow" of molten metal is being referred to here, not a process of refining; this is the wrong word and/or commentary. Nothing about Christ needs "refining"! RSV, NRSV, and ESV agree with NKJV.
Rev.2:22a *Behold, I will cast her into a **bed**, and them that commit adultery with her ...* **bed**— SC 2825: <u>couch</u>	*Indeed I will cast her into a **sickbed**, and those who commit adultery with her ...* "**Sick**" is not in the Greek. Yet, it isn't indicated as supplied, and it isn't correct. The "bed" here is a harlot's bed! NASV, RSV, ESV, HCSV, ERV and NIV agree with NKJV.

Problems upon problems with the NKJV

King James	New King James
Rev.10:6 *And swear by him that liveth for ever and ever, who created heaven, and the things that therein are, and the earth, and the things that therein are, and the sea, and the things that are therein, that there should be* **time** *no longer.*	*and swore by Him who lives for ever and ever, who created heaven and the things that are in it, the earth and the things that are in it, and the sea and the things that are in it, that there should be* **delay** *no longer,*
time— SC 5550: a space of time ... <u>opportunity</u> Lex: Time, era, epoch, duration	"**Time**" is used over 30 times in the KJ New Testament in the normal sense of "**time**" and never as "**delay**".

Rev.10 is the center of the Revelation. It is the hub of the wheel, so to speak—the heart of THE REVELATION OF JESUS CHRIST. It is very difficult for any translator's personal (and limited) understanding, or especially his theological bias, not to affect how he translates a given word or verse—unless he knows both languages very well indeed and holds himself to a rigorous literal translation which must mesh simply with the context. This is the end of God's purposes in "**time**" begun in Gen.1:1, John 1:1. Note carefully the next verse, that "*in the days* [days are time] *of the voice of the seventh angel*" extend all the way from the midpoint of the Tribulation to "*the time of the dead that they should be judged ...*" (Rev.11:14-19; 20:5-15; 1000 years are still time), where, apparently, "**time**" as we know it ends—"*for there shall be no night there*" (Rev.21:25b). Doesn't "**delay**" throw out the wheel bearing off the hub, so to speak, of our understanding of THE REVELATION?

NASV, RSV, NRSV, ESV, and NIV agree with NKJV; HCSV says, "*there will no longer be an interval of time*".

King James	New King James
Rev.18:2 *And he cried mightily with a strong voice, saying, Babylon the great is fallen, is fallen, and is become the habitation of* **devils**, *and the hold of every foul spirit, and a cage of every unclean and hateful bird.*	*And he cried mightily with a loud voice, saying, "Babylon the great is fallen, is fallen, and has become a dwelling place of* **demons**, *a prison for every foul spirit, and a cage for every unclean and hated bird!*
devil— SC 1142: a supernatural spirit (of a bad nature), from: to <u>distribute</u> fortunes [Rev.12:9 The Devil = Satan] Webster's Collegiate Dict**:** (1.)"demon"**:** a guarding divinity, an attendant power (2.) "devil": a lesser evil spirit, a malignant spirit	Different (and not just New Age) dictionaries define "**demons**" as "Guiding Spirits", gods or demigods; yet define "**devils**" as those which "fight against the truth." This is precisely how the KJ refers to "**devils**", as evil spirits which "fight against the truth".

To translate Rev.18:2 "**devils**" as "**demons**" is allowed, but the KJ is not archaic here; isn't it a big BETTER? (1) Isn't calling Satan's demonic servants "**devils**" communicating better to people, especially in this so-called "Age of Aquarius" where most **demons** are said to be good and even to be served for the "fortunes" they will promise you. (It's called the "magician's bargain"—[evil] power in exchange for your soul!) (2) Couldn't this cause confusion in the Christian Battle? Knowing your enemy can make the difference between victory and defeat. Also, (3) even to the reader who properly understands demonology from the Bible, using the word "**devils**" (small d) would not be misleading.
NASV, RSV, NRSV, ESV, HCSV, and NIV agree with NKJV.

King James	New King James
Rev.19:8 *And to her was granted that she should be arrayed in fine linen, clean and white: for the fine linen is the* **righteousness** *of saints.*	*And to her it was granted to be arrayed in fine linen, clean and bright, for the fine linen is the* **righteous acts** *of the saints.*
Righteousness— SC 1345: <u>equitable deed</u>, from: 1344 <u>just</u>, <u>innocent</u>	This NKJV translation has serious incorrect doctrinal implications. Our wedding dress is purchased and provided by the Lamb, not by **righteous acts**/works we could do!

"... All our righteousnesses are as filthy rags ..." Isa. 64:6. *"He hath clothed me with the garments of salvation, he hath covered me with the robe of righteousness ..."* Isa. 61:10.

   "Rev.19:8 refers to that blessed Marriage of the Lamb and His wife the Church; and, on what I believe to be sound Scriptural grounds, I cannot believe for one moment that on this blessed occasion the bride would be, or even wish to be, covered with anything but that perfect Robe of Righteousness provided at such infinite cost by her Beloved Husband; most certainly I would loathe to be clothed with my own filthy rags." (D. K. Madden, Ref.2, p.17.)

   NKJV Editor James Price gives a defense of the NKJV "righteous acts" based on the special Greek word used here which could refer to "righteous acts", <u>but it is referring to the "righteous acts" of Christ,</u>

   " ... by the righteousness (righteous acts) of one the free gift came upon all men unto justification of life" (Rom. 5:18).

NASV, RSV, NRSV, ESV, HCSV, ERV and NIV agree with NKJV.

King James	New King James
Rev.20:13,14 *And the sea gave up the dead which were in it; and death and* **hell** *delivered up the dead which were in them: and they were judged every man according to their works. (14) And death and* **hell** *were cast into the lake of fire. This is the second death.*	*The sea gave up the dead who were in it, and Death and* **Hades** *delivered up the dead who were in them. And they were judged, each one according to his works. (14) Then Death and* **Hades** *were cast into the lake of fire. This is the second death.*
hell— SC 86: <u>unseen</u>, the place of departed ones	

Death and what? Both Greek words translated "**hell**" in the KJ New Testament refer to where those who "spit in his face" (Matt.26:67) go to await their everlasting swim in the Lake of Fire. NKJV just doesn't translate one of these words the 10 times it occurs. NKJV leaves it in the Greek—which is Greek to most readers—diluting God's gracious warning regarding a sure and terrible future judgment to those who reject Jesus. Basically, the NKJV has pulled down one-half of the warning signs to hell in the Bible.

Origen, Hort and J.B. Phillips say hell is "figurative". Westcott agrees, calling hell a "state" not a place. The Merriam Webster dictionary defines "Hades" as the "abode of the dead in Greek mythology". <u>A mythological place is different from the deadly reality of hell</u>, and the NKJV transliteration of "Hades" is especially dangerous because of how some New Agers, and Jehovah Witnesses find hope of just a "grave" (the NIV translates "Hades" as "the grave" most of the time, implying some second chance or, just oblivion?)

NASV, RSV, ESV, HCSV, and NIV agree with NKJV—including the Capital "H" which is not in the Greek or Hebrew.

OLD TESTAMENT

In one way this ENOUGH is not being entirely fair to the NKJV because we have not listed the many places where the NKJV accurately modernized word spelling where the progress of orthography (spelling) have required it. (Oh, that they would have just made such simple straight substitutions—as they had said initially was all they intended—and not thousands of <u>textual</u> changes. Please see inside of back cover about the King James 1611/2011 ("KJ2011") where this publisher has endeavored to do just that.)

Apart from many learned Jewish people who speak Hebrew, real Hebrew scholars are more rare than good Greek authorities. If Hebrew was the directly God-given language of Adam and Noah, it would be the most profound language on earth and would require greatness and humility to truly translate. We should expect the separation of the amateurs from the professionals when it comes to Bible translation of the O.T, especially since poor translation is more of a problem in the O.T. than the textual differences found in the N.T. battle for the Bible.

Let's see how KJ and NKJV do:

King James	New King James
Gen.2:4a [many other verses] *These are the **generations** ...* **generations—SC 8435:** descent, family Isn't "generations" a fine word for "generations"?	*This is the **history** ...* The word is "descent", "family" — more than **history**. (The NKJV translates this same Hebrew word "genealogy" in Gen.5:1.) The creator God appears to measure His program by the "family" of man. NASV and NIV say "account"; HCSV says "record".
Gen.2:7 [and many other verses] *And the LORD God formed man of the dust of the ground, and breathed into his nostrils the breath of life; and man became a living **soul**.* **soul— SC 5315:** a breathing creature i.e. (abstractly) vitality; from: "breath"; (passively) to be breathed upon, i.e. refreshed as if by a current of air The "soul" of man is a basic building block of the Bible—the same Hebrew word is translated "soul" in the KJ over 500 times. The NKJV's seemingly random substitution of synonyms seems to be distracting from this common theme.	*And the LORD God formed man of the dust of the ground, and breathed into his nostrils the breath of life; and man became a **living being**.* KEY COMPARISON COMMENT: Actually, the different synonyms substituted for "soul" are only in the beginning of many NKJV Bible books. Then the NKJV translates this word as "soul" towards the end, as if the translators got tired of changing out so many references —not because of any language or contextual reasons. "Soul" isn't the only word so changed. Really, the NKJV Old Testament sometimes seems to be a superficial revision of the English KJ, not an original translation of Hebrew—a revision that actually overall loses a lot. NASV, RSV, NRSV, ESV, NIV and HCSV agree with NKJV.

King James	New King James
Gen.2:13 *And the name of the second river is Gihon: the same is it that compasseth the whole land of* **Ethiopia**.	*The name of the second river is Gihon; it is the one which goes around the whole land of* **Cush**.
Ethiopia— SC 3568: <u>Cush</u> or <u>Ethiopia</u>, the name of a son of Ham, and his territory	

The "easier to understand" NKJV obscures simple geography here by not translating the Hebrew word (this is called "transliterating" = writing the Hebrew word in English). In 17 other occurrences of this Hebrew word in the Old Testament, NKJV translates it "Ethiopia". The KJ says "Ethiopia" all 19 times. There is no apparent textual reason for the NKJV to say "Cush" here, or in Isa. 45:14.
(NASV, RSV, HCSV, and NRSV agree with NKJV even to translating the same word "Ethiopia" in the other 17 places. NIV is at least consistent, translating "Cush" all 19 places.

King James	New King James
Gen.5:2 *Male and female created he them; and blessed them, and called their name* **Adam**, *in the day when they were created.*	*He created them male and female, and blessed them and called them* **mankind** *in the day they were created.*
Adam— SC 120: <u>ruddy</u>, i.e. a <u>human</u> <u>being</u>, an individual of the species <u>mankind</u>; from: "to <u>show blood</u>" (in the face) i.e. <u>flush</u> or <u>turn rosy</u> Eve had no name until Gen.3:20.	Doesn't this seem a bland translation? It really loses a lot— God's name for "mankind". NASV, RSV, NRSV, ESV, HCSV, and NIV agree with the NKJV.
Gen.6:5 *And God saw that the wickedness of man* <u>was</u> *great in the earth, and* <u>that</u> *every* **imagination** *of the thoughts of his heart* <u>was</u> *only evil continually.*	*Then the LORD saw that the wickedness of man* <u>was</u> *great in the earth, and* <u>that</u> *every* **intent** *of the thoughts of his heart* <u>was</u> *only evil continually.*
imagination— SC 3336: a <u>form</u>, <u>conception</u> (purpose); from: to <u>determine</u>, to form by <u>squeezing</u> into shape Thayer's Lex: frame, formation; meditation	(In Gen.8:21 the NKJV does translate this word "imagination".) "**Intent**" is a poor rendering of this imaginative Hebrew word picture. NASV agrees with the NKJV.

56

King James	New King James
Gen.16:6 *But Abram said unto Sarai, Behold, thy maid is in thy hand; do to her as it pleaseth thee. And when Sarai dealt hardly with her, she fled from her* **face**.	*so Abram said to Sarai, "Indeed your maid is in your hand; do to her as you please." And when Sarai dealt harshly with her, she fled from her* **presence**.
face— SC 6440: the <u>face</u> (as the part that <u>turns</u>) The Hebrew word picture here is of Hagar fleeing from an angry-faced Sarai. See Psalm 32:8. The <u>eyes</u> say it.	The word is "**face**". Of course, to flee from her **face** is to flee from her **presence**; but to say "**presence**" is paraphrase—not translation.. NASV, RSV, NRSV, ESV, NIV, and HCSV agree with the NKJV.
Gen.18:3; 24:2,45 *And said, My Lord, if now I have found favor in thy sight, pass not away,* **I pray thee**, *from thy servant*:	*and said, my Lord, if I have now found favor in Your sight, do not pass on by Your servant.*
I pray thee— SC 4994: a primary particle of incitement or entreaty, which may be rendered <u>I pray</u> Thayer's Lex: particle used in submissive and modest request Lex: respectful entreaty or exhortation	"**I pray thee**" is missing! Or is NKJV using a different Hebrew text than the Masoretic? Abraham would teach us how to talk to Almighty God—"in submissive and modest request". NASV, RSV, NRSV, ESV, NIV agree with the NKJV.
Gen.18:6b *... make cakes* **upon the hearth**.	*... and make cakes.*
upon— SC 5921: <u>above</u>, <u>over</u>, <u>upon</u>	"**Upon the hearth**" is deleted by the NKJV translators, or they are using a different Hebrew text. NASV, RSV, NRSV, ESV, NIV, and HCSV agree with the NKJV.

Please note the continuous litany of problems with the NKJV.

King James	New King James
Gen.18:11 *Now Abraham and Sarah were old and well stricken in age; and it ceased to be with Sarah* **after the manner of women**.	*Now Abraham and Sarah were old, well advanced in age; and Sarah had passed* **the age of child bearing**.
manner— SC 734: a well trodden road **women**— SC 802: ishshah, woman	This is not translation but is, rather, paraphrase or even commentary. The NKJV is supposed to be a Bible, not a commentary NASV, HCSV, and NIV agree with NKJV.
Gen.19:5 *And they called unto Lot, and said unto him, Where are the men which came in to thee this night? bring them out unto us, that we may* **know them**.	*And they called to Lot and said to him, "Where are the men who came to you tonight? Bring them out to us that we may* **know them carnally**."
know— SC 3045: to know; to ascertain by seeing; used in a great variety of senses	**"Carnally"** is indicated as supplied, but is it needed to translate the Hebrew? This seems commentary, true commentary, but not literal translation. NASV, HCSV, and NIV agree with NKJV.
Gen.19:15 *And when the morning arose, then the angels hastened Lot, saying, Arise, take thy wife, and thy two daughters, which are here; lest thou be consumed in the* **iniquity** *of the city.*	*When the morning dawned, the angels urged Lot to hurry, saying, "Arise, take your wife and your two daughters who are here, lest you be consumed in the* **punishment** *of the city."*
iniquity— SC 5771: perversity, evil	**"Punishment"** is the wrong word. NASV, RSV, NRSV, ESV, NIV, and HCSV agree with NKJV.

King James	New King James
Gen.22:14 *And Abraham called the name of that place* **Jehovah-jireh**: *as it is said <u>to</u> this day, In the mount of the* LORD *it shall be* **seen**.	*And Abraham called the name of the place,* **The-LORD-Will-Provide**; *as it is said <u>to</u> this day,* "*In the Mount of the* LORD *it shall be* **provided**."
Jehovah—jireh— SC 3070: <u>Jehovah will see</u> [to it], a symbolized name for mount Moriah. **jireh**— SC 7200: <u>to see</u> **seen**— SC 7200: <u>to see</u>	

The NKJV translators made a number of decisions not to translate certain words, but to transliterate them into English—such as "Sheol" for hell and "Cush" for Ethiopia (though they did this inconsistently, sometimes translating and sometimes not, without apparent textual reason). However, when it came to these names (see also Ex.17:15, Judges 6:24), which would seem to need to be given in Hebrew as proper names, they translate them into English—even though the immediate context of each name gives the meaning, as above. Furthermore, the NKJV "**provided**" is not the same as "**seen**". This is Mount Moriah, a very important place, with a proper name!
NASV, RSV, NRSV, ESV, HCSV, and NIV agree with NKJV.

King James	New King James
Gen.33:18a *And Jacob came to* **Shalem**, *a city of Shechem*,	*Then Jacob came* **safely** *to the city of Shechem*,
Shalem: Lex: this word is a proper name ["*Shalem, a city of Shechem*", not an adverb "safely"—quite different meanings.]	This seems mis–translation or translation from the wrong Hebrew.

KEY COMPARISON COMMENT: We do need to choose our "holy men" (and Bible translators) carefully. They make many important decisions that we are affected by. If we choose as our Bible virtually any of the modern Bible versions, then we are accepting as fact (because these versions do) that there is not a completely reliable Greek and Hebrew Bible available to translate from today. That is not true, as will be documented in Part II, "Scrollduggery", of this ENOUGH.
NASV, RSV, NRSV, ESV, NIV, and HCSV agree with NKJV.

King James	New King James
Gen.34:30a *And Jacob said to Simeon and Levi, Ye have troubled me to make me to **stink** among the inhabitants of the land,*	*Then Jacob said to Simeon and Levi, "You have troubled me by making me **obnoxious** among the inhabitants of the land,*
stink— SC 887: to <u>smell</u> bad	The word is "**stink**"; "**obnoxious**" is paraphrase, not translation. NASV, RSV, HCSV, and NRSV agree with NKJV.
Gen.37:28a *Then there passed by Midianites merchant-men; and **they** drew and lifted up Joseph out of the pit, and sold Joseph to the Ishmaelites for twenty **pieces** of silver:*	*Then Midianite traders passed by; so **the brothers** pulled Joseph up and lifted him out of the pit, and sold him to the Ishmaelites for twenty **shekels** of silver.*

"**The brothers**" is incorrectly supplied by the NKJV translators. The Hebrew is even more clear, "*Came Midianite traders and drew up and took Joseph and sold*". No previous "they" to find the antecedent for; but the antecedent for the KJ "they" is logically the Midianites. In the NKJV, just what do the "*Midianite traders*" do if not lift Joseph and sell him to the Ishmaelites? Furthermore, Gen.37:36 actually says that the Midianites sold him "*into Egypt*" (by selling him to the Ishmaelites who "*brought Joseph into Egypt*" Gen.37:28 & 39:1). Also, if **the brothers** had sold Joseph into Egypt, wouldn't they have even expected to find him there, instead of being totally surprised (Gen.42:8ff)?

  Some Bible commentators try to resolve the apparent contradictions here as to who sold Joseph down to Egypt by saying that Midianites and Ismaelites are two names used interchangeably for one group. However then, besides the fact that Midian and Ishmael were from two different lines of Abraham, it would appear to have the Midianites selling Joseph to themselves!

  "***Shekels*****" is not in the Hebrew** and is not needed or allowed. The "*shekel of the Sanctuary*" (Num.7:13) was a Jewish standard weight and amount of money; it is highly unlikely that it would be a medium of exchange between Midianites and Ishmaelites. Also, did Jacob use shekels at that early date hundreds of years before God initiated the sheckel of the sanctuary through Moses? "So what!" some will say— just that this is God's Word here. Change one place and much more is changed because of the infinitely interrelated self-consistent nature of the Word of God. THIS IS A KEY COMPARISON COMMENT: change anything and the Bible is "broken" (literally, "blows up" John 10:35). A $5000 Persian rug is only worth a few hundred dollars if it has one strand of the tapestry out of place! How much more with God's Word? It is priceless as given—or worth-less if knowingly changed anywhere—and especially so if systematically edited as in the modern bibles.

NIV agrees with NKJV about "the brothers";
NASV, RSV, NRSV, ESV say "shekels".

Gen.39:7 *And it came to pass after these things, that his master's wife* ***cast*** *her eyes upon Joseph; and she said, Lie with me.*	*And it came to pass after these things that his master's wife* ***cast longing*** *eyes on Joseph, and she said, "Lie with me."*
cast— SC 5375: to <u>lift</u> (great variety of applications)	

"**Longing**" isn't in the Hebrew; it isn't indicated as supplied by the NKJV translator as necessary to fully communicate the Hebrew, and it shouldn't be in a literal translation of the Bible. It seems true, but true commentary.
NASV and HCSV agree with NKJV.

Gen.49:6b ... *for in their anger they slew a man, and in their selfwill they* ***digged down a wall***.	... *For in their anger they slew a man, and in their self-will they* ***hamstrung an ox***.

digged— SC 6131: <u>pluck</u> up,
  (especially by the roots),
Thayer's Lex: to root out
wall— SC 7791: wall [the wall
  of Shechem]
	The word is "**digged**" dirt, not cut "**hamstring**" tendon. The difference between "ox" and "wall", in the Hebrew, is the placement of a dot in the center letter—kind of like what the Lord said about not a jot or a tittle passing until all be fulfilled (Matt.5:18).

Again, we must choose our holy men carefully, perhaps judging them by their faith or disbelief in God's promises to have inspired and preserved His Word!
NASV, RSV, NRSV , ESV, NIV, and HCSV agree with NKJV.

King James	New King James
Ex.3:22a *But every woman shall* ***borrow*** *of her neighbor, and of her that* ***sojourneth*** *in her house,*	*But every woman shall* ***ask*** *of her neighbor, namely, of her who* ***dwells*** *near her house,*

borrow— SC 7592: <u>request</u>, <u>demand</u> [The basic Hebrew word for <u>loan</u>, "shelah", from which came the English "Star Chamber" of political intrigues.] **sojourneth**— SC 1481: to <u>turn</u> aside, from: the road, <u>sojourn</u> (as a guest), to <u>shrink</u>, <u>fear</u> (as in a <u>strange</u> place) also to <u>gather</u> for hostility (as "<u>afraid</u>")	They were to "**borrow**"—maybe on the credit the Egyptians owed them for hundreds of years of slavery. Doesn't this NKJV rendering seem clumsy at best?

"*Sojourneth in her house*" perhaps pictures Egyptians (in terror of the plagues) moving in with Jewish families for safety. The (KJ) Bible indicates <u>two</u> sources of enrichment: neighbors and sojourners, in contrast with the NKJV just neighbors. (Of course a "*neighbor ... dwells near*"; this goes without saying, and the Bible never says anything without import.) This verse In the NKJV appears to have been cut to fit the translator's (incomplete) understanding of the situation, not the dictates of the Hebrew text!
NASV, NRSV, HCSV, and NIV agree with NKJV.

Ex.7:13a *And he* ***hardened*** *Pharaoh's heart,*	*And Pharaoh's heart* ***grew hard***,

hardened— SC 2388: to <u>fasten</u>; hence to <u>seize</u>, <u>be strong</u>, obstinate; to <u>bind</u>, <u>restrain</u>, <u>conquer</u> Lex: 3rd person singular: "he hardened"	The Hebrew says the Lord did it. In Ex.4:21 the Lord said, "*I will harden his heart*". It didn't just <u>grow hard</u>.

Using the primary means of Scripture interpretation as stated in I Cor.2:13 wherein the Holy Ghost teaches by comparing "*spiritual things with spiritual*"—that is by <u>comparing true parallel passages of Scripture</u>—properly uses the Bible as it's own best commentary on itself. Let's deal straight with what the Bible says about Divine sovereignty and human free will. The modern versions seem to want to create God according to their image or to translate the Bible after their own theology. THIS IS A KEY COMPARISON COMMENT. The modern versions seem to imply that God wouldn't violate Pharaoh's free will (harden his heart) or, on the other flank of theology, that Pharoah had no free will. But, see Rom.9:17-24, and note how graciously God hardened Pharaoh's heart—by enduring "*with much long suffering*" (Rom.9:22) Pharaoh's broken promises to God about letting Israel go.

NASV, RSV, HCSV, and NIV agree with NKJV.

Ex.9:32 *But the wheat and the rie were not smitten*: *for they <u>were</u> not grown up*.	*But the wheat and the spelt were not struck, for they <u>are</u> **late crops**.*
not grown up— SC 648: <u>unripe</u>	"**Late crops**" is cute and true commentary, not literal translation. NASV, NRSV, ESV, HCSV and NIV agree with NKJV.
Ex.10:19a *And the* Lord *turned a mighty strong west wind, which took away the locusts, and **cast** them into the Red sea;*	*And the* Lord *turned a very strong west wind, which took the locusts away and **blew** them into the Red Sea.*
cast— SC 8628: to <u>clatter</u> i.e. <u>slap</u> (the hands together), <u>clang</u> (an instrument); by analogy, to <u>drive</u> a nail or tent-pin	"**Blew**" is a very weak or wrong word. The Hebrew almost lets you hear all those hard hoppers <u>crashing</u> into the sea. HCSV agrees with NKJV.

King James	New King James
Ex.15:2b ... *he* <u>*is*</u> *my God, and I will prepare him an* **habitation**;	*... He* <u>*is*</u> *my God, and I will praise him*;
habitation— SC 5115: <u>rest</u> (as at home); Lex: to rest, settle down God's people live with Him.	Again, we seem to be losing a beautiful Hebrew word picture of Israel just leaving their home in Egypt and going <u>to live with God</u> in the promised land. Note: NKJV translates the same Hebrew word as "habitation" in Ex. 15:13. NASV, RSV, NRSV, ESV, NIV, and HCSV agree with NKJV.
Ex.32:34b ... *nevertheless in the day when I* **visit** *I will* **visit** *their sin upon them.*	*... Nevertheless, in the day when I* **visit** *for* **punishment**, *I will* **visit punishment** *upon them for their sin.*
visit — SC 6485: <u>visit</u>, with friendly or hostile intent; to <u>oversee</u>, <u>muster</u>, <u>charge</u>, <u>care for</u>, <u>miss</u>, <u>deposit</u>. Lex: to come to see This is a simple infinitive in both occurrences in this verse. That this is a visit upon their sin is stated, but the translation is just to "visit".	This is commentary; "**punishment**" isn't in the Hebrew, and it isn't even indicated as supplied in the NKJV. NASV, NRSV, HCSV, and NIV agree with NKJV.

"My house is <u>your</u> house, Oh my God!"

"Mi Casa es Su Casa o Dios Mio.

Exodus 15:2b

64

	King James	New King James
	Ex.34:13 *But ye shall destroy their altars, break down their **images**, and cut down their **groves**:*	*But you shall destroy their altars, break their **sacred** **pillars**, and cut down their **wooden images***
	images— SC 4676: something stationed, by anal, an <u>idol</u> Thayer's Lex: a statue, for example, "the image of an idol" See also Ex.23:24; II Kings 3:2; 10:26; Micah 5:13. **groves**— Lex: <u>groves</u>. Dict: a small (stand of) wood, usually without underbrush The **groves** were usually cut down as trees are cut down and are forbidden to be "planted" (Deut.16:21 KJ and NKJV). People did bad things in "the groves" (I Kings 15:13). Also note the repeated contrast made between the "images" (idols) and the "groves": I Kings 21:7; Ex.34:3 (above); Deut.7:5; II Chron.31:1; all of chapter 33; Isa.17:8; 37:9.	The NKJV's uniform translation of "**images**" as "**pillars**" (supplying "sacred") seems a poor if not strange translation for the "image" of an idol. To call "groves" = "**wooden images**" also is confusing. There is no "wooden" in the Hebrew; it seems commentary perhaps based on the context that the groves are to be burned. We have here a blurring of the translation of this often repeated, and therefore very important problem of idolatry. God says *"And I will pluck up* ["by the roots", "root out"] *the groves out of the midst of thee"* (Micah 5:14).

Groves are growing trees, not some sort of totem poles—secretive gardens (of trees) where the priestesses used their assets to seduce (God's) people. Is it not critical that these commands from God be clearly given regarding how to deal with idols (anything or anyone more important to us than God)?! John thought so; see I John 5:21.
NASV, RSV, NRSV, ESV, NIV, and HCSV agree with NKJV.

King James	New King James
Lev.8:15 *And he slew it; and Moses took the blood ....*	*And Moses killed it. Then he took the blood....*
The Hebrew says, **"He ... Moses";** it appears from v.14 that Aaron killed it. Doesn't it seem that it was Aaron's job as the High Priest to kill the animals?	Strange translation. RSV, NASV, and NIV agree with NKJV.

King James	New King James
Num.33:52 *Then ye shall drive out all the inhabitants of the land from before you, and destroy all their **pictures**, and destroy all their molten images, and quite pluck down all their high places*:	*then you shall drive out all the inhabitants of the land from before you, destroy all their **engraved stones**, destroy all their molded images, and demolish all their high places*;
pictures— SC 4906: a <u>figure</u> from: to <u>observe</u> Lex: <u>image</u>, <u>figure</u>	What?

This NKJV translation unfortunately deletes an inspired warning of one of the most pervasive and powerful last days' threats of mind manipulation and control—"**pictures**". Archeology verifies that "pictures" have always been a key part of false religion; should we be surprised if this intensifies? "*But as the days of Noe were, so also shall the coming of the Son of man be*" (Matt.24:37). The word is "**pictures**", not "**engraved stones**". "**Engraved stones**" just isn't in the Hebrew except as a commentary as to one way "figures" were portrayed. The "neurobiological theory of cerebral dissociation" indicates that T.V. with its soothing, repetitious sounds, monotonous 20 frames per second fixation of the eyes, usually experienced in a passive relaxed state of mind, is the perfect instrument for producing a light hypnosis and thereby causing a highly increased suggestibility". (Could this be why they call it T.V. "programing"?) Then consider how many Christians spend so much more time with the T.V. and videos than with the Bible.
NASV, RSV, NRSV, ESV, HCSV, and NIV agree with NKJV.

King James	New King James
Ruth 2:14b ... *And she sat beside the reapers*: *and he reached her parched* <u>corn</u>, *and she did eat, and was sufficed, and* **left**.	... *So she sat beside the reapers, and he passed parched* <u>grain</u> *to her, and she ate and was satisfied, and* **kept some back**.
left— SC 3498: to <u>exceed</u>, <u>remain</u>, <u>be</u> <u>left</u>

KJ is literally correct but not clear what was "left". | (Compare Ruth 2:18, "*and she brought forth, and gave to her that she had reserved after she was sufficed*".) NKJV seems better translated here.
NASV, NRSV, ESV, HCSV, and NIV agree with NKJV. |
| Ruth 3:3a *Wash thyself therefore, and anoint thee, and put thy* **raiment** *upon thee*, | *Therefore wash yourself and anoint yourself, put on your* **best garment**. |
| **raiment**— SC 8071: <u>dress</u>, <u>mantle</u> (a <u>cover</u>, as assuming the shape of what is under it)

Ruth was not told (as implied in the NKJV) to deck herself up and try to impress Boaz as someone other than just who she was—a fresh, clean young woman with fresh clean faith in God appealing to her Kinsman Redeemer. | "**Best**" is supplied in the NKJV. This is supposed to mean that the word is supplied by the translator because he felt that it was necessary in order to convey the Hebrew meaning in English. However, the Hebrew doesn't imply "best". This is misleading commentary.
NASV, RSV, NRSV, NIV, and HCSV agree with NKJV. |
| Ruth 3:9 *And he said, Who art thou? And she answered, I am Ruth thine hand maid:* **spread therefore thy skirt** *over thine handmaid; for thou art a* **near kinsman**. | *And he said, "Who are you?" So she answered, "I am Ruth, your maidservant. Take your maidservant* **under your wing**, *for you are a* **close relative**." |
| **skirt**— SC 3671: an edge, <u>extremity</u> (of a bird or army), a wing, (of a garment or bed-clothing) a flap
kinsman— SC 1350: to redeem (according to the oriental law of kinship), to be the next of kin (and as such) to <u>buy back</u> a relative's property and marry his widow. | "**Under your wing**" is a picturesque paraphrase which loses the picture of the Hebrew here. Verses 7 and 8 tell us that she "uncovered his feet". This was her appeal for redemption. His response, if willing, was to spread the hem of his robe over them both, which he did. There is nothing immoral here needing NKJV censorship.
(cont.→) |

Whether the present owner wanted to sell or not—he had to according to this ancient law of God, even as Satan must loose anyone who comes to Christ, our "**near kinsman**" (our "Kinsman Redeemer") for redemption.

What an awesome truth to translate as poorly as the NKJV does here. KEY COMPARISON COMMENT: A "Kinsman Redeemer" is also a "Kinsman Avenger". Will He not judge those who mess with His Words (Rev.22:18,19)?

"**Close relative**" throws the entire story out of focus. Yes, a "near kinsman" is a "close relative", but the "near kinsman" has the <u>right to redeem</u>—as the Lord Jesus, by His humanity, as our "Kinsman Redeemer", alone had the <u>right</u> to redeem the human race if He was willing to pay such a price. And He was and He did! HALLELUJAH!

NASV says "close relative" also.

Ruth 3:9

King James	New King James
Ruth 3:14 ... **a** woman ...	... **the** woman ...
	"**The**" doesn't make sense here. NASV, RSV, NRSV, and ESV agree with NKJV.
I Sam.1:5a *But unto Hannah he gave a* **worthy** *portion*; **worthy**— SC 639: to breathe hard [a portion that takes the breath away]	*But to Hannah he would give a* **double** *portion,* "**Double**" is a poor translation; it fogs the Hebrew word picture here. NASV, NRSV, ESV, NIV, and HCSV agree with NKJV.
I Sam.1:16b ... *A daughter of* **Belial**; ... **Belial**— SC 1100: without profit, worthlessness, destruction [Transliterated from the Hebrew into English because it is a proper name] "**Belial**" is a name for Satan and Company throughout the Word.	... *a* **wicked** *woman*, ... This is another Dynamic Equivalent paraphrase translation, which the NKJV prefaces said they did not do. NASV, RSV, NRSV, ESV, NIV, and HCSV agree with NKJV.
I Sam.2:1 *And Hannah prayed, and said, My heart rejoiceth in the LORD, mine horn is exalted in the LORD: my mouth is* **enlarged** *over mine enemies; because I rejoice in thy salvation.* **enlarged**— SC 7337: broaden, literally or figuratively Lex: to open wide as the mouth [to receive], to make room for This is a graphic word picture which could include smiling but obviously is much more.	*And Hannah prayed and said:* "*My heart rejoices in the LORD; my horn is exalted in the LORD. I* **smile** *at my enemies, because I rejoice in Your salvation.* "**Smile**" is an ingenious paraphrase —but it is a paraphrase, not a literal translation. Inserting "smile" into the other 20 places where 7337 is used in the Old Testament makes non-sense. The word refers to increasing capacity, stability, blessing. This would tend to cause a smile, but the literal translation is "enlarge over", not "smile at". RSV and HCSV agree with NKJV.

King James	New King James
I Sam.2:25a *If one man sins against another, the **judge** shall judge him: but if a man sin against the LORD, who shall entreat for him?*	*If one man sins against another, **God** will judge him. But if a man sins against the LORD, who will intercede for him?*
judge— SC 430: (elohiym) <u>gods</u> (with the article is the supreme God); occasionally applied by way of deference to <u>magistrates</u> [as here]	This translation of "**elohiym**" as "**God**", and not "**judge**", is wrong here. NASV, RSV, ESV, HCSV, and NIV agree with NKJV.
I Sam.5:9b *... and he smote the men of the city, both small and great, and they had emerods in their **secret parts**.*	*... and He struck the men of the city, both small and great, and tumors **broke out on them**.*
secret parts— SC 8368: to break out (as an eruption) Septuagint: "tumors in the groin"	Another example of censorship— not wanting to mention the "secret parts"? NASV, RSV, NRSV, ESV, NIV, and HCSV agree with NKJV.
I Sam.10:24 ***God save** the King*	***long live** the King*
Also see I Kings 1:25, 34, 39; II Kings 11:12; II Chron.23:11. Literally, from the Hebrew, the phrase is "you save the king" with "you" as the grammatically implied subject of this imperative sentence. There is <u>nothing</u> implied about how "long" he should live. A pronoun usually refers back to the last proper name or noun (which was Samuel). But, who saves? If the KJ didn't say "God", the reader might think that Samuel was being ordered to "save the King". The KING JAMES gives the glory to God, who alone can save anyone. NASV, RSV, NRSV, ESV, HCSV, and NIV agree with NKJV.	

King James	New King James
I Sam.14:14 *And that first slaughter, which Jonathan and his armorbearer made, was about twenty men, within as it were an half acre of land, <u>which **a yoke** of oxen might plow</u>.* **yoke**— SC 6776: <u>yoke</u> or <u>team</u> (a pair) (a day's task for a yoke of cattle to plough)	*That first slaughter which Jonathan and his armorbearer made was about twenty men within about half an acre of land.* Where's the "**yoke**"? This is not translation, or NKJV translated from the wrong Hebrew. It also loses the picture and flavor of the Hebrew —which is as if Jonathan and his aid were just plowing a field of the enemies of God. NASV, RSV, NRSV, ESV, NIV, and HCSV agree with NKJV.
I Sam.17:20 *and he came to the trench, as the host was going forth to fight, and shouted for the battle.* Isn't the Hebrew sense here that David was shouting for the battle, not as in the NKJV that the soldiers were shouting?	*And he came to the camp as the army was going out to the fight and shouting for the battle.* Realizing that David was the one shouting, the last NKJV sentence in this verse isn't good English. RSV, NRSV, ESV, HCSV, and NIV agree with NKJV.
I Sam.17:39 *And David girded his sword upon his armor, and he **assayed** to **go**; for he had not proved it. And David said unto Saul, I cannot **go** with these; for I have not proved <u>them</u>. And David put them off him.* **assayed**— SC 2974: to <u>undertake</u> as an act of will Lex: to be <u>willing</u>, <u>contented</u> **go**— SC 3212: primary root, <u>walk</u>—translated 40 different ways in the O.T. in a great variety of applications. To force this primary root meaning, "to walk", in this context seems superficial linguistically.	*David fastened his sword to his armor and **tried to walk**, for he had not tested <u>them</u>. And David said to Saul, "I cannot **walk** with these, for I have not tested <u>them</u>." So David took them off.* The pathetic picture we get is this spindly kid under a pile of armor (Saul's), <u>unable even to walk</u>. NKJV says "walk" twice, but "walk" doesn't make sense in this context. This very verse states twice the problem was not an inability to "walk", but that David hadn't proved armor in actual battle or at least wasn't proficient with it. What a shame to mess up this strategic introduction to David! NASV, RSV, NRSV, ESV, NIV, and HCSV agree with NKJV.

King James	New King James
I Sam.17:45 *Then said David to the Philistine, Thou comest to me with a sword, and with a spear, and with a **shield**:*	*Then David said to the Philistine, You come to me with a sword, with a spear, and with a **javelin***
shield:— SC 3591: something to <u>strike</u> with:–shield, spear, target.	What is the practical difference between a "spear" and a "**javelin**"?
Note that I Sam.17:6 describes Goliath as having "a target [same SC3591] of brass between his shoulders". This was a shield of some sort probably covering his back (possibly with a point in the center to strike with?).	I Sam.17:6 in NKJV says he had "a bronze **javelin** between his shoulders"; this doesn't even make sense.

Get the picture here: David's weapon was a sling. 17:7 says "one bearing a shield went before [Goliath]". This was certainly to protect Goliath from archers; and this shield bearer probably could deflect David's stone also. It looks as if David used psychological warfare here—he brought a shepherd's staff and no armor (or visible weapons) to so shame Goliath that he would at least make the contest one to one, i.e. no shield bearer. 17:47 does seem to set the conditions of the "duel"—"sword and spear", no shield. Also, if the shield bearer was there, David would not have been able to run up and finish Goliath off with Goliath's own sword. It worked; David won. The poor NKJV translation misses the fine points of the contest here. KEY COMPARISON COMMENT: This seems to be another place where the NKJV translators are over their heads in the Hebrew.

   We are not detracting from the wonder of God's deliverance of Israel here by portraying a fictitious superman David. Rather, think of the wonder of a faithful young man who so loved God that he so gave himself to whatever job God gave him to do, even the lowest job of caring for the sheep (and notice how he redeemed the time), that he practiced slinging stones <u>on the run</u> (17:48) when the only onlookers were sleepy sheep. That wasn't just a lucky shot!

King James	New King James
I Sam.18:21b ... *Wherefore Saul said to David, Thou shalt this day be my son in law **in <u>the one of the twain</u>**.*	*...Therefore Saul said to David **a second time**, "You shall be my son–in–law today."*
These verses are quite different. Does God's Word allow for such variety of reading? No! It seems to us that the context and a careful translation of each word yields the version found in the KJ—that Saul would keep his promise to give David one of his two daughters. RSV, HCSV agree with NKJV.	
I Sam.24:3a *And he came to the sheepcote by the way, where <u>was</u> a cave; and Saul went in **to cover his feet**:* **cover**— SC 5526: <u>fence in</u>, <u>protect</u>, <u>cover</u> **feet**— SC 7272: (plural of) <u>foot</u> Saul was sleepy.	*So he came to the sheepfold by the road*, where <u>was</u> a cave; *and Saul went in **to attend to his needs**.* This is pure (and inaccurate) Dynamic Equivalent paraphrase. NASV, RSV, NRSV, ESV, NIV, and HCSV agree with NKJV.
I Sam.25:12a *So David's young men **turned their way**, and went again,* **turned**— SC 2015: to turn about **way**: 1870 <u>road</u> (as <u>trodden</u>) <u>course</u>	*So David's young men **turned on their heels** and went back*; The NKJV seems better here.

73

King James	New King James
I Sam. 25:22 *(I Kings 16;11 also)* *So and more also do God unto the enemies of David, if I leave of all that <u>pertain</u> to him by the morning light **any that pisseth against the wall**.* **pisseth**— SC 8366: <u>make</u> <u>water</u>, i.e. <u>urinate</u> **wall**— SC 7023: a <u>wall</u>	"*May God do so, and more also, to the enemies of David, if I leave one **male** of all who <u>belong</u> to him by morning light.*" What is this, censorship? It is Dynamic Equivalent translation, changing a Hebrew clause into a noun, "**male**". NASV, RSV, NRSV, ESV, NIV, and HCSV agree with NKJV.
Ps.10:5 *His ways are always **grievous**; thy judgments <u>are</u> far above out of his sight: <u>as for</u> all his enemies, he **puffeth** at them.* **grievous**— SC 2342: to <u>twist</u>, <u>writhe</u> in pain (as in giving birth), or as in fear **puffeth**— SC 6315: <u>puff</u>, <u>blow</u>, <u>fan</u>, <u>utter</u>, <u>scoff</u>	*His ways are always **prospering**; Your judgments are far above, out of his sight; As for all his enemies, he **sneers** at them.* The Hebrew seems to say that the wicked are continuously in the throes of "giving birth" (to evil), not "**prospering**". Therefore, this first phrase is <u>mistranslated</u>. "**Sneer**" doesn't nearly capture the Hebrew here. NASV, RSV, NRSV, ESV, NIV, and HCSV agree with NKJV.

King James	New King James
Ps.11:6a *Upon the wicked he shall rain* **snares**,	*Upon the wicked He will rain* **coals**;
snares— SC 6341: a metallic sheet, a spring net Thayer's Lex: a net, a snare (especially of a fowler)	The Hebrew says "**snares**". RSV, NRSV, ESV, HCSV, NIV agree with NKJV; NASV allows "coals" in the footnotes.
Ps.12:5b *... now will I arise, saith the LORD; I will set* <u>him</u> **in safety from him that** *puffeth at him*.	*... Now will I arise," says the LORD;* "*I will set* <u>him</u> **in the safety for which he yearns**."
puffeth— SC 6315: to puff, to scoff (see Ps.10:5) Thayer's Lex: "to rail against anyone" Lex: to puff at, to rail at	This is a very different meaning. NASV, RSV, NRSV, ESV, NIV, and HCSV agree with NKJV.
Ps.12:8a *The wicked* **walk** *on every side, when the vilest men are exalted.*	*The wicked* **prowl** *on every side, When vileness is exalted among the sons of men.*
walk— SC 1980: to walk (in great variety of applications, literal and figurative) This is a pivotal Psalm and merits very careful study and translation because of the Scripture preservation promise in 12:6,7. Who could be more "vile" than those who understand the truth about God's preserved Word, but then try to contradict it or even give misinformation—as often done by many in the battle for the Bible.	This is the same Hebrew word translated "walk" by the NKJV in I Sam.17:39 where it seems so wrong. NASV, RSV, NRSV, ESV, NIV, and HCSV agree with NKJV.

King James	New King James
Ps.17:10 **They are enclosed in their own fat**: *with their mouth they speak proudly.*	**They have closed up their fat _hearts_**; *with their mouths they speak proudly.*
Thinking only about satisfying themselves—like eating (v.14 "... *whose belly thou fillest...");* they can only do proudly.	What does this mean "**closed up their fat hearts**"? Notice that the main word "hearts" had to be supplied to get the NKJV rendering. NASV, RSV, NRSV, ESV, NIV, and HCSV agree with NKJV.
Ps.17:13b, 14a ... *deliver my soul from the wicked,* **which is** *thy sword*: (14a) *From men* **which are** *thy hand, O LORD, from men of the world,* <u>which</u> <u>have</u> *their portion in <u>this</u> life,*	... *Deliver my life from the wicked* **with** *Your sword,* **With** *Your hand from men, O LORD, from men of the world* <u>who have</u> *their portion in <u>this</u> life,*

No, NOT "*from the wicked with Your sword*", BUT "*from the wicked, which is thy sword.*" God uses the wicked <u>as</u> His sword. ALSO, NOT "*with your hand from men*" (which makes non-sense) BUT,"*from men which are thy hand*". God <u>uses</u> these men of the world "*which have their portion* [only] *in this life*" as His hand, and so He certainly will keep them from preventing His willing servants from doing His will.

The second NKJV "With" is capitalized because it begins a stanza. This unfortunate NKJV practice injects thousands of capitalized words into sentences, sometimes with disastrous results. (See Dan.9:27 in this ENOUGH.)
NASV, RSV, NRSV, ESV, and NIV agree with NKJV.

| Ps.17:15 *As for me*, I will behold thy face in righteousness**:** *I shall be satisfied, when I awake,* **with** *thy likeness.* | *As for me, I will see Your face in righteousness*; *I shall be satisfied when I awake* **in** *Your likeness.* |

David doesn't seem to be saying he will be "in" God's likeness, but be satisfied "with" His likeness—with Him.

King James	New King James
Ps.30:4 *Sing unto the* Lord, *O ye saints of his, and give thanks at the remembrance of his* **holiness**.	*Sing praise to the* Lord, *you saints of His, And give thanks at the remembrance of His* **holy name**.
holiness— SC 6944: a <u>sacred</u> place or thing; from: <u>clean</u>	There is no "**name**" in the Hebrew, and it's not even indicated as supplied. NASV, RSV, NRSV, ESV, NIV, and HCSV agree with NKJV.
Ps.31:11a *I was a reproach among all mine enemies, but especially among my neighbors, and a* **fear** *to mine acquaintance: they that did see me without fled from me.*	*I am a reproach among all my enemies, But especially among my neighbors, And* <u>am</u> **repulsive** *to my acquaintances; Those who see me outside flee from me.*
fear— SC 6343: a (sudden) <u>alarm</u>; properly, the object feared; from: to <u>be startled</u>; to <u>fear</u> in general	Where did "**repulsive**" come from? It changes the message of this verse and is very different from "fear"—note those fleeing in fear in the last phrase. NIV and HCSV agree with NKJV.
Ps.32:4 *For day and night thy hand was heavy upon me:* *my* **moisture** *is turned into the drought of summer.* *Selah*	*For day and night Your hand was heavy upon me; my* **vitality** *was turned into the drought of summer.* *Selah*
moisture— SC 3955: <u>juice</u> (fresh)	"**Vitality**" sadly blurs the Hebrew word picture of a <u>dried up life</u>.
The true Bible is Almighty God's inspired and preserved Words. Let us find the literal translation of that Hebrew and Greek Bible in our language and then hang on His every Word. He says exactly what He means and means exactly what He says. NASV, HCSV, RSV, HCSV, and ESV agree with NKJV.	

King James	New King James
Ps.32:9 *Be not as the horse, or as the mule, which have no understanding: whose* **mouth** *must be held in with bit and bridle,* ***lest they come near unto thee***.	*Do not be like the horse or like the mule,* <u>*which*</u> *have no understanding, Which must be harnessed with bit and bridle,* ***Else they will not come near you***.
mouth— SC 5716: <u>headstall</u> [a part of a bridle] Thayer's Lex: many attribute to this word the significations of <u>mouth</u> **bit**— SC 4964: to <u>curb</u>, a <u>bit</u>; Dict: The part of a bridle that is placed in a horse's mouth **lest**— SC 1077: <u>not</u>, <u>lest</u>; Dict: for fear that	The last phrase of these two verses are <u>opposite</u> in meaning. The "mouth" has the metal "bit" so the animal can't come near the rider and bite him—or other "horse play"; and so they can be steered. The modern versions lack horse sense (horse lore) here. NASV, RSV, NRSV, ESV, NIV, and HCSV agree with NKJV.
Ps.35:11 **False** *witnesses did rise up; they laid to my charge* <u>*things*</u> *that I knew not.*	***Fierce*** *witnesses rise up; They ask me* <u>*things*</u> *that I do not know.*
false— Thayer's Lex: wrong or false	In the Hebrew, this verse says that the Psalmist was accused of things which he "knew not". If he didn't know what they were talking about, then the witnesses were **false** (not **fierce**). So different! Please leave the Psalms alone!. NASV, NRSV, ESV, HCSV, and NIV agree with NKJV.

King James	New King James
Ps.36:1 *The transgression of the wicked **saith** within my heart, that there is no fear of God before his eyes.*	*An **oracle** within my heart concerning the transgression of the wicked: There is no fear of God before his eyes.*
saith— Lex: to utter, speak, declare	**oracle**: Dict: one held to give divinely inspired answers or revelations
NKJV translates this same Hebrew word as "says" over 800 times. This KJ rendering seems clear— as in Proverbs 3:7 *"Fear the Lord and depart from evil."*	What is this "voice" in the heart? This poor paraphrase makes almost no sense, or sinister sense. NASV, RSV, NRSV, ESV, NIV, and HCSV agree with NKJV.
Ps.36:2 *For he flattereth himself in his own eyes, until his iniquity be found to be hateful.*	*For he flatters himself in his own eyes, When he finds out his iniquity and when he hates.* The NKJV verse is non-sense and doesn't follow the thought from v. 1 (through into v. 3). Some NKJV people really seem to be over their depth in the Hebrew language. NASV, RSV, NRSV, ESV, NIV, and HCSV agree with NKJV.
Ps.37:3 *Trust in the LORD, and do good; so shalt thou dwell in the land, and verily thou shalt be fed.*	*Trust in the LORD, and do good; dwell in the land, and feed on his faithfulness.*

Here the KJ is supplying a word. If the Hebrew requires the translator to supply a word in order to communicate in English, it must be done. The NKJV loses the progression of Psalm 37 by not supplying the word "so": "1. trust.... 2. do good.... 3. dwell... 4. be fed... ." Also, where does this "feed on His faithfulness" come from? It definitely doesn't seem to be in the Hebrew, which is talking about trusting God for our food (basic physical needs).
NASV agrees with NKJV.

King James	New King James
Ps.37:20 *and the enemies of the LORD* <u>shall be</u> **as the fat of lambs**: *they shall consume; into smoke shall they consume away.*	*And the enemies of the LORD,* ***like the splendor of the meadows***, *shall vanish. Into smoke they shall vanish away.*
fat— SC 3733: <u>plumpness</u>, a <u>ram</u> (as <u>fully grown</u> and <u>fat</u>), a <u>meadow</u> as <u>for sheep</u> Thayer's Lex: a lamb fattened and well fed Note how the wicked's selfish fatness makes their judgment hotter. Apparently God's just rewards work both ways—in blessing and in cursing.	This is another mixing of metaphors. Although the Hebrew allows "meadow," the message here is that the fat, in the fire on the altar of judgment, "into smoke … consumes(s) away—as the fat of rams was offered on the altar (Lev.3:14-16), and not like a brush fire! Besides, when a meadow is so dry that it will burn, the **splendor** is past. NASV, NRSV, ESV, HCSV, and NIV agree with NKJV.
Ps.50:1 *The mighty* **God**, <u>even</u> *the LORD, hath spoken,*	*The Mighty* **One***, God the LORD, Has spoken*
God— SC 430: <u>elohiym</u>, with the definite article (as here) the supreme <u>God</u>.	Where did this "**One**" come from? Not the Masoretic Hebrew text!
"**One**", with its New Age connotations is substituted for "**God**" in the NKJV. NASV, RSV, NIV agree with NKJV; NRSV and ESV agree with NKJV, but don't capitalize "one".	

King James	New King James
Ps.56:1,2a *Be merciful unto me, O God: for men would* **swallow** *me up; he fighting daily oppresseth me. (2a)Mine enemies would daily* **swallow** _me_ *up:*	*Be merciful to me, O God, for man would* **swallow** *me up; Fighting all day he oppresses me. (2a)My enemies would* **hound** _me_ *all day,*
swallow— SC 7602: <u>inhale</u> eagerly; figuratively to <u>covet</u>; by implication to <u>be angry</u>; also to <u>hasten</u> [same Hebrew word in verses 1 and 2.] Lex: <u>to draw in</u>, hence (1.) <u>to pant</u>, <u>gasp</u> (2.) <u>to breathe in, snuff up</u> the air, wind; <u>to pant for</u>, <u>desire</u> <u>eagerly</u>; of savage enemies, <u>to swallow up</u>, <u>destroy</u>	The modern versions often seem to carry to extremes translating the same word in the original with the same English word, irregardless of the context; but here the NKJV changes the second "**swallow**" into "**hound**" with no apparent textual reason.
There is no "hound" or "trample" here.	NASV, RSV, NRSV, ESV, HCSV, and NIV all say "trample" for "swallow" in v. 2—which seems similarly poor.

Ps.64:6b ... *both the inward* <u>thought</u> *of every one* <u>of them</u>, *and the heart* <u>is</u> *deep.*	*Both the inward thought and the heart of men are deep.*

The context here is that it is these "wicked" (v. 2) whose "heart" and "thought" is deep, not NKJV "of men" in general. Also, "men" isn't in the Hebrew, yet it is not indicated as supplied in the NKJV, and where is the KJ "every one" in the NKJV?
NASV, RSV, NRSV, ESV, and NIV agree with NKJV.

Ps.64:8a *So they shall make their own tongue to* **fall** *upon themselves:*	*So he will make them* **stumble** *over their own tongue;*
fall— SC 3782: to <u>totter</u>, <u>stumble</u>, <u>fall</u>	

"**Stumble**" is allowed here, but doesn't it blur the graphic Hebrew picture here of the tongue they "pointed" like a sword (in v. 3), which now falls upon them somewhat as Saul died by falling on his own sword (1 Samuel 31:4)—not "stumble over their own tongue".
NASV, RSV, NRSV, ESV, HCSV, and NIV agree with NKJV.

King James	New King James
Ps.68:30a *Rebuke the **company of spear men**, ... scatter thou the people <u>that</u> delight in war.*	*Rebuke the **beasts of the reeds**, ... Scatter the peoples <u>who</u> delight in war.*
company— SC 2416: <u>alive</u>, <u>strong</u> Lex: a living thing; a people, band, troop [Note: both KJ and NKJV translate this same word as "congregation" in v.10 of this same Psalm.] **spear men**— SC 7070: <u>reed</u>, (as <u>erect</u>), <u>rod</u>, <u>shaft</u>, [spear] That this verse is referring to "spearmen" is confirmed by the context of the verse which says *"scatter thou the people that delight in war."*	This translation seems quite off. KEY COMPARISON COMMENT: Dear reader: we who are making these comments don't doubt that we know less Hebrew than the NKJV scholars who translated these passages. Please continue to bear in mind that this is a comparison of the KJ and the NKJV—not the writers of this ENOUGH and the NKJV—to discover which translation communicates God's Words most clearly and most truly, and which version is using the preserved TR text. NASV, RSV, NRSV, ESV, NIV, and HCSV agree with NKJV.
Ps.68:35a *O God, <u>thou art</u> terrible **out** of thy holy places:*	*O God, <u>You are</u> more awesome **than** Your holy places.*
out— SC 4480: <u>from</u> or <u>out of</u> We note that the problem passages seem to be grouped together—see v.13 and v.30 (above) also; yet many Psalms have no problems noted. It is as if some parts of the NKJV are handled better than others. This is a KEY COMPARISON COMMENT. Remember that the KJ was independently translated by 14 different scholars in each passage, with the translations compared, and the best selected (as well as all the English people who knew Greek or Hebrew being able to make comments), thus catching poor or inaccurate translations.	This doesn't make sense. The immediate context refers to our God sending out His voice (v.33), His strength being seen in the clouds (v.34), and His giving "strength and power" (v.35) "from" or "out from" Him. In the early 1600's, a young preacher felt he had a better translation than the KJ. However, one of the KJ translators in the congregation explained that the translators had considered his rendering <u>and six others</u> and then explained why they translated the KJ the way they did.

King James	New King James
Ps.69:1 *Save me, O God; for the waters are come in unto* <u>*my*</u> ***soul***.	*Save me, O God! For the waters have come up to my* ***neck***.
soul— SC 5315: <u>soul</u>, <u>vitality</u>, <u>a breathing creature</u>

It is the basic Old Testament word for "soul", used over 500 times. The Psalm refers to "waters", "mire", and "the pit".   It's not talking about H_2O, nor waters rising to a physical "neck". | "**Neck**" does not seem indicated in the Hebrew.   This is a cute paraphrase, but it loses a lot. The human "soul" is the battleground.

NASV, RSV, NRSV, ESV, NIV, and HCSV agree with NKJV. |
| Ps.74:11 *Why withdrawest thou thy hand, even thy right hand? pluck* <u>*it*</u> *out of thy bosom.* | *Why do You withdraw Your hand, even Your right hand?* <u>*Take it out of Your bosom*</u> ***and destroy them***.

"**(A)nd destroy them**" is a commentary Dynamic Equivalent <u>addition</u> to the Words of God.

NASV, HCSV, and NIV agree with NKJV. |

King James	New King James
Ps.76:10 *Surely the wrath of men shall praise thee: the remainder of wrath shalt thou* **restrain.**	*Surely the wrath of man shall praise You; with the remainder of wrath You shall* **gird** *yourself.*
restrain— Thayer's Lex: can be translated "restrain" Lex: to <u>bind</u>...<u>straighten</u>...<u>dismay</u>	Does the second half of this verse make sense? Certainly not in the immediate context of v.12, "*He shall cut off the spirit of princes: he is terrible to the kings of the earth.*"

Please note, unless a person is a better Hebraist even than as a second language, he is dependent on second-hand sources such as the Strong's Dictionary, and Gesenius' Lexicon. This does seem to be the linguistic level of translation in many of these places where the KJ and NKJV differ—as here. Especially in the depth of expression of the Psalms and Proverbs is a total familiarity with both languages necessary. The writers of this ENOUGH see this grasp of the Hebrew language, overall, in the KJ. The NKJV was apparently done by a number of different people for the different books of the Bible—some of them obviously more competent and or careful than others—as the batching of problem passages is apparent even in this brief comparison. Also, please note that this verse has a very strategic message—one which must be clearly sounded forth. The message is that God uses even human wrath to His praise—and **restrains** that which is not part of His plan. KEY COMPARISON COMMENT: It is interesting where the confusion in translations often happens—in strategic passages! NASV, HCSV and NIV agree with NKJV; NRSV and ESV get lost altogether.

King James	New King James
Ps.77:2a *In the day of my trouble I sought the LORD:* **my sore ran in the night,** *and ceased not:*	*In the day of my trouble I sought the LORD;* **My hand was stretched out in the night** *without ceasing;*
sore— SC 3027: a "primary word" translated into over 70 different English words in the KJ O.T. Lex: <u>hand</u>; <u>power</u>, <u>strength</u>, <u>might</u>; <u>care</u>, **ran**— SC 5064: to <u>flow</u>; causatively, to <u>pour</u> out or down. [How does a "hand" "flow"?]	"**My hand was stretched out**" communicates the interesting idea of a person lifting his hands in worship, which seems foreign to the Hebrew picture being painted here in this context of a depleted, poured-out person. These "primary" Hebrew words require the full art of the Hebraist in order to paint the <u>true</u> picture. NASV, RSV, NRSV, ESV, NIV, and HCSV agree with NKJV.

King James	New King James
Ps.81:6 *I removed his shoulder from the burden: his hands were delivered from the* **pots**. **pots**— SC 1731: <u>pot</u> for <u>boiling</u>; from: to <u>boil</u>	"*I removed his shoulder from the burden; His hands were freed from the* **baskets**. Try to boil in a **basket**! Which is a heavier burden, a pot or a basket? NASV, RSV, NRSV, ESV, NIV, and HCSV agree with NKJV.
Ps.81:15 *The haters of the* LORD *should have submitted themselves unto him*: *but their* **time** *should have endured for ever.* **time**— SC 6256: <u>time</u>, <u>now</u>,<u>when</u>	*The haters of the* LORD *would* **pretend** *submission to Him, But their* **fate** *would endure forever.*
NKJV loses it here with this "**pretend**" (which, if appropriate, should be indicated as supplied since it isn't in the Hebrew). The context indicates that the haters <u>would</u> submit, not "**pretend**" to! The word "**fate**" is a mistranslation of "**time**". "Their time" refers to Israel, not to the "*haters of the* LORD"(see the next verse). KEY COMPARISON COMMENT: Our God's poems are so easily spoiled by clumsy translation. NKJV follows NASV in inserting "pretend". Even RSV, HCSV, and ESV don't "pretend", but the RSV does say "fate" instead of "time"; NRSV says "doom".	
Ps.84:5b *in whose heart* <u>are</u> *the* **ways** <u>of them</u>. **ways**— SC 4546: a <u>thoroughfare</u>; lit. a <u>viaduct</u>, a <u>staircase</u>; from: a <u>mound</u> [as a <u>high</u>way]	*Whose heart is set on* **pilgrimage**. This NKJV "**pilgrimage**" is para-phrase. It misses the inspired message that the man who relies for strength from the Lord deals from his heart. NASV, RSV, HCSV, and NIV agree with NKJV; NRSV and ESV comment: "*in whose heart are the highways of Zion*"—??
Ps.89:22a *The enemy shall not* **exact upon** *him*; **exact upon**— SC 5378: to <u>lend</u> on interest, to <u>dun</u> for a debt Thayer's Lex: a <u>creditor</u>, to "exact" or collect interest on a loan	*The enemy shall not* **outwit** *him*, "**Outwit**" is simply the wrong word and, therefore, drops the ball on the message which is that David would prosper (vs. 19-21), not be a debtor. NASV, RSV, NRSV, ESV, and HCSV agree with NKJV.

King James	New King James
Ps.94:19 *In the multitude of my* ***thoughts*** *within me thy comforts delight my soul.*	*In the multitude of my* ***anxieties*** *within me, Your comforts delight my soul.*
thoughts— SC 8312: <u>cogitation</u> (thinking, thoughts); from: <u>sentiments</u> A mind meditating on the Word has no room for "anxieties".	The word is "**thoughts**", not "**anxieties**". If your mind is full of anxieties, is there any room for comfort? This verse is meant to be a blessed testimony of the power of meditating ("cogitation ... thoughts") on the Word for comfort in crisis. NASV, RSV, NRSV, ESV, and HCSV agree with NKJV.
Ps.107:8a,15,21,31 *Oh that* <u>*men*</u> *would* ***praise*** *the* L<small>ORD</small> <u>*for*</u> *His goodness,*	*Oh, that* <u>*men*</u> *would give* ***thanks*** *to the* L<small>ORD</small> *for His goodness,*
praise— SC 3034: to <u>revere</u> or <u>worship</u> (with extended hands)	The Hebrew says "**praise**" more than "**thanks**"
We **thank** the Lord for His works; we **praise** Him for Himself—His "goodness", power, wisdom.... This seemingly minor difference is the heart of this Psalm (used four times). It is therefore very important to get it exactly right—in this Psalm, and in our lives! NASV, RSV, NRSV, ESV, NIV, and HCSV agree with NKJV.	
Ps.128:3 *Thy wife* <u>*shall be*</u> *as a fruitful vine* ***by the sides of thine house***: *thy children like olive plants round about thy table.*	*Your wife* <u>*shall be*</u> *like a fruitful vine* ***In the very heart of your house***, *Your children like olive plants All around your table.*
sides— SC 3411: <u>flank</u>, <u>rear</u> Lex: <u>side</u> of a tent, <u>a</u> side of a country, of a building	Vines need **sides**, to climb. The Hebrew word picture is of a God-blessed house like a bountiful garden with luxurious vines covering the walls. A vine in the center of the room couldn't go anywhere but be in the way underfoot. NASV, RSV, NRSV, ESV, NIV, and HCSV agree with NKJV.

King James	New King James
Ps.144:12 *... our daughters may be as* **corner stones***, polished after the similitude of a palace***:	*... our daughters may be as* **pillars***, sculptured in palace style;*
corner stone— SC 2106: a prominence, an angle (as projecting) a cornerstone	**Pillars** is off the mark for the women being the "cornerstone" of the family.
The cornerstone was for shooting the angles of the adjacent walls. It set the major direction of the building as the daughters, who will become wives and mothers, do to the family.	NASV, RSV, NRSV, and ESV agree with NKJV.
Prov.1:6a *To understand a proverb, and the* **interpretation***;*	*To understand a proverb and an* **enigma***,*
interpretation— SC 4426: a satire; from**:** to make mouths at (from effort to say a foreign language); to intercede, interpret	This is a poor translation— "**enigma**" is another name for a "proverb", not its **interpretation**.
	NASV, RSV, ESV, HCSV, and NRSV agree with NKJV.
Prov.6:13 *He winketh with his eyes, he* **speaketh** *with his feet, he* **teacheth** *with his fingers;*	*He winks with his eyes, He* **shuffles** *his feet, He* **points** *with his fingers;*
speaketh— SC 4448: speak (mostly poetically), say **teacheth**— SC 3384: to flow as water, to point out (as if aiming the finger), to teach	The NKJV translator here seems to be just seeing the physical surface of the words, not the word picture being painted.
This "wicked man" (v.12) is a contagious plague, "speaking" and "teaching" error in his every movement.	NASV, RSV, NRSV, and NIV agree in "points" and "shuffling"; except NIV and ESV say "signals" instead of "shuffles".

King James	New King James
Prov.8:30a *Then I was by him, <u>as</u> one* **brought up** <u>with him</u>: **brought up**— SC 539: <u>"amen"</u>, to <u>build up</u> or <u>support</u>, to <u>foster</u>, to <u>render</u> (or <u>be</u>) <u>sure</u>, <u>firm</u> or faithful, to <u>trust</u>, <u>permanent</u>, <u>true</u>	*Then I was beside Him, <u>as</u> a* **master craftsman**; A "master craftsman" isn't "*daily his delight*". The Hebrew word picture in this key Christological proverb is of a faithful son by the side of his father. NASV, RSV, NRSV, ESV, HCSV, and NIV agree with NKJV.
Prov.11:6 & 13:2,15 *The righteousness of the upright shall deliver them: but* **transgressors** *shall be taken in <u>their own</u> naughtiness.* **transgressor**— SC 898: to <u>cover</u> (with a garment) <u>act covertly</u>, to <u>pillage</u>	*The righteousness of the upright will deliver them, But the* **unfaithful** *will be caught by <u>their</u> lust.* "**Unfaithful**" is simply the wrong word. NIV agrees with NKJV.
Prov.12:26a *The righteous <u>is</u> more* **excellent** *than His neighbor.* **excellent**— SC 8446: <u>meander</u> (<u>guide</u>) about, especially for trade or reconnoitering	*The righteous should choose his friends carefully,* The NKJV has lost its way in verse 26 in this strange rendering. NIV and HCSV agree with NKJV.
Prov.14:23 *In all labor there is profit: but the* **talk** *of the lips <u>tendeth</u> only to penury.* **talk**— SC 1697: from a primary <u>word</u>; a <u>matter</u>, <u>cause</u>:- translated almost 100 different ways in the Old Testament.	*In all labor there is profit, but* **idle chatter** <u>leads</u> *only to poverty.* "**Idle chatter**" is too specific—poor translation. It's not just idle chatter, but talking in general instead of labor, that the warning is given here as leading to poverty. NASV, RSV, NRSV, ESV, NIV, and HCSV agree with NKJV.

King James	New King James
Prov.16:10 *A **divine sentence** is in the lips of the King: his mouth transgresseth not in judgment.*	***Divination** is on the lips of the king; his mouth must not transgress in judgment.*
divine sentence— SC 7081: to <u>determine</u> by <u>lot</u>, <u>divination</u> (including it's <u>fee</u>), <u>oracle</u>; from: to determine	This verse is a very important verse to get right! Again, we have a strategic promise messed with.
There is nothing in the NKJV rendering about the guaranteed divine direction to the one whom God puts in charge (of a family, a church, or a kingdom). God promises that his mouth need not transgress in judgment (but not that it cannot or "must not"). NASV and NIV agree with NKJV.	
Prov.17:26 *Also to punish the just is not good, nor to strike princes for **equity**.*	*Also, to punish the righteous is not good, Nor to strike princes for <u>their</u> **uprightness**.*
equity— SC 3476: the <u>right</u>; from: <u>straight</u> or <u>even</u>, <u>pleasant</u> (fair)	This NKJV verse misses the whole concept of "**equity**": matters of (personal) judgment or fairness— versus cases of law. NASV, NRSV, ESV, HCSV also
Prov.18:1 *Through desire a man, having separated himself, seeketh and **intermeddleth** with all wisdom.*	*A man who isolates himself seeks his own desire; He **rages** against all wise judgment.*
These are drastically different; they aren't both right. Certainly this man is separating himself from the will of the majority, but the majority is usually wrong. The KJ is clearly instructing us that to satisfy a longing often requires great (even violent) action and wisdom—a very positive and strategic message. The Hebrew doesn't say it's his "own (selfishness implied) desire". The Hebrew doesn't say he fights "against" wisdom, but acts "with" her. "*Seeketh and i**ntermeddleth**", not "*seeks his own desire; he **rages**". Both versions have the same basic words, but the NKJV rendering is so negative, as if the NKJV translator of Proverbs 18 just couldn't reconcile a Godly man "raging"—but remember what happened to those vendors in His Father's "House of Prayer", against whom Jesus had truly righteous indignation. We warmly invite any true Hebraists to enter the ring with insights on this text. NASV, RSV, NRSV, ESV, HCSV, and NIV agree with NKJV.	
Prov.18:8, & 26:22 *The words of a talebearer <u>are</u> as **wounds**, and they go down into the innermost parts of the belly.*	*The words of a talebearer <u>are</u> like **tasty trifles**, And they go down into the inmost body.*
wounds— SC 3859: to <u>burn</u> in; <u>rankle</u> Dict: "rankle"— a festering sore, serpent bite, to cause anger, bitterness	"**Tasty trifles**" have nothing to do with "**wounds**". This warning against gossip is gutted by this NKJV miss-translation. NASV, RSV, NRSV, ESV, NIV, and HCSV agree with NKJV.

89

King James	New King James
Prov.19:18 *Chasten thy son while there is hope, and let not thy soul spare for his* **crying**. **crying**— SC 4191: to <u>die</u>, to <u>kill</u>	*Chasten your son while there is hope, And do not set your heart on his* **destruction**.
NKJV apparently was misled by the word "**crying**", which usually is translated "to die". Isn't the message here that he <u>sounds</u> like he is dying when you punish him? Don't stop or "spare" the rod until he is corrected – and you may deliver his soul from Hell! (See Prov.23:13,14.) NASV, RSV, NRSV, ESV, HCSV and NIV agree with NKJV.	
Prov.19:22 *The desire of a man <u>is</u> his kindness*:	*What is desired in a man is kindness,*
Very different. Is not the message here that to help a person with what he "desires" is considered a kindness by him, as in the KJ. A "poor man" has many ways to be helped— and he will tend to appreciate the kindness. NASV, RSV, NRSV, ESV, HCSV, and NIV agree with NKJV.	
Prov.21:28 *A false witness shall perish*: *but the man that heareth speaketh* **constantly**. **constantly**— SC 5331: a <u>goal</u>, the bright object at a distance traveled towards; hence <u>splendor</u>, <u>truthfulness</u>, <u>confidence</u>	*A false witness shall perish, But the man who hears <u>him</u> will speak* **endlessly**. This NKJV verse makes no sense; the word "**constantly**" means "truthfully"—not "**endlessly**". A false witness doesn't speak constantly; his stories will (eventually) contradict themselves and catch him up in his lies, and so he perishes. NASV and NIV agree with NKJV; HCSV "successfully"

King James	New King James
Prov.25:14 *Whoso boasteth himself of a* **false gift** *is like clouds and wind without rain.*	*Whoever* **falsely** *boasts of* **giving** *Is* like *clouds and wind without rain.*

false— SC 8267: <u>untruth</u>, a <u>sham</u>;
  from: a <u>cheat</u>
gift— SC 4991: a present;
  from: to <u>give</u>

There's quite a difference in many of these verses. We need translators who are true Hebraists, as their first language, or the words sometimes swirl into arrangements where God's message is damaged (or even reversed as in Prov.18:1).
  Isn't this verse about judgment against "sham" people who promise life (water, "rain") to people, but don't have it to give and so can't deliver? (See Jude 12b.) Some of their followers even die!

King James	New King James
Prov.27:16 *Whosoever* **hideth** *her* **hideth** *the wind, and the* **ointment** *of his right hand, which* **bewrayeth** <u>*itself*</u>.	*Whosoever* **restrains** *her* **restrains** *the wind, and* **grasps oil** *with his right hand.*

hideth— SC 6845: to <u>hide</u>
 (by <u>covering</u> over), to <u>protect</u>
ointment— SC 8081: <u>oily</u>; as
  olive oil, (often perfumed)
bewrayeth— SC 7121: to <u>call</u>
  out, <u>accost</u>

Bomb out for NKJV on this verse. The word is "**hide**", not "**restrain**"; and "**grasps oil**" is nonsense. This scripture refers to the impossibility of hiding the stench of being related to a contentious woman (see preceding verse) as it is impossible not to smell perfume when it's on your own hand.
NASV, RSV, NRSV, ESV, NIV, and HCSV agree with NKJV.

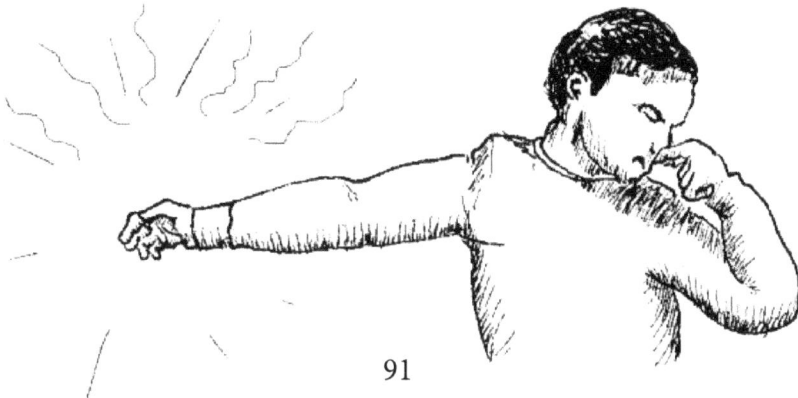

King James	New King James
Prov.29:7 *The righteous considereth the cause of the poor: but the wicked* **regardeth not to know it**.	*The righteous considers the cause of the poor,* **But** *the wicked* **does not understand** **such** **knowledge**.
regardeth— SC 995: to separate, distinguish, understand	Doesn't it seem as if the NKJV "does not understand" the Hebrew?
Isn't the message, as in the KJ, that the wicked choose not to look—so they won't have a guilty conscience when they do nothing to help.	NASV, RSV, NRSV, ESV, and HCSV agree with NKJV.
Prov.29:9 *If a wise man contendeth with a foolish man, whether he rage or laugh, there is no rest.*	*If a wise man contends with a foolish man, whether the fool rages or laughs, there is no peace.*
NKJV says in Prov 29:9b that it is the fool who is "raging or laughing". "The fool" is indicated as supplied in order to say this interpretation. However, since it is the wise man who is "contending" in this verse, it would be he who is trying to resolve the issues; if he gets angry or tries to be friendly, it's no good with a fool. Again, NKJV seems over their depth in the Hebrew. NASV, RSV, NRSV, ESV, HCSV, and NIV agree with NKJV.	
Prov.29:18 *Where there is no vision, the people* **perish**: *but he that keepeth the law, happy is he.*	*Where there is no revelation, the people* **cast off restraint**; *But happy is he who keeps the law.*
perish— SC 6544: loosen, expose, dismiss:– avenge, (make) naked, perish Thayer's Lex: Niphil stem (passive voice) make lawless, from: naked	**"Cast off restraint"** is not correct since it is active voice. The Hebrew here is passive voice. This action is done to the people. Lawlessness is worthy of perishing before the Holy God, but the word of the "vision" of God's servants shows how the law breaker can be forgiven and then how to keep the law and so be happy.
	NASV, RSV, NRSV, ESV, NIV, and HCSV agree with NKJV.

King James	New King James
Prov.29:24 *Whoso is partner with a thief hateth his own soul:* **he heareth cursing***, and bewrayeth* it *not.*	*Whoever is partner with a thief hates his own life; he* **swears to tell the truth***, but reveals nothing.*

cursing— SC 423: <u>imprecation</u> (= to pray against)
 	
   Again, notice how certain localized NKJV texts have lots of problems—as if they weren't "translated" as well as others: Prov.29:7,9,10,18,24.
   Changing "heareth cursing" into a clause *"he swears to tell the truth"* is pure Dynamic Equivalency (and incorrect) interpretation translation, changing the Masoretic text.
	This NKJV verse doesn't wash. Isn't the message, as in the KJ, that he hears the "cursing" of those who have been robbed, or any other wrong, and knows who the thief is but says nothing— and thereby is a "partner", an accessory, to the crime. Having broken down justice, he will find none himself when he is wronged; so he hates his own soul to not see that justice is done.

Ecc.5:20 *For he shall not much remember the days of his life; because God* **answereth** <u>him</u> *in the joy of his heart.·*	*For he will not dwell unduly on the days of his life, because God* **keeps** <u>him</u> **busy** *with the joy of his heart.*

answereth— SC 6030: to <u>eye</u>,
   to <u>heed</u>, <u>pay</u> <u>attention</u>, <u>begin</u>
   to speak	

Talk about taking poetic licence—this NKJV translation apparently reverses the message here. The KJ (and the Hebrew) says that which lasts are the "heart" matters. The NKJV says just keeping busy with the temporal stuff is the joy of the heart.
   In translating poetry, both languages must be known by heart. This often doesn't seem to be the case with the NKJV.

NASV, RSV, NRSV, ESV, HCSV, and NIV basically agree with NKJV's "keep(ing) busy" idea.

King James	New King James
Isa.1:12 *When ye come to appear before me, who hath required this at your hand, to **tread** my courts?*	*When you come to appear before Me, Who has required this from your hand, To **trample** My courts?*
tread— SC 7429: <u>tread</u> upon (as a potter) in walking or abusively	"**Trample**" is an allowed translation, but it <u>violates</u> the entire context of Isa.1:10-15 which says that they are very religious and outwardly pious with solemn sacrifices (v.11), assemblies (v.13), feasts (v.14) and prayers (v.15). So they aren't trampling His courts, but are frequenting them without worship. NASV, RSV, NRSV, ESV, NIV, and HCSV agree with NKJV.
Isa.1:29,30 *For they shall be ashamed of the **oaks** which ye have desired, and ye shall be confounded for the gardens that ye have chosen. (30) For ye shall be as an **oak** whose leaf fadeth, and as a garden that hath no water.*	*For they shall be ashamed of the **terebinth trees** Which you have desired; And you shall be embarrassed because of the gardens Which you have chosen. (30) For you shall be a **terebinth** whose leaf fades, And as a garden that has no water.*
oak— SC 424: an <u>oak</u> or other strong tree; from: <u>strength</u>, hence anything <u>strong</u>	What is a **terebinth tree**?

NKJV translates the same Hebrew word "**oak**" in Isa.2:13,6:13 and 44:14. What is the point and authority for diverting the attention of the reader to this interesting specific name of a tree, when "**oak**" seems an accurate translation, used over 20 times in the Old Testament?
  Introducing this botanical curiosity is confusing in many passages.

King James	New King James
Isa.6:13b ... *and as an oak, whose* **substance** *is in them, when they* **cast** *their leaves*: ... **substance**— SC 4678: something <u>stationary</u>, the <u>stock</u> of a tree [not necessarily a "stump"] **cast**— SC 7995: a <u>felling</u>; from: <u>throw</u> out, down or away	... *or as an oak, Whose* **stump** <u>*remains*</u> *when it is* **cut** *down*. The point seems to be that life will still be there even when Israel is in deep spiritual winter—a bare winter tree, as in the KJ. "Cutting" down doesn't allow the sap to retreat down into the trunk, so the life could be lost. NASV, RSV, NRSV, ESV, NIV, and HCSV agree with NKJV.

Isaiah 6:13b

95

King James	New King James
Isa.7.2a *And it was told the house of David, saying, Syria is **confederate** with Ephraim.*	*And it was told to the house of David, saying, "Syria's forces are **deployed** in Ephraim."*
confederate— SC 5117: <u>rest</u>, <u>settle</u> down, used in a great variety of applications Lex: <u>place</u>, <u>deposit</u>	This is a striking statement, but not a literal translation at all! This is the Bible, the Word of God, not a screen play written for effect. Verse one says that Syria had joined forces with "Israel" to attack Jerusalem—not that they had formed battle lines ("deployed") in Ephraim ("Israel" is "Ephraim"). NASV and HCSV agree with NKJV.
Isa.7:4b ... *Take heed, and be quiet; fear not, neither be fainthearted for the two **tails** of these smoking firebrands, ...*	*... Take heed, and be quiet; do not fear or be faint hearted for these two **stubs** of smoking firebrands, ...*
tails— SC 2180: (<u>flapping</u>) <u>tail</u>; from: to <u>wag</u>	Where did NKJV get "**stubs**" from? The Word says "**tails**"; "**stubs**" don't "flap" or "wag". NASV, RSV, NRSV, ESV, NIV, and HCSV agree with NKJV.
Isa.14:15 *Yet thou shalt be brought down to **hell**, to the sides of the pit.*	*Yet you shall be brought down to **Sheol**, to the lowest depths of the Pit.*

Hell has no vengeance like the wrath of a woman—**Sheol** get even! Why this Hebrew lesson here, and only randomly in 13 of the 32 occurrences of this Hebrew word in the Old Testament? Even in v. 9 of this same chapter "**sheol**" is translated "**hell**" in NKJV. Also, note that "**sheol**" and "pit" are personalized (as in pantheism) by being capitalized. This is a commentary since it isn't capitalized in the Hebrew. (Do see comparison of Rev.20:13,14 for the New Testament discussion of this same problem.)
NASV, RSV, NRSV, ESV, and HCSV agree with NKJV.

King James	New King James
Dan.9:27 *And he shall confirm the covenant with many for one week:* *and in the midst of the week he shall cause the sacrifice and oblation to cease, and for the overspreading of abominations **he** shall make it desolate, even until the consummation, and that determined shall be poured upon the desolate.*	*Then he shall confirm a covenant with many for one week; But in the middle of the week He shall bring an end to sacrifice and offering. And on the wing of abominations shall be **one** who makes desolate, Even until the consummation, which is determined, Is poured out on the desolate.”*

Please consider the following three problems with NKJV here: (1) Who is this second party, this "**one**", in this NKJV verse? This "**one**" is the Anti-Christ; so "**he**" that shall confirm the covenant for 7 years would then have to be the Messiah of v.26a. Whoa there! There is no second party in this verse. It's all done by the Anti-Christ, and this man-handled Hebrew by NKJV crashes the precise, complex prophetic picture God gave to Daniel. (2) See comparison of Ps.50:1 for what is terribly wrong with this "**one**". (3) Note that "that determined" to be poured upon "the desolate" is not the "consummation".

Is this poor Hebrew and/or translating from the wrong Hebrew text? Whichever accounts for these miss-translations, the effect is, at best, confusion of an absolutely strategic prophetic text.

Finally, in the light of the NKJV commentary capitalization of pronouns they judge refer to God, see the serious confusion caused since the NKJV also capitalizes thousands of other words at the head of each of the poetic stanzas into which they have recast the entire book of Psalms and other texts . When these texts are quoted in regular text format, we find a lot of capitalized words in the middle of sentences. (See NKJV Ps.77:2a; Ps.81:6 in this ENOUGH, where the Psalmist appears deified.) Here in Daniel 9:27 "... *in the middle of the week He shall bring an end to sacrifice ...*" —by the capitalized He, the Antichrist is apparently called God!

NASV, HCSV, and RSV agree with NKJV's "*one who makes desolate*"; NRSV and ESV seem hopelessly lost.

King James	New King James
Zech.3:8b ... *For they are men* **wondered** *at*: ...	... *For they are a* **wondrous** *sign*; ...
wonder— SC 4159: conspicuousness, a <u>miracle</u>, a <u>token</u> or <u>omen</u>	This NKJV translation obscures a beautiful and important message—that the faithful co-workers (the team) of God's servants are a great testimony in their own right! NASV, HCSV, and NIV agree with NKJV.
Zech.13:6 *And <u>one</u> shall say unto him, What <u>are</u> these wounds in thine* **hands?** *Then he shall answer,* <u>*those*</u> *with which I was wounded <u>in</u> the house of my friends.* **hands**— SC 3027: <u>hands</u>	*And <u>one</u> will say to him, "What are these wounds* **between your arms?**" *Then he will answer, '<u>Those</u> with which I was wounded in the house of my friends'.*

What are wounds "**between your arms**"? <u>Then notice the chaos of the clones.</u> In this text, the clones only agree in disagreeing with the KJ. NASV agrees with NKJV; RSV and ESV say "wounds in your back"; NRSV "wounds in your chest" with a footnote giving "wounds between your hands" as an alternate; NIV "wounds on your body" and the same footnote as NRSV; HCSV "wounds on your chest".

♫

"In Heaven the only thing made by man are the wounds in the Saviour's hands." ♪

BIBLE BUSTERS BEWARE:

"I LIFT UP MY HAND TO HEAVEN, AND SAY I LIVE FOR EVER.
IF I WHET MY GLITTERING SWORD, AND MINE HAND TAKE
HOLD ON JUDGMENT; I WILL RENDER VENGEANCE TO MINE
ENEMIES, AND WILL REWARD THEM THAT HATE ME."

DEUTERONOMY 32:41

AND

"I TESTIFY UNTO EVERY MAN THAT HEARETH THE WORDS
OF THE PROPHECY OF THIS BOOK, IF ANY MAN SHALL ADD
UNTO THESE THINGS, GOD SHALL ADD UNTO HIM THE
PLAGUES THAT ARE WRITTEN IN THIS BOOK: AND IF ANY MAN
SHALL TAKE AWAY FROM THE WORDS OF THE BOOK OF THIS
PROPHECY, GOD SHALL TAKE AWAY HIS PART OUT OF THE
BOOK OF LIFE, AND OUT OF THE HOLY CITY, AND FROM THE
THINGS WHICH ARE WRITTEN IN THIS BOOK."

REVELATION 22:18,19

SO,

"Don't mess with Textus (Receptus)".

("Don't Mess with Texas" is an anti-litter campaign in Texas)

TIME-TESTED ANSWER

Illustration was adapted for this ENOUGH.

PART II: SCROLLDUGGERY[*]

The New King James Version (NKJV) doesn't have the old English, but please join us as we examine it, together with its prefaces and footnotes, for faithfulness to the "Originals", in the light of:

1.) God's contract (covenant) promises to preserve His Word;
2.) the established principles of manuscript copying through time;
3.) the readings of 98% of ancient manuscripts (the "majority" text);
4.) the 3:1 testimony of the Church Fathers for the K J manuscripts;
5.) the 2:1 testimony of the 1st-3rd Century Papyri in favor of the KJ;
6.) the overwhelming support for the KJ by the oldest translations;
7.) the proper application of the Laws of Evidence themselves.

This is a trial for fraud—"Scrollduggery". (Please see Appendix G, p. 181, to appreciate the courtroom drama here.) God has made many covenants (contracts) with mankind. One of those contracts guarantees that His Words will be preserved. The **modern Bible** versions change the "language" (the precise words signed) of those contracts. Any attorney or judge will tell you that unilateral changing of contract language is fraud.

In the process of "canonization" (= the Divinely supervised selection of which books belong in the Bible), early believers were simply obeying the command given in II Peter 3:2, "*That ye may be mindful of the words which were spoken before by the holy prophets,*[the Old Testament] *and of the commandment of us the apostles of the Lord and Saviour* [the New Testament]". Notice that Peter said "words", as did Paul in II Tim.1:13—the precise words of inspired, preserved written Scripture. God knew that these words would be under attack: "*That ye be not soon shaken in mind, or be troubled, neither by spirit, nor by word, nor by letter as from us,....*"(II Thess.2:2). God foresaw the brash lawlessness of Westcott and Hort and those who chose to follow them. While the Apostle Paul still lived, there were those who forged his name on their letters. "*For I know this, that after my departing shall grievous wolves enter in among you, not sparing the flock. Also of your own selves shall men arise, speaking perverse things, to draw away disciples*

---

[*]A play on "skullduggery: underhanded or unscrupulous behavior"

after them. Therefore watch, and remember, that by the space of three years I ceased not to warn everyone night and day with tears" (Acts 20:29-31). Church Father Irenaeus said concerning Marcion the Gnostic: "Wherefore also Marcion and his followers have betaken themselves to mutilating the Scriptures, not acknowledging some books at all; and, curtailing the Gospel according to Luke, and the epistles of Paul, they assert that these alone are authentic, which they have themselves shortened" (Ref.16,p.187). Jude challenged believers to *"earnestly contend for the faith which was once delivered unto the saints"*s (not to the scholars; some "saints" are scholars, but certainly not all scholars are saints). Isn't the Bible here commanding us to make an issue of where the promised preserved Bible is today?

We sincerely suggest that the general question being addressed here in this entire book: "Have God's Words been preserved to our day?" must be answered "yes!" for any search or defense of the Truth to be successful. The Remnant *"sheep of my pasture"* (Jeremiah 23:1-3) **expect** Him to keep those many promises to preserve His Words: Psalm 12:6,7; 78:1-7; 105:7-11; 119:89,152,160; Pro.22:20,21; Eccl.3:14; Isa.40:7,8; Matt.4:4; 5:17,18; 24:35; John 10:35; 14:26; 15:26,27; 16:12,13; Col.1:17; I Peter 1:23–25.... If you don't, maybe you aren't!

Scrollduggery is a supernatural plot that has been thickening since Satan so effectively perpetrated the first "Dynamic Equivalency" (Appendix F, p. 179) perversion of the Words of God in the Garden of Eden when he deceived Eve (Gen.3). This won't be a trivial trial since Satan can get the best justice money can buy from most people; for *"the love of money is the root of all evil"* (1 Tim. 6:10). There will be a lot of pro and con testimony, and the Lord Jesus warns us four times in the Olivet Discourse about not being "deceived". (We who respect the Lord, pay close attention whenever He repeats something just <u>once</u>!)

THE PROPHETICALLY AUTHORIZED REFINING PROCESS

The resolution to this seemingly endless back and forth "bible, bible, who's got the Bible?" con game seems to have been right before our eyes all along: Psalm 12:6, "*The words of the Lord are pure words: as silver tried in a furnace of earth, purified seven times*" prophesies that the preservation of the inerrant Words of God will be by a historical "seven"-fold refining process of the majority manuscripts (of course, ignoring the 1% of obviously deviating and/ or adulterated "refuse" copies)—1-3.)Erasmus then 4.) Stephanus, 5.) Beza (augmented by his receiving the Waldensian "Italia" MSS), 6.) King James translators (who made 190 more refinements on Beza)...with the 7th revision (signifying "completion") ongoing until Jesus returns. Psalm 12:7 promises that God will "preserve" ("maintain") these pure words pure ("preserve" agrees in person grammatically with "words" in v.6).

This refining process acknowledges that some impurities have gotten into even the majority manuscripts, (no two of them are exactly alike). This is the 99.9999% fine "Textus Receptus" Hebrew and Greek Traditional Text that was used in 1604 – 1611 for the King James Bible. Today if someone can demonstrate a possible textual problem with the Traditional Text, let him set forth the evidence based on comparisons (collation) of all the 20,000+ extant MSS (98% of which are amazingly all TT). It's not that easy to find problems now that the TT is so close to Original Scripture. If he is right, the TT will be further refined.

This "Scrollduggery" will now observe and document the contrast between the <u>Scripturally refined</u> TT and the Origen/Vaticanus/Vulgate/Westcott&Hort/Nestle-Aland "Critical Text" (CT) used for virtually every English bible version since 1881, including to a significant degree the NKJV. Also, note that the 99.9999% fine TR is getting **better** with each refinement; the 85% poor CT becomes **less** pure by each textual variant added (60,000+ variant readings so far). Isn't this "take" on inerrancy both Scriptural and defendable?

Let's pray: Dear Heavenly Father, please use this exposé of "Scrollduggery" to bring total confidence in Your Words, for tactical readiness to complete <u>our</u> end times missions from You. In your name Jesus, Lord of the harvest. Amen.

We will look first at the:

OLD TESTAMENT, KING JAMES (KJ)

From the Hebrew "Tanakh" (the "Jewish Bible", the Christian Old Testament) to the Dead Sea Scrolls, there is basically only one Hebrew text, commonly called "The Masoretic Text". The Hebrew appears to have been so well maintained that no 7-fold refining was necessary. This is the text which was every word translated into English by the KJ translators, who "were almost as familiar with the languages of the Bible as with their native English" (**NKJV Preface**). By 1600 the English language was fully ripe; Shakespeare, Spenser, and Handel, ... were writing then; yet, just turn the page from the Elizbethan style KJ Preface, and read the simplicity of Genesis 1. The style of the KJ translators was not Elizabethan; it was simple faithful and proficient translation of the Preserved God-spoken Original Hebrew and Greek: <u>it is God's style</u>. SELAH! Contrast the "Formica flat" Dynamic Equivalent translation of the abbreviated Vaticanus (Classical Attic, not Koine Greek) text found in the NIV, NASV, ESV (see Appendix I, page 187, before using the ESV), RSV, NRSV, and to a considerable extent in the NKJV.

The KJ translators believed in "Verbal" (the words, not just the thoughts) "Plenary" (all of those words) Inspiration of the Bible. They also believed in Preservation of Scripture, (that the very words were preserved, not just "The Message"). They believed "that the manuscripts [the Hebrew Old Testament] were providentially handed down and were a trustworthy record of the inspired Word of God" (**NKJV Preface**).

The preservation of the Hebrew text was a part of "*the covenant of Levi*" (Mal.2:7,8); the almost verbatim agreement in the book of Isaiah between the Masoretic Text and the Dead Sea scrolls, which are over 1000 years older, testifies as to how well they did. (They had help, obviously; God is intensely involved in all of this, in blessing **and cursing**.)

OLD TESTAMENT, NEW KING JAMES (NKJV)

The **NKJV Preface** states that its translators used "the Stuttgart edition of Biblia Hebraica ..." ("BHS", underline added).   This Masoretic text was primarily edited by Gerhard Kittel, "German rationalistic higher (subjective) critic, rejecting Biblical inerrancy and firmly devoted to evolutionism" [and anti-Semitism!] (THE NEW DEFENDER'S STUDY BIBLE, World Publishing, 2006, p. 2149). The over 25,000 variant readings of the Critical Apparatus "footdoubts" (footnotes questioning what the actual Original Text is) of the BHS, the "New Kittel" (Ref.21, Vol.2, p.112), reveals that Kittel's footnotes have more questions about what the very Hebrew Bible text is than there are verses in the Old Testament! How is any translator going to produce an accurate Bible if he has to guess at what God originally said over 25,000 times?

Obviously the NKJV didn't buy into most of these Critical Apparatus footnotes, but their study Bibles still have over 400 "footdoubts" which cite "Significant Variations" in the Hebrew text itself! Also, it is important to recognize that NKJV translator confidence in the Masoretic Text had to have been seriously shaken. A translator who does not believe he has a Bible manuscript from which he can accept each word of God as "*forever ... settled in heaven*" (Psalm 119:89) will tend to exercise originality—illegal in both Bible translating and accounting.

Then the **NKJV Preface** says that they sometimes made changes to the Masoretic Hebrew text when it differed from the "Septuagint", a Greek translation of the Hebrew Old Testament. To see if this Septuagint has the authority it would need to correct the Masoretic Hebrew, see Appendix B: "The Goods on the (BC/ AD?) Septuagint", p.154. Just the facts given in Appendix B destroy the Septuagint's relevance to this ENOUGH, and we say shame on the NKJV for "sometimes" changing the Masoretic Hebrew to agree with the Septuagint. We are amazed at how 1) the loosely paraphrased Septuagint Greek 2) Dynamic Equivalent translation of 3) a highly edited Hebrew text is accepted as authoritative over the TR Hebrew Old Testament in supposedly **conservative** circles!

The Lord Jesus Christ Himself said, "*the scripture cannot be broken*" (= obliterated, atomized), John 10:35b. Therefore, if you translate or teach from a broken (unpreserved) Scripture, or knowingly accept bibles prepared by those who don't believe "*the record*", you are therefore calling God a liar (I John 5:10)! Then the **Holy Bible disappears for you** (is "broken", in the Greek, literally, it "blows up" in your face), becoming just another good book to you, because **you will not bet your life on it!** ("[T]*hey overcame him* [Satan, because]...*they loved not their lives unto the death*" Rev.12:11.)

NEW TESTAMENT, KING JAMES

The New Testament is the main textual battleground (although the Old Testament is coming under increasing biblical critical fire, as mentioned in the seeming Septuagint scam, Appendix B). The issue of PRESERVATION of the inspired texts explains much of the difference between the KJ and the NKJV. The writers of this **ENOUGH** are here dealing in the Scripture promises and evidence that convinced them that God did preserve His inspired Word, and that the Textus Receptus (TR) Masoretic Hebrew, and Traditional Greek used in the 1611 KJ Bible, are that perfectly inspired and that promised preserved Text. If the KJ manuscripts aren't the preserved copy of the "Autographs", where is the promised text that can even claim to be? The Autographs—none of which seem still to be in existence—were the actual fragile first copy penned by the different inspired authors and were the eternal words of God "*forever ... settled in heaven*" (Ps.119:89), which God not only preserved after the Autographs wore out but which actually preceded the Autographs! (Ref.8, p.509)

The King James New Testament is a literal, every-word-accounted-for, translation of the refined "Greek text used by Greek speaking churches [like today's Greek Orthodox] for many centuries" (**NKJV Preface**). As we will see, the pre-TR "Traditional Text" also predominates in the Papyri, early Church Father Scripture quotes, the absolutely earliest translated versions, together with the vast majority of the earliest extant manuscripts. (We use the term "Pre-TR" because, technically, the term "TR"—Textus Receptus— wasn't coined until the 1630s by the Elzevir brothers, but it refers to the same "Traditional Text", "TT".)

The **NKJV Preface** states that there have been revisions made to the KJ Bible. However, "The King James Version of 1611, the myth of early revisions" (Ref.6, pp.14-29) convincingly argues that this is not so. There were some 400 original printing errors corrected (80% of them by the third printing in 1638), the Gothic type was changed to the much more readable Roman type, and (direct replacement) spelling standardization was made in thousands of places—but no <u>textual</u> revisions. Dr. James Price, senior editor of the NKJV Old Testament, evidently sees no difference between the almost 800 (eight hundred!) textual variant footnotes in the NKJV (questioning every twentieth word in the Greek and English texts) and the 10-15 <u>textual variant</u> footnotes in the entire original 1611 KJ Bible. (See "Witness #4" on p.140.)

Consider the "Report of the Committee on Versions" to the Board of Managers of the American Bible Society in 1852, by Dr. James W. McLane, Chairman, pp.7,11: "The English Bible as left by the translators [in 1611] has come down to us unaltered in respect to its text ... [no changes have been made] with the exception of typographical errors and changes required by the progress of orthography [spelling] in the English language."

Now, nothing men touch is perfect, (apart from when God chooses to do something like breathe His Words through man into the Autographs), and the TR seems to be only 99+% accurate to the Originals. The 10-15 legitimate Greek textual questions in the entire TR have been resolved by reference to the over 98% of the 6000+ extant manuscripts of the Greek New Testament, the Papyri, earliest translations, and over a million (1,000,000) Church Father Scripture quotes which agree with the TR 2:1 (3:1 in key texts) over B. Compare that to the the 36,000+ "variant readings" in the Critical Text New Testament.

PROBLEM TEXTS, by Dr. Peter Ruckman (Ref.7) gives significant answers, if in a polemic and direct way, to hundreds of the most asked (apparent) questions about the KJ translation. Read Ruckman! His discourteous (I Peter 3:5), unclothed with humility (I Peter 5:5) manner is used as an **excuse** to try to ignore him. Dr. Ruckman's analysis of problem texts generally doesn't leave much else to say to those for whom the Bible is "the Final Authority", so some people who are not determined to find the truth, follow the dictum "deny everything, then make accusation!" However, Dr. Ruckman believed that the English KJ translation, not the preserved TR Masoretic Hebrew and Greek texts it literally translates, is the final standard for faith and conduct. This would imply that God spoke through the 47 KJ translators just as he did to Moses, Jeremiah, John etc. There is no Scriptural prophecy or historical record that He did or would. (See Ref.19, pp.42-45 for more on this.) Dr. Ruckman so vociferously argues his take on preservation that this analytical genius but angry prophet is not the best representative of the "standard" God has raised up to stem the flood of "Dynamic Equivalent" (see Appendix F, p.179) paraphrased bibles attacking the reliability of His Word. (Do see Isa.59:16-19.) However, consider the historical fact, which Dr. Ruckman agreed with, that God has providentially and practically superintended, used, and blessed literal translations of the inspired and preserved manuscripts throughout His-story: The Syrian Peschito, the Old Latin ("the Italia"), Olivetan French, Italian Diodati, Martin Luther's German, Dutch Statenvertaling,... but especially—for number of copies, accuracy, and years used—the English KING JAMES translation.

Practically speaking, there is not much difference to be found between the preserved TR/KJ Greek and Hebrew texts and the English KJ itself, the last and best literal English translation of those texts. Also, in a brotherly attempt to soften our criticism of Dr. Ruckman (but not to endorse everything this prolific scholar says), wouldn't it be appropriate to say that the KJ English Bible represents the preserved text to English speakers who do not have access to the TR/KJ Hebrew and Greek? It is the firm position of most informed "Remnant" Christians that it is the TR/KJ Hebrew and Greek texts

that have been preserved, but there isn't much difference; so what is the big battle all about? ACTUALLY THERE IS NOT NEARLY THE BATTLE THAT THERE SHOULD BE!   Most Christian churches are just using paraphrased translations of strangely edited "bibles".   However, when the Remnant starts looking at the facts and asking questions about the promised, preserved Word of God, which these non-Bibles obviously are <u>not</u>, then the flies (who are not of the Remnant in their hearts, as revealed by their reactions when exposed to the facts of preservation—these children of "Beelzebub" = "the dung-god", "the lord of the flies") hovering around the piles of corrupted "bibles", really begin to BUZ-Z-Z-Z: **"KING JAMES ONLY"! ... "RUCKMAN"! ... "THE SCHOLARS SAY...."** The flies know that they can't answer the Remnant's Biblical questions; but
• they also know that the extreme "King James Only" people have an Achilles Heel, which is the claim that the King James <u>English translation</u> has been re-inspired—not, that the TR/KJ Hebrew and Greek has been preserved.
• They tell the Remnant that "good, godly, conservative scholars" hold that the TR/KJ manuscripts are "late and secondary" compared to (the Roman Catholic, Council of Trent decreed, 1% textually supported, and actually "later") Vaticanus.
• There is often such zealousness but unbiblical impoliteness on the part of some who support the KJ, that discussion or even debate becomes virtually impossible—and usually the Remnant gets sidetracked, so that the real questions don't even get asked.

However, if these "real questions" do get asked, answers are offered such as the following: "Nothing in biblical statements such as *'All Scripture is inspired of God'* (II Tim.3:16) or *'until heaven and earth pass away, not the smallest letter ... shall pass ....'* requires that every inspired word must be likewise preserved <u>outside</u> of the autographs." (SEARCHING FOR THE ORIGINAL BIBLE, by Randall Price, p.207; we attempted to talk with Dr. Price about these matters, but were not received.) Let's discuss this faulty answer:
1.) To speak of preservation only in the Autographs, as the NKJV translators all signed that they believed, is no preservation at all,

since we no longer have any of the Autographs (= the first, inspired "Original" Manuscripts).

2.) If words mean anything, could the Lord have been more emphatic in Matthew 5:18; 24:35 that His words, down to the very letters, would last until *"heaven and earth"* pass away, not just as long as the Autographs lasted?

3) As we previously stated, it is <u>essential</u> that the "language" (the very wording) of Jesus' covenants/contracts be 100% preserved for them to be <u>legally</u> binding. The Lord <u>signs His name</u> in contractual obligation, (making His honor "security"!). *"Thus saith the* LORD*"* is found in various forms over 2000 times in the Bible, as well as statements such as, *"the word of the* LORD *came"*, *"this is the word of the* LORD*..."*, and ultimately, *"Jesus said ..."*. To change **a word** in a signed contract is fraud! If any dispute remains as to exact wording (and there can be very little at this "99.9999% fine" point of preservation), it must then be resolved by examining the overwhelming textual support that God has provided for His Word.

4.) I Peter 1:23 says *"Being born again, not of corruptible seed, but of incorruptible, by the word of God, which liveth and abideth for ever"*. So, if you have a corrupted bible, are you *"born again ... for ever"*? You don't have a *"helmet of salvation"* (Eph.6:17) and can be cold-conked spiritually any time because the <u>promise even of your salvation is not sure</u>!

5.) The bible/Bible battle has been called a "non-issue". Actually, this issue of religion without (inerrant) Revelation ("Final Authority") is THE ISSUE, Ground Zero here near the end of time; *"in the latter days ye shall consider it perfectly"* (Jer.23:20) :

A) "The idol shepherd" of Zech.11:15-17 (the Anti-Christ) who consumes and does not "visit" the sheep, is pre-figured by

B) *"the pastors that destroy and scatter the sheep of my pasture! saith the* LORD*"* and *"have not visited them"* Jer.23:1&2. ("Visit" = "to care for" the sheep of His pasture—by giving them God's pure words.

NEW TESTAMENT, KING JAMES   111

C) A human-edited bible is required for Humanism, as propounded by Zeno, Aristotle, and Alexander the Great, to take over. (Alexander's evil Principality is apparently coming AGAIN: "*even he is the eighth, and is of the seven*," Dan.8:21-26; Rev.17:11.) The Bible must be effectively destroyed in the minds of most people for the Beast to be democratically elected by the World.

6.) "Men today perhaps do not burn the Bible.... They destroy it in the way they deal with it. They destroy it by not reading it as written, ... by ignoring historical-grammatical exegesis, by changing the Bible's own perspective of itself as propositional revelation in space and time, ..." (Francis A. Schaeffer, DEATH IN THE CITY, p.78, Crossway Books, 2002).

7.) Dr. Schaeffer also called the issue of the reliability of the Bible "the watershed of Evangelicalism" and "within evangelicalism there are a growing number who are modifying their views of the inerrancy of the Bible so that the full authority of Scripture is completely undercut." (Dr. Schaeffer, THE GREAT EVANGELICAL DISASTER, p.44, Crossway Books, 1984)

8.) Dr. E.F. Hills asks,

"How can we know whether the King James Version is a correct translation or not? Don't we have to rely on dictionaries, such as Brown-Driver-Briggs, Thayer, Kittel, and Liddell-Scott? And for grammar don't we have to go to the great authorities in this field, such as Gesenius, Bauer, and Blass-Debrunner? .... For our knowledge of the New Testament manuscripts are we not obliged to depend almost entirely on the writings of experts, such as Gregory, Kenyon, Colwell, Metzger, and Aland? When we study the Bible ... how can we begin with God? Must we not rather begin with men? With the information provided by scholars, most of whom are unbelievers? Questions like these cause many conservative seminary students to panic and become virtual unbelievers in their Biblical studies. In order, therefore, to prevent such catastrophes, we must always emphasize the Christian starting point that all our thinking ought to have. If we are Christians, then we must begin our thinking not with

the assertions of unbelieving scholars and their naturalistic
human logic, but with Christ and the logic of faith."
(Dr. Edward F. Hills, Ref.14, pp.113-114; do see this **ENOUGH**'s
"Closing Arguments", page 149, for Dr. Hill's explanation of "The
logic of faith".)

9.) Appendix E, p.177 makes a case for there being no
scientifically supportable reasons for not receiving the Received
Text (TR) as the preserved text of the Bible (and for what's wrong
with the "scientism" of Westcott and Hort).

10.) To not believe that the Words of God have been preserved to
our day as promised is to make the Lord Jesus Christ a liar—or at
least confused! (See I John 5:10.)

Again, we ask, the Lord Jesus Christ signed many contracts in
the Bible, good until Heaven and Earth pass away—**didn't He?** *"My
covenant will I not break, nor alter the thing that is gone out of my
lips"* (Psalm 89:34). We accept these promises and find that the
only Bible that can even claim to be preserved is the KJ Hebrew and
Greek "TR" text.

Loud voices arise challenging the TR/KJ text as the 99.9999%
fine Bible, but with no convincing proof yet offered. The KJ
manuscripts did have 10-15 problem texts, which were resolved
hundreds of years ago *"as silver tried in a furnace of earth"* (Psalm
12:6). The other text (there are really just two: TR or CT), CT
(B) has less than 1% textual support—every new possible variant
reading is added to the bramble of textual apparatus, and the CT
text gets more uncertain, not "refined" as God prophesied in Psalm
12:6. What is going on here?

For refreshing objectivity vs scrollduggery, turn to Appendix
C, p.160. There you will find some of the basic facts which have
been put on the table in the literature, but which haven't been given
the hearing they deserve—being ignored or subjected to a lot of
unbalanced treatment as, we feel, in James White's book, THE KING
JAMES ONLY CONTROVERSY (Ref.10). White says that most textual
variants are "not significant" and, "no textual variants in either the
Old or New Testaments... materially disrupt or destroy any essential
doctrine of the Christian faith" (Ref.10, p.40). Wait a minute Dr.

White, did God dictate that man shall not live by bread alone, but by every <u>doctrine</u> that proceeds out of the mouth of God, or by *"every word"* (Matt.4:4, "each and every word" lit. from Greek); yea by every written <u>letter</u> (Matt.5:18)?   KEY COMPARISON COMMENT: **What is the Holy Bible to these people?** Do they think the Bible is just a doctrinal statement that can be "Dynamic Equivalently" paraphrased and then "lawyered" back into shape, just a creed ...? Almighty God has magnified His Word above all His name (Ps.138)!

Please, if you love Him, you will (re)consider your awe of His Words!

NEW TESTAMENT, NEW KING JAMES

Those who do not trust God to preserve His Word do not have the power of God in their lives for service through the authority of His Word. If you realize your need for God's power in your life, then you must resolve this bible/Bible battle!

The NKJV translators all signed a document affirming they each believed in "the Verbal Plenary Inspiration of Scripture as originally written" (**NKJV Preface**). This "as originally written" disclaimer is a sophistry—a subtle deception, participated in knowingly or unknowingly—since there are no original "Autographs" extant today. To say you believe every word of a document no one can hold in his hand today is irrelevant as a stand for inerrancy of the Bible today.

Also, isn't it a **fundamental contradiction** (hypocrisy) on the part of those who claim to still be "fundamentalists"? They claim to believe what the Bible says about its own **inspiration** while virtually ignoring the equally direct Biblical statements concerning **preservation**. If Jesus is your Lord, you will do what He says (Luke 6:46). The Lord Jesus said at the beginning of His earthly ministry, that *"Man shall not live by bread alone, but by every word that proceedeth out of the mouth of God"* (Matt.4:4). How can anyone live by each and every word of God if every word of God has not been preserved? That statement, by itself, makes all Bible versions based on the Critical Text unacceptable because they are missing tens of thousands of words. Furthermore, in John 12:48, the Lord Jesus warned that we will be judged by *"the word that I have spoken"*— unfair if that word hasn't been preserved for us. Again consider Matt. 24:35 (Jesus' statement in simple and clear words that His words would never pass away, could not be plainer—verbal preservation); Matt.5:18 (The Lord here promises sub-verbal—the very letters—preservation); Prov.30:5,6; Eccl.3:14. (Ref.19, Chapt. 4, expounds on all of these texts, in context, not as "proof texts".)

The "Fruit Inspection", part I of this book, showed that, where the NKJV differs from the KJ, the NKJV is in clonish collusion over 80% of the time with up to seven popular modern versions which are heavily influenced by the CT "Critical Greek Text". Let's examine this Critical Text and find:

THE NAKED TRUTH about

the crowning masterpiece of God's creative skill—
the God-spoken and preserved Textus Receptus Bible

—vs—

the "Critical Text"— based on just a couple of man-
mutilated manuscripts

Once upon a time, the vain Emperor of a country was always searching for fancier clothes to wear. A shrewd sales-man got the Emperor to trade the Crown Jewel of the country for an (imaginary) invisible suit. The Emperor couldn't wait to ride through the city to show it off to his people, who loved his vanity. All these people were so impressed; but a poor little boy yelled out in amazement, "The Emperor has no clothes on!"

In our story the Emperor represents the leaders of the"Protestant" Church, the shrewd salesman is Cambridge professor Dr. Fenton J.A. Hort, the Crown Jewel is the inerrant Holy Bible, the invisible suit is a bible that's not the Bible, the people are those who obviously don't appreciate the treasure of the Holy Bible or they wouldn't tolerate such a trade, and the little boy represents the writers of this book.

The Emperor had been foolishly and tragically seduced (II Cor. 11:2-4)—*just* as people have no Holy Bible who accept holey "cloud-land" bibles; and, <u>that's the naked truth!</u>

Now, with the help of Oxford Dean John Burgon, let's see if this CRITICAL TEXT is "just so" (as in Kipling's fairy tales):

There is little debate about the fact that the Critical Text is <u>the basis of every major English bible version since 1881</u>. John William Burgon (the Dean of Chichester, Oxford University) in his book, THE REVISION REVISED (Ref.17), point for point rebuts Dr. Hort's mythological justification for changing over 10,000 words in the Textus Receptus (the Traditional) Greek New Testament (hereinafter TR) to form this Critical Greek Text (CT). (Most of these changes take words out of the TR. The NIV, for example, is "Bible lite", lacking over 50,000 words!) In <u>hundreds</u> of places the CT reduces titles of "the Lord Jesus Christ" by dropping out "Lord", or "Christ", or "Jesus", or combinations of these titles. Is it simply coincidence that the two major heresies of the last 2000 years, the Arian and the Gnostic, also omit certain titles of the Lord Jesus Christ? The Arians wouldn't call Him "Lord" and "Christ", and the Gnostics wouldn't call Him "Jesus". Isn't Vaticanus actually a handbook of heresy rather than the "oldest and best"?

The Alexandrian love for the shorter, more terse, classical "Attic Greek" also seems to have played a part in Origen's revision of the New Testament which is mostly the text found in Vaticanus ("the shorter text".)

Burgon's proof was never rebutted—and for the best of reasons: his arguments are apparently unanswerable. In the preface to THE REVISION REVISED, Dean Burgon says: " 'Cloud-land' having been duly sighted..." when Dr. Hort's INTRODUCTION TO THE NEW

TESTAMENT IN THE ORIGINAL GREEK (hereinafter, INTRODUCTION) was published. (Ref.17 p. xxvii)

WHY SHOULD THIS PROOF DEMAND YOUR ATTENTION?

1.) "(T)he country has been flooded with two editions of the [New Testament] Greek Text, and thus the door has been set wide open for universal mistrust of the Truth of Scripture to enter." (Ref.17 p. xxx)

2.) This unfounded Critical Text was printed **for school boys** in the CAMBRIDGE GREEK TESTAMENT FOR SCHOOLS.

3.) The Bible Society has permitted its Translators, who are "unacquainted with the dangers which beset this delicate and difficult problem [Biblical Textual Criticism][1], to determine...what *is* inspired Scripture, and what *not*" and then to sow this bad seed in countries which have not heard about Jesus. (Ref.17 p. xxxi)

(4.) Hundreds of bible versions have been translated from this Critical Text by translators who are unsure of what the original inspired Words of God are, **on an average, twice in every verse of the Bible**, because of alternative readings given in the "footdoubts" (footnotes) of the Critical Text. Just how true can the translations be when there is this much doubt about the text being translated? [For those who object that the modern Critical REM (Reasoned Eclectic Method) Text is not basically the same as Westcott and Hort'sText, Kurt Aland says, in the introduction to his 24th edition of the NESTLE-ALAND GREEK NEW TESTAMENT, "This [REM] Text, built upon the work of the 19th Century, has remained as a whole unchanged." The "NESTLE-ALAND" is the definitive modern Critical Text Greek New Testament, the CT.]

We will now attempt to summarize Dean Burgon's case against Dr. Hort's "scientific Theory" of the Critical Text (and for the Traditional ["TR"] Text). Actually, Dean Burgon calls W&H's Text "UnCritical" because "It dispenses with proof. It furnishes no evidence. It asserts when it ought to argue. It reiterates when it is called up to explain....I venture to style [this] the *unscientific* method...." (In this discussion, Burgon's proof will

---

[1] Words within [brackets] are basically the writer's comments, not those of Hort or Burgon.

rest on "the combined verdict of Manuscripts, Versions, Fathers" [and Lectionaries] (Ref.17 p. xxvii) because "...the ancient Fathers collectively (AD 150 to AD 350),—inasmuch as they must needs have known far better than [modern scholars]...what was the Text of the New Testament in the earliest ages, are perforce more trustworthy guides than they." (Ref.17 p. 377)   As we proceed, do observe how Burgon's documentary basis of proof is in stark contrast to Hort's conjectures, preferences, instincts, apparent "dread of *facts*" and (as we shall observe) occultic guidance.

"But, it is high time to unfold [the INTRODUCTION (Hort's book)] at the first page and begin to read" says Dean Burgon. (Ref.17 p. 248):

  Pages 1-11 (of Hort's INTRODUCTION) deal with "Transmission" (copying) of manuscripts, but fail to mention the most important problem—errors of transmission. These break down into 1) errors by accident and 2) errors by design. [Vaticanus ("B") manuscript is over 92% the total textual support where the Critical Text differs from the TR.] B disagrees with the TR in **35,000 words**, and most of these are <u>differences by design</u> (aka "Recension"=heavy revision). "Wondrous few of these *can* have been due to accidental causes." (Ref.17 p. 249) Therefore, Burgon tells the reader he is going to prove that B exhibits a "Rescinded" (=revised) Text when the B/TR differences are evaluated by "collation" (=word by word comparison) of 1) Manuscripts, 2) (translated) Versions, ... and 3) Fathers. (Ref.17 p. 249 gives an example of Burgon's rigorous collation.) Collation is essential for scientific textual scholarship. Westcott and Hort did no collation!

Page 13 Hort incorrectly says that earlier critic Lachmann's Text was "the first founded on documentary authority". Burgon asks, "on *what* then" were the Texts of Erasmus founded? (Ref.17 p. 250) [This appears an initial move by Hort to exalt, in the mind of the reader, the Lachmann, Tregelles, Tischendorf, Westcott and Hort (hereinafter W&H) minority Text over the 99:1 more manuscript-supported majority text refined by Erasmus, Stephanus, Beza, KJ translators, from which came the TR.]

Pages 20-30 Burgon says, "The dissertation on '**INTRINSIC**' and '**TRANSCRIPTIONAL PROBABILITY**'...—being *unsupported by one single instance or illustration*—we pass by." (Ref.17 p. 251[**bold** and CAPS ours, indicating key parts of the W&H Textual Theory]) Most serious B errors are by design (revisions of God's Word). However Hort perpetually mentions "Scribal" and "Copiest" errors [which would be "accidental", apparently as a cover for the fact (as we shall see) that B was <u>revised</u>—not faithfully <u>copied</u> from the Originals.] The fact that Hort declares that "Transcriptional Probability is incontestable" doesn't make it so—W&H often disagreed. Burgon notes that "W"(Westcott) and "H"(Hort) are written next to marginal notes on "many and serious occasions" where they couldn't agree. (Ref.17 p. 251) [How can you have "incontestable" guidance of W, and opposite for H?]

Pages 30-32 Dr. Hort says "When one of the documents is found habitually to contain morally certain or at least strongly preferred, Readings...we [W&H] can have no doubt that the Text of the first has been transmitted in comparative purity...." Burgon replies, "Are we...seriously invited to admit that the 'STRONG PREFERENCE'... is to be the ultimate standard of appeal?" (On p. 61, Hort prefers *"Readings which...*[subjective] *Internal Evidence pronounces to be right, in opposition to formidable arrays of Documentary Evidence"*. Burgon states, "Dr. Hort is for setting up what his inner consciousness 'pronounces to be right' against 'Documentary Evidence,' however multitudinous....Can he be in earnest?") (Ref.17 p. 253) [Also note that Hort is here subtly introducing a concept key to his Theory; he prefers to **WEIGH** than to <u>count</u> manuscripts—giving **much** heavier weight to those he "prefers".] We see Dean Burgon patiently dealing with each point, proving that Hort is proving nothing. Hort usually gives no citations in favor of his readings in comparison to the overwhelming majority of textual support for the TR readings presented by Burgon. Also, amazingly, some of Hort's <u>meager</u> citations are simply <u>**wrong**</u>. (Ref.17 p. 359(b))

It is impossible to adequately convey the thoroughness of Burgon's arguments in this summary; however, here is a good example:

W&H chose to delete the essential words, "without a cause" (Matt.5:22) spoken by the Lord, just because B does. Now look at Burgon's evidence: With the exception of B, every Uncial (early manuscript written in all capital letters), the oldest versions, and Church Fathers (Burgon actually cites 30 of them) have these words. (Ref.17 pp. 358-362, arguments a-h) [Comparing Burgon's scholarship with W&H's must raise questions about the rest of W&H's Critical Text for anyone truly seeking the truth. READ at least pages 358-362 of THE REVISION REVISED to see Burgon's tireless diligence!]

W&H said that there is "irrecoverable error" in Scripture [imagine that!] and that there is an apparent need for them to resort to the spirit world to fill the gap with what they call "The [BLACK] Art of **CONJECTURAL EMENDATION**"! Burgon comments: "Yes, the Nemesis of Superstition and Idolatry is ever the same. General mistrust of all evidence is the sure result...(W&H)...invent a ghost to be exorcised in every dark corner." (Ref.17 pp. 351-357) [Can their blind adherence to B be understood as anything else but "Superstitious Reverence"? See Ref.17 p. 244] Hasn't Hort "doubted what is *demonstrably* true: has rejected what is *indubitably* Divine"? (Ref.17 p. 350) [W&H obviously have no faith in the Divine Promises of either Inspiration or Preservation of Scripture.] Hort says, "We dare not introduce considerations which could not reasonably be applied to other ancient texts". (BELIEVER'S BIBLE STUDY by Dr. Edward Hills, p. 227) [However, other "ancient texts" don't declare Divine inspiration and promise Divine preservation!] Westcott and Hort formed a group called "The Ghostly Guild" in 1851—"for the investigation of ghosts and all supernatural appearances...." (Ref.8, p. 619) This was in the same time frame (and for Conjectural Emendation in?) their thirty-year project to rewrite the Greek N.T. to replace the "villainous" Textus Receptus. (LIFE OF HORT, Vol.1, p. 211)]

Then Dean Burgon makes other significant observations challenging the whole Revision: 1.) Most of the men on the Revision Committee were scholars capable of revising an English translation but not trained in the delicate art of "Biblical Textual

Criticism". Since the Revision Committee was only authorized by the Church to examine the English Authorized Version for "necessary" improvement, this was fine. What actually happened, however, was that they arrived at a new Greek Text for the New Testament. In this "Textual Criticism", most of them were over their heads and were so easily steered by "oracle" Hort—actually being seriously dishonest to their pledge to abide by the charge of the Church which had entrusted the ENGLISH Bible to them. They lied to the Church! 2.) W&H had devised their own private New Testament Greek Text over the preceding thirty years. In a comparison of that Text with what the Revision Committee came up with, we find a "fatal...sympathy between the labors of Drs. Westcott and Hort and those of our Revisionists". That is, there didn't seem to be much revision going on at all. W&H were basically giving the world their private New Testament. For example, *"whatever those Editors* [W&H] *rejected from their Text, these Revisionists have rejected also". "Whatever* [W&H] *have shut up within double brackets, the latter are discovered to have branded with a note of suspicion..."*(Ref.17 p. 77)—wholesale thousands of precious utterances of the Holy Spirit!

Pages 39-59 In INTRODUCTION, p. 43 Hort says, "total change in the bearing of the evidence" is "made by the introduction of the factor of **GENEALOGY**"—that is, the study of the history of a Manuscript, as distinguished from the evidence for or against their Readings. Burgon asks if such a thing is feasible since there is not *"one single instance* of a known MS (manuscript) copied from another known MS....All talk about 'Genealogical evidence', where *no single step in the descent* can be produced,—in other words, *where no Genealogical evidence exists,*—is absurd...moonshine". [Also, the Genealogical Method is valid only when there has not been intentional tampering. Only those who reject what the Bible has to say about Satan can believe that the Bible has not received much attack never experienced by Classical ancient literature. Tampering was going on even while Paul was alive (II Cor.2:17; II Thess.2:2). The Lord spoke of "an enemy" "sowing tares" amidst the good seed of the Word (Matt.13). Isn't it amazing that in supposedly "scientific work", in most seminaries the Genealogical Method continues dominating the handbooks as the canonical method of "restoring" the text of the New Testament (Ref.1b p.84).] Then Burgon gives an illustration:

"The living inhabitants of a village, congregated in the church yard where the bodies of their forgotten progenitors for 1000 years repose without [grave stones] of any kind,—is a faint image of the relation which subsists between extant copies of the Gospels and the sources from which they were derived. That, in either case [Bibles and bodies], there has been repeated mixture is undeniable; but since the Parish-register is lost, and not a vestige of tradition survives, it is idle to pretend to argue on *that* part...." Burgon concludes, " '*The factor of Genealogy*', in short, in this discussion, represents a mere phantom of the brain: is the name of an imagination—not of a fact...." (Ref.17 p. 256)

"Nothing of this kind however is what Drs. Westcott and Hort intend to convey,—or indeed seem to understand." (Ref.17 p. 257)

Page 94 Hort says he is now going to "determine the Genealogical relations of the chief ancient texts". (Ref.17 p. 257) He will build a structure on top of his apparently imaginary Genealogy foundation and claim that he has traced B back almost to the Autographs with "perfect certainty". Yet Dr. Ernest Cowell, expert in Biblical Manuscripts, asks, "Where are the charts which start with the majority of late manuscripts and climb back through diminishing generations...they are nowhere...." (Ref.23, p.192). Hort lied again!

[Kurt Aland, of the NESTLE/ALAND Greek Text says the Genealogical method "cannot be applied to the New Testament"—THE BIBLE IN MODERN SCHOLARSHIP, p.341. This NESTLE/ALAND is the definitive modern edition of the Critical Text, and the Preface to the 23rd edition says that it is "basically unchanged" from W&H's 19th century Critical Text.]

Hort must somehow put the pre-TR later than B, and an imaginary Genealogical Father-Son relationship between manuscripts would do that. Dr. Frederick Kenyon, who sort of wrote the handbook on textual criticism, said, "If it can be shown that the readings which Hort called 'Syrian' (the pre-TR text) existed before the fourth century, the keystone would be knocked out...of Hort's theory." (Ref.8 p. 34) Note regarding the early date of the pre-TR that 1.) the Papyrii, which are the absolutely oldest NT manuscripts, are 2:1 TR over B (Ref.8 p. 488). 2.) The 1,000,000+ Patristic (Church Fathers) Scripture quotes are 2:1 TR, 3:1 in critical passages (Ref.8 p. 488); 3.) the earliest translated version, the Peschito, is translated from the TR says Dr. Bruce Metzger (no friend of Dean Burgon) (Ref.15 p. 136); (4) the head of W&H's Revision Committee, Bishop Ellicott said, "It is no stretch of the imagination to suppose that portions of the Peschito might have been in the hand of St. John." That's a pretty early N.T. translation!

So much for Genealogy, but behold! Hort will now build on this imaginary "moonshine" Genealogical order. Hort says that the reason B is shorter than the TR is that shorter manuscripts were **CONFLATED** (=combined) together by some church council. (There is, however, no historical record of any such momentous Council, called the Lucian Recension, and Lucian was an outspoken Arian and would have rejected the pre-TR text because it refutes the Arian Heresy.) "Today Textual scholars are reluctant to appeal to conflation" writes a noble scholar and faithful missionary of the Gospel. (Ref.12A p. 29) If TR Manuscripts were derived from one 400 AD revision, they would show "family tree", father-son similarities—but they don't. They do have remarkable similarity, which one would expect of the Traditional majority text, but throughout there are minor but distinct differences which *couldn't* be in manuscripts derived from one manuscript. In thirty years of research, Westcott and Hort could only find eight possibly conflated verses.   There would have to be thousands of these conflations to account for the thousands of words in the TR which are not found in B. [Do observe that this is the same fundamental flaw in Darwin's Theory of Evolution—not even one probable example of evolution in the entire fossil record!) However, at last Hort gives us actual Scripture references to evaluate. Dr.Edward Miller (CAUSES OF CORRUPTION, pp.271-278) and Dean Burgon discuss all eight of them in exhaustive scholarly detail (Ref.17 pp. 258-262), and Burgon's conclusion is that only #7 could, without challenge, possibly be conflated. BUT based on this poor showing of conflation, W&H "have gratuitously built up the following extravagant and astonishing theory". (Ref.17 p. 263) Dr. Hort had said that these verses are "The clearest Evidence" producible for "The Theory of Conflation". Dean Burgon says therefore, "The whole matter is demonstrably a weak imagination, a dream, and nothing more.... In the meantime, Drs. Westcott and Hort, instead of realizing the insecurity of the ground under their feet, proceed gravely to build upon it and to treat their hypothetical assumptions as well ascertained facts". (Ref.17 p. 265)

Page 105 Hort says, "We have found reason to believe" B "to be the original Readings...." Burgon says, "*No reason whatever* have they assigned to their belief." (Ref.17 p. 266)

Page 106 Hort says, "*It is certain*...The proved actual use of [shorter] documents in the **CONFLATE** Readings...." Burgon asks, "*Where* and *what* is the proof referred to?" [Here is some proof against the shorter texts like B: Heretics historically delete more words than they add, apparently because deleted words are less obvious to a reader than added words.] Burgon: "May a plain man, sincerely in search of Truth,—after wasting many precious hours over these barren pages [Hort's INTRODUCTION]—be permitted to declare that he resents such solemn trifling."(Ref.17 p. 266)

Pages 107-116 " Patristic evidence *has shown* that...[B] must have already existed early in the third century" says Hort. Burgon remarks, "*no single appeal* has been made to the evidence supplied by *one single ancient Father!* ...again we are 'shown' absolutely nothing: although we are treated to the assurance that we have been shown many wonders." (Ref.17 p. 267)

Hort states, "Another step is gained by a close examination of all Readings distinctively Syrian." Burgon replies, "And yet we are never told which the 'Readings distinctively Syrian' *are*,—although they are henceforth referred to in every page. Neither are we instructed how to recognize them when we see them; which is unfortunate, since (Hort continues:) 'it follows,'—(though we entirely fail to see from *what,)* [says Burgon]—'that all distinctively Syrian Readings [pre-TR] may be set aside at once....' " (Ref.17 p. 267)

Page 119 Hort says "it follows from what has been said above,... that all Readings in which the Pre-Syrian texts concur, *must be accepted at once as the Apostolic Readings:*" and that "all distinctively Syrian Readings *must be at once rejected....*" Burgon: "It becomes apparent that we have to do with a Writer [Hort] who has discovered a summary way of dealing with the Text of Scripture, and who is prepared to impart his secret to any who care to accept—without questioning—his views." (Ref.17 p. 268) Burgon cynically labels all this, "Textual Criticism made easy". (Ref.17 p. 25)

Page 133 What is Dr. Hort driving at? He says "The Syrian Text [the pre-TR] must in fact be the result of a **RECENSION**... performed deliberately by Editors, and not merely by Scribes." Burgon says, "One of the two [TR or B] has been fabricated. Granted." (Ref.17 p. 272) The question is, which one?

Pages 133-149 Hort here writes a poor historical novel about some mythical church council editing actual Bible manuscripts to produce some "Received Text". This is a poor novel because "good" historical novels mesh well with actual history, and there is <u>no</u> historical record of such a momentous "church council" ever happening.

Pages 150-end Hort continues to stack cards, on this playing card house, to an incredible height. Burgon says:

> "(T)he entire discussion becomes...within the compass of a nutshell....We are invited to make our election between the Fathers of the Church, A.D. 250 and A.D. 350,—and Dr. Hort, A.D. 1881. The issue is really reduced to *that.* The general question of THE TEXT OF SCRIPTURE being the matter at stake; (not any particular passage, remember, but *the Text of Scripture as a whole;*)—and the *conflicting parties* being but *two;*...Shall we accept the august testimony of the whole body of the Fathers? or shall we prefer to be guided by the self-evolved imaginations of one who confessedly has nothing to

offer but conjecture?...We are invited to make our election between FACT and FICTION...." (Ref.17 p. 293)

[Bear in mind that Dean John W. Burgon, without a computer, word-for-word compared (collated) over 1,000,000 Scripture quotes from almost 90,000 extant Patristic documents (sixteen large volumes now residing in the British Museum, England), absolutely documenting that they used the pre-TR over B "2:1, 3:1 in key texts". W&H quite apparently lie again by denying that the early Church Fathers quote (predominantly) from the TR text (Ref.11, p.66 and Ref.23, p.192). Who, beside Dean Burgon, could speak more authoritatively from the ancient Church Fathers?] Burgon continues:

> "Reject it (the Recension of the TR), and the entire fabric (of W&H's Textual Theory) is observed to collapse, and subside into a shapeless ruin. And with it, of necessity, goes the 'New Greek Text', —and therefore the *'New English Version'* [**and virtually every version since 1881**]...which in the main have been founded on it." (Ref.17 p. 294)

[The whole historical novel about some "conflation" Revision of the TR, being put forth as actually having happened, must be considered as another lie. W&H's credibility approaches zero—their testimony should be thrown out of Court.]

The Oxford Dean summarizes:

> "Thus then, at last, at the end of exactly 150 weary pages, the secret comes out! The one point which the respected Editors are found to have been all along driving at:—the one aim of those many hazy disquisitions of theirs about '**Intrinsic and Transcriptional Probability**,'—'**Genealogical evidence**, simple and divergent,'—and 'the study of Groups:'—the one reason of all their vague terminology,—and of their baseless theory of '**Conflation**,'—and of their disparagement of the Fathers:—the one *raison d'être* of their fiction of a '**Syrian**' and a '**Pre-Syrian**' and a '**Neutral**' text:—the secret of it all comes out at last!...All is summed up in the curt formula—*Codex* B! [Vaticanus]...A coarser,—a clumsier,—a more unscientific,—a

more *stupid* expedient for settling the true Text of Scripture was surely never invented!" (Ref.17 p. 301, **bold** ours)

"The only indication we anywhere meet with of the actual *ground* of Dr. Hort's certainty, and reason of his preference, is contained in his claim that,—'Every... group [of manuscripts] *containing* B is found to offer a large proportion of Readings, which, on the closest scrutiny, have THE RING OF GENUINENESS...'. Thus we have, at last, an honest confession of the ultimate principle which has determined the Text of the present edition of the N.T. '*The ring of genuineness*'!" (Ref.17 p. 307)   However, "the most signal deformities" in B are "*instances of Omission*"—how can you hear a "ring of genuineness...where there is nothing to ring with"? (Ref.17 p. 310)

Finally, there is a staggering statement made by W&H regarding their "**endstinktive**" edition of the N.T. They said that it would need "perpetual correction and recorrection" (Ref.17 p. 307, Introduction, p. 66)   Also, note that the NKJV has been continuously revised in thousands of places since copyrighted in 1982. The average person has been led to believe that the Critical Text is an honest endeavor to fix (assumed) problems with the text. (It is our conviction based in part on the evidence contained in this book, that God has preserved the TR, and so there are virtually no textual problems to correct.) This Critical Greek Text is **a veritable attack against any confidence in the Bible at all!** The faithless questions they raised about the reliability of the Bible **generate "Perpetual" questions leading to "universal mistrust of the Truth of Scripture."** (Ref.17 p. xxx preface). Burgon continues:

"Our Revisionists; who under the plea of *amending our English Authorized Version* have...*falsified the Greek text* of the Gospels in countless places,—often...without notice" [marginal notes are <u>required</u> when deleting parts of a manuscript. (Ref.17 pp. 89,110,118,361(f)) How can a reader verify the correctness of an omission if no marginal note records that the omission was made?]   "Will the...Church suffer herself to be in this way defrauded of her priceless inheritance, [her true crown jewel!]—through the irreverent bungling of...utterly misguided men?" (Ref.17 p. 92))

[A better introduction to W&H is in order:

1.) Were Westcott and Hort simply two naive scholars with a speculative textual theory which has, however, been falsified by scholarly hands, especially of Oxford Dean John Burgon? Or, were they "bloody" Westcott and Hort? (British queen Bloody Mary, trying to bring England back under the control of the Roman Catholic Pope, slaughtered over 300 good Christian leaders.) W&H have slaughtered the faith of millions in what they scorningly called "The Paper Pope"—the inerrantly inspired and preserved Word of God. To them, the Paper Pope had to go! (There is no question historically that W&H were active members of the Anglican Church party who favored a return of England to Rome.)

2.) Dr. Westcott said, "I reject the word infallibility of Holy Scriptures overwhelmingly." (LIFE OF WESTCOTT, Vol.1, p. 207); Dr. Hort said, "Evangelicals seem to me not just wrong, but perverted....There are, I fear, still more serious differences between us on the subject of authority, especially the authority of the Bible." (LIFE OF HORT, Vol.1, p. 400) (My, but doesn't Westcott speak straight to the point compared to Hort?)

3.) Hort also said, "my feeling is strong that (Charles Darwin's) Theory is unanswerable. If so, it opens up a new period." (Ref.16 p. 189) [WHAT "PERIOD"? IT SEEMS W&H SENSED THAT, IN THE LIGHT OF DARWIN'S SUCCESS IN OVERTHROWING SO MUCH BELIEF IN GOD AS CREATOR, THE TIME WAS RIPE TO ATTACK THE CITADEL OF THE FAITH—THE PRESERVATION OF THE INSPIRED WORD OF GOD!]

4.) Also, see THE THEOLOGICAL HERESIES OF WESTCOTT AND HORT: AS SEEN IN THEIR OWN WRITINGS, available from Ref. 5).

These two men who have given us the Critical Text would imply to us that the Lord has let mankind down if the "true Text" of the New Testament was lost for 1500 years, but they rediscovered it —Vaticanus, "B", in the Vatican library. The fourth part of the lie is this myth "that the true New Testament text was lost for more than 1500 years and then restored by Westcott and Hort" (Ref.23, p. 193).

In contrast to this negative nonsense, let us wind up with a positive picture of how "Biblical Textual Criticism" actually works. First, consider, "The worst corruptions to which the New Testament has ever been subjected, originated within a hundred years after it was composed" Prebendary Scrivener (Ref.17 p. 317). THEREFORE, the older manuscript is by no means guaranteed to be better. In contrast with the unscientific speculations of subjective (called "higher") Textual Criticism, the <u>Science</u> of "Biblical Textual Criticism" is based upon certain facts:

1.) No "perpetual miracle" of preserving sacred manuscripts against depraving influences was ever promised.

2.) As a matter of observable historical fact, the Biblical Church purged herself of those shamefully depraved copies, by not using them (so B was not worn out by use, surviving to our day).

3.) Now these blind guides, who have no faith in God's repeated promises to preserve His Words, want to dig up those manuscripts that had been quarantined, thus <u>re-infecting</u> the Remnant Church with a disease it had been healed of centuries ago.

4.) We hear W&H, speaking like some heathen oracle in "magisterial statements, unsupported by a particle of rational evidence", that B is virtually the Apostolic Autographs (Ref.17 p. 247). Burgon says,

> "A safer, the *only* trustworthy method in fact, of ascertaining the Truth of Scripture,...without prejudice or partiality,— simply ascertains WHICH FORM OF THE TEXT ENJOYS THE EARLIEST, THE FULLEST, THE WIDEST, THE MOST RESPECTABLE, AND—above all things—THE MOST VARIED ATTESTATION....(T)hat Copies, Versions, and Fathers should all three concur in sanctioning....It will be perceived therefore that the method we plead for consists merely in <u>a loyal recognition of the whole of the Evidence</u>...."

[The "evidence" is the vast majority of manuscripts, preserved at the cost of millions martyred as the Origen/Arian Church tried to <u>change</u> the manuscripts, and then the Dark Ages Church tried to <u>burn</u> the true manuscripts along with those martyrs who copied and evangelized the world with them.]

Let us admire (worship) the Lord Jesus Christ's actual handiwork in inspiring <u>and preserving</u> His Words:

"The ample and highly complex provision which Divine Wisdom hath made for the effectual conservation of that crowning master-piece of His own creative skill,—THE WRITTEN WORD.... The good Providence of the Author of Scripture is discovered to have furnished His household, the Church, with..." (Ref.17 p. 338-341)[over 6000 manuscripts of the Greek N.T., almost 90,000 Patristic documents quoting over 1,000,000 Scripture texts, over 20 ancient translated versions, and much more—a thousand times more textual support than any other ancient writing—which has produced the majority "Traditional Text" (supported by 98% of these documents)].

There was then an actual historical successive refining basically via collation: Erasmus, Stephanus, Beza, King James translators, Elzevirs, ... with the 7th (or completion) ongoing. Compare the TR to the less than 1% textually supported, internally mutually self-contradictoring, subjectively conjectured, Dynamic Equivalently paraphrased, ghostly Critical Text.

Now that the issues are so much clearer, you will still choose what you really want. However, do take note that the Critical Text's attack on the preservation of the Inspired Word of God is thrown out of a just court, and the case challenging our faith in God's Words can be closed.

NOTE: For anyone wanting an in depth course on REVISION REVISED, Triune Biblical University is offering a graduate level Course. online.   www.tbuworldwide.com (425)829-0431

So, we see that the (Nestle-Aland) Critical Text is the illegitimate offspring of Westcott and Hort's mythlogical theory. (It never even earned theory status, but was really an extremely clever chess strategy, to destroy any faith in the preservation of Holy Scripture by causing doubts in the TR.) Yet, it is strangely still the primary text used for virtually every new English bible version since 1880, including to a large extent the NKJV—by those who are unaware of the facts (as greatly summarized above), and among <u>snakes</u> (the "seed" of the serpent Gen. 3:15), "the children of the wicked one" (Matt.13:38). So, WHAT'S NEW WITH SNAKES? They will stop when they are stopped.

This **ENOUGH** is prayerfully dedicated to (1.) making the facts in this matter available and understandable so those who are seeking the truth can come to truthful conclusions, and (2.) blowing the cover of those whose intent it is to deceive.

B is the bible that drove the entire human race into the Dark Ages—only stopped when the Scripturally refined and thereby preserved Textus Receptus Words of God were translated into Latin, German, English ..., and too many copies were printed on the newly invented printing presses for the Inquisition Church to confiscate and burn them all. This caused what is called "The Reformation". (Appendix J, "The *Counter*-Reformation", warns of the desperate danger of accepting back the Dark Ages bible.)

DEAR READER: Since the NKJV reads the same as the Nestle-Aland Critical Text (the current form of the Westcott & Hort Vaticanus) in over 80% of the places where NKJV differs from the KJ (see Part I, "Fruit Inspection"), we really should consider this simple resolution to what is, practically speaking, the basic issue in this battle for the Bible: conclude that the Vaticanus manuscript (B and the NKJV!) are, at best, simply historical curiosities, of no major use in finding God's inspired and preserved Words. To assist you in arriving at this conclusion, please consider the next section carefully.

VATICANUS EXPOSED

To decide whether B should be the manuscript from which your Bible is translated, consider the following:

A.) "B" EDITED AND NOT OLDEST: We have demonstrated that B is by no means the oldest of over 6000 manuscript witnesses to the Bible, but which began its existence being heavily edited by Origen, then Eusebius. (What man should edit God's Word at all?) Then thousands of scribal overwritings, erasures, and notes demonstrate that B was repeatedly systematically and randomly further edited. Note also that it is the earliest manuscript which contains the Apocrypha. (See "J" below for fraudulent hypocrisy.)

B.) "HIGHER" TEXTUAL CRITICISM HIGHLY SUBJECTIVE: Modern textual critics re-created B, by unreasonably and subjectively grossly over-weighing it in comparison to the overwhelming majority of manuscripts, in order to change the Bible to agree with B. They deleted many thousands of words from the Bible, alleging that those who were pious added these words to the Word of God. (See Appendix K, page 191. This is called "Expansions of piety", but it is a very <u>impious</u> thing, being in violation of the Word's command to not change anything.) Another example of "higher" textual criticism is to choose a minority manuscript (= fewer manuscripts in existence with that reading, often 2:6000!) over a majority manuscript, because of some nonsense like the style of the minority reading seemed more "Marken" than the other (sounded more to the critic like what he felt Mark would write). A further example is second-guessing how one reader *might* have appended a margin comment to a manuscript, and then a subsequent copyist *might* mistakenly put that comment into the text, so, clip! the sentence or the entire passage being questioned by the critic is deleted from the Bible— such subjective deadly attitudes for editing the Word of God!

These Critics must think something like "If I can't understand it, or if it doesn't say what I think it ought to say, I have the right to change it, because it must be a scribal error or a bad copy...." (Things That Are Different Are Not the Same, Dr. Mickey Carter, p.161)

C.) CRITICAL TEXT RADICALLY UNSUPPORTED:

If we apply Biblical textual criticism, which is the comparing of extant manuscript readings to find a majority reading, we would legitimately eliminate virtually all of the 35,000 B word changes to the TR because <u>truly</u>, actually, factually, most of these changes are based only upon B readings.

D.) B NOT SCIENTIFIC: This "higher" textual criticism is a very subjective comparing of scholars' opinions, not scientifically comparing manuscripts. "Individual idiosyncrasy, not external evidence, readings strongly preferred, not attested, and always using as the standard Vaticanus" (Ref.17, pp.307, 308).

E.) B THE BASIS OF CRITICAL TEXT: The [Critical] text of Westcott and Hort is practically the text of B [Vaticanus] (Ref.8, p.546) says Dr. Sir Herman Hoskier, who was perhaps the world's pre-eminent Greek New Testament manuscript expert, whose collation with other key manuscripts of Vaticanus ("B") in CODEX B AND IT's ALLIES, is unsurpassed to this day (Ref.8, p.550).   Sir Hoskier also said that B is "disfigured".

F.) OLDEST NT MSS SUPPORT TR: Based on cutting-edge research on <u>the most ancient</u> New Testament texts, the Papyri, Wilbur Pickering, ThD, PhD, said, Its [B] "respectability quotient hovers near zero .... In particular I fail to see how anyone can read Hoskier's CODEX B AND ITS ALLIES with attention and still retain respect for" B as witness to The New Testament. In addition, Pickering said, "The modern Critical and eclectic texts are based precisely on B ... and they have been found wanting." The Papyri— such as P66, dated 150 AD in contrast with 350 AD for B forced almost 500 changes in the "New Greek" Text, back to the TR/KJ readings, just between the 26th to 27th editions of the Nestle-Aland Greek New Testament. (However, that is out of over 36,000 variant readings—too little too late.)   Dr. Pickering also said, "there has been an open disavowal— one might call it a debunking—of Westcott and Hort methodology and textual theory." (Ref.8, p.550) Take Vaticanus off the table of discussion and everything Westcott & Hort said and wrote loses cohesion—and all that is left is the TR, supported by 98% of all textual data.

G.) B FABRICATED/MUTILATED: Moody Bible Institute Vice President Dr. Alfred Martin called B "depraved"; it exhibits "a fabricated text ... [which is] shamefully mutilated."

H.) B BASIS OF ARIAN HERESY: Floyd Jones, ThD, PhD, has this to say: "The most significant fact regarding these MSS is that in ... Vaticanus B John 1:18 reads that Jesus was the only begotten 'God' instead of the only begotten 'Son'—which is the original Arian Heresy! This means that God had a little God named Jesus who is thus a lesser God than the Father .... But at the incarnation A GOD WAS NOT BEGOTTEN. God begot a son who, in so far as his deity is concerned, is eternal (Micah 5:2). This reading [in John 1:18] renders these MSS as UNTRUSTWORTHY and DEPRAVED! This Arian heresy resulted from Origen's editing the Greek manuscripts and appears in Vaticanus B which was derived from copying his work." (Ref.1b, p.11, Footnote 1.) Imagine! The Arian Heresy, which so totally derailed "The Holy Roman Empire" and some 1200 years of human history, was possibly conceived when Origen changed John 1:18. If one wonders if this little change makes so much difference, note that after Constantine, the Arian Roman Catholic Church took over from the Roman emperors in brutal persecutions of the true Body of Christ, amassing a body count of millions of Christian martyrs murdered! (See FOXE'S BOOK OF MARTYRS.)

I.) B CHALLENGES CHRIST'S DEITY: Dr. Jack Moorman sees this resurrection of the Gnostic denial of the true humanity of The Lord Jesus Christ, coupled with the denial of the Deity of Jesus, as the "dark secret" in the new bibles. However they try to explain these omissions, they can't deny that these omissions exist. The new versions change "The Lord Jesus Christ" to "the Lord Jesus", to "Jesus" to "He" in hundreds of places. Early heretics could not get their hands on all of the manuscripts so they couldn't systematically change all references, but do note that B has this heretical reading in John 1:18 and these thousands of deletions from the KJ/TR (Ref.12A, pp.14-16).

J.) B HAS THE REJECTED APOCRYPHA: B contains the Apocrypha (Tobit, Bel and the Dragon, the Maccabees ....) The NASV, RSV, NRSV, ESV, HCSV, NIV, ... virtually every English translation since 1881 are basically from the B Westcott and Hort text. Yet all fundamental Christians (and Bible-believing Jews for the OT), reject the Apocrypha from the Canon of Scripture. **It would be hypocritical for those who accept B as their highest Bible Text authority to not include the Apocrypha in their bible. Yet, none does; they all are!**

K.) BIBLE TRANSLATION AFFLICTED WITH CRITICAL TEXT: Dr. Merrill C. Tenney, in NEW DIMENSIONS IN NEW TESTAMENT STUDY, p.19, says, "the recent United Bible Society's Greek New Testament (UGT) [the"U" in the NKJV "NU" text] has moved even closer to Westcott and Hort (B)", (underline added). Imagine, missionaries putting their lives on the line to translate from a non-Bible! No translation is perfect, but if it uses intentionally changed manuscripts and then paraphrases (Dynamic Equivalence) God's Holy Words, the Holy Spirit will not own and empower that book! A veteran Bible Translator stated, "...incredible amount of translations that have been done by sweet young people, [were] printed, but hardly even used by the tribesman." This translator left Wycliffe Bible Translators because he was required to use 1.) "a theory of translation more radical than anything promoted by UBS [United Bible Society], and 2.) the dynamic equivalency approach". He observed that,"The age of the quick, easy paraphrase has replaced trembling at the very thought of changing the smallest aspect of a verse." The writers of this ENOUGH went to Wycliffe Florida headquarters prayerfully seeking to discuss the issue of literal/formal (literal = every word accounted for; formal = identical grammar whenever possible) translation of the preserved inerrant Bible vs the paraphrases of the UGT, but were not received in any way.

Anyone interested in Bible Translation for Bible-less people should verify that the starting point is God's preserved Words (as found in the TR), and that translation is literal/formal equivalence instead of dynamic equivalence. Trinitarian Bible Society and Baptist Bible Translators have remained faithful in this and would be a strategic help for true translations of God's Words. NOTE: in addition, a list of Bibles which have been translated into foreign languages based on the TR can be found at the William Carey Bible Society (www.wcbible.org). What a challenge and calling to convey God's Words! In a sense every Christian is called to be a translator! Do see "APPENDIX F" on page 179 in this context.

L.) B ISSUED BY THE INQUISITION: Vaticanus was re-discovered in 1481 in the Vatican library, but the Vatican was bringing mankind the horrendous "Inquisition" in the same time frame!   So, Vaticanus was issued from the Inquisition, which brutally murdered, some say as many as 70,000,000 Christians! Be careful who you run with; has the Roman Catholic Church changed significantly since that blood flood, or is it just lacking opportunity?

M.) MAJORITY MSS RULE: Dean John Burgon word for word collated over 1,000,000 (one million) of the scripture texts quoted in almost 90,000 ancient extant Greek documents by the early Church Fathers. He said "Strange as it may appear, it is undeniably true, that the whole of the controversy may be reduced to the following narrow issue: does the truth of the text of scripture dwell with the vast multitude of copies,... concerning which nothing is more remarkable than the marvelous agreement which subsists between them? Or is it rather to be supposed that the truth abides exclusively with a very little handful of manuscripts [that is Vaticanus and its few allies] which at once differ from the great bulk of witnesses, and among themselves.

The main answer the B proponents give against the above argument is that Byzantinia was the only place that still spoke and wrote Greek, so of course, there would be more Greek manuscripts from there—but they would be "late". Well, a balanced scholarly treatment must consider that the earliest Byzantine manuscripts are at least as old as B, and the 1,000,000+ church Father quotes are before 300AD (that is before B), the "Lectionaries", the early versions, and the Papyri are all predominately TR type; and most of them are much earlier than B! Granted the number of TR type manuscripts is less around the fourth century, but this was the height of the Arian controversy when the Arian Catholic Church was "writing" FOXES BOOK OF MARTYRS—in blood, and destroying all martyr manuscripts they could find! Also, if B was the true copy, nothing, including the Moslem conquest, would have kept it from multiplying. (In order to stabilize their empire, the Moslems got along with other religions and usually didn't destroy their literature. B is old, yet physically in good condition precisely because it was not used or copied. It was rejected—soon even in Alexandria. [See P.) for several scientific implications of these facts presented in M.)]

N.) THE TRUE CHURCH ALWAYS HAS THE TRUE BIBLE: If Divine preservation of the Bible text is believed to be true, as unequivocally promised by Christ, accepting B as a serious text flies in the face of God's promises and His character. Would He leave His Church without the true text of the Bible for 1500 years until rediscovered in the Pope's Palace library?

O.) B SIMPLY THE WORST MSS: "(W)ithout a particle of hesitation, that ℵ B D are *three **of the most scandalously corrupt copies extant:**—*exhibit **the most shamefully mutilated** texts which are anywhere to be met with:— have become, by whatever process (for their history is wholly unknown), the depositories of the largest amount of **fabricated readings,** ancient **blunders,** and **intentional perversions of Truth**, which are discoverable in any known copies of the Word of GOD." (Dean John Burgon, Ref.17, p.16, **bold ours**)

P.) ACCEPTING B REJECTS SCIENTIFIC PROBABILITIES: "What modern textual critics are *really* affirming—either implicitly or explicitly—constitutes nothing less than a wholesale rejection of [transmission] probabilities on a sweeping scale." (Ref.11, p.166) This is so because the B manuscript which theoretically would have been copied one for one with the TR predecessor manuscripts, was not—because it historically was rejected by everyone except the Catholic Church until Hort and Co. resurrected it in the 1800's.

Therefore, you be the judge. Strike Vaticanus as "corrupted evidence", "inadmissible", and the jury's verdict at the end of this trial will be for the (King James) TR manuscripts, beyond all reasonable doubt! However, this verdict is as acceptable to some people as is Creation to a devoted believer in Evolution. Not that most true scientists or scholars (those who do original work) believe this incredible stuff, but the only alternative—God—is just not allowable to them. Nobel Prize winner and Harvard biology professor Dr. George Wald said, "Spontaneous generation [of life] was scientifically disproved 120 years ago by Louis Pasteur and others, but that leaves us with only one other possibility ... that life came as a supernatural act of creation of God, but I can't accept that philosophy because I do not want to believe in God." ("The Origin of Life," SCIENTIFIC AMERICAN, December 1978).

But watch the fur fly, and the real sheep separate themselves from the wolves in sheep's clothing over any challenge, however factual and documented, to this non-Bible (B); there are those who have been wholly taken in by this masterful Scrollduggery and others who apparently delight to use it in their long war against God (Ref.9). (Let us observe alertly those who continue to defend this manuscript after this exposé is put into their hands!) SO:

I Peter 5:8 Be sober, be vigilant, because your adversary, the devil, as a vicious scholar, walks about seeking whom he may devour.

Jer.17:5 Cursed be the man that trusteth in man (because he has a PhD!) and maketh flesh his arm, and whose heart departeth from the Lord.

Footnote: this is known as "Scholarolatry"

Paraphrased Puns

Put it back, Tischendorf!
(*See Appendix L, p, 193*)

16 PROSECUTION WITNESSES:

The following are **mostly in NKJV's own words**—impeccable witnesses.

1.) The 1992 NKJV preface stated that it is translated from the TR, yet in the words of a Nelson NEW KING JAMES STUDY BIBLE **Preface:** The Greek text used for the NKJV was "an eclectic text comparing the Byzantine Text [largely supporting the Textus Receptus] with the Alexandrian Text [basically Vaticanus] and all other available manuscripts". "NKJV uses less than 10% Greek manuscripts based on TR." (www.PocketDoctrines.com)

2.) "The New Testament translator ... does not deal with the manuscripts themselves. He works indirectly through the use of the modern Greek text" [the Nestle-Aland, Westcott & Hort,

Origen/Eusebius "Critical Text"—not near the TR!], said NIV/ NKJV translator Louis Foster ("SELECTING A TRANSLATION OF THE BIBLE", pp.14,15). **Eight other NKJV translators also translated the NIV** which used vastly different translation principles than the KJ; that has to have affected the translation of the NKJV.

3.) A **NKJV Preface** states: "readers may be assured that the textual debate does not affect one in a thousand words in the Greek and English New Testament" (.1%). However, in the footnotes of both the NKJV Scofield and Nelson Study Bibles over 1000 "Significant Variations" in the New Testament Greek Text, each having a calculated average of 10 words are found; 1000 variations x 10 words each = 10,000 words affected by the "textual debate" in the 200,000 word Greek or English New Testaments, or 10,000/200,000 = (simplifying the fraction) 1/20 words (5%) affected. Wow! Not "1 in 1000", but 1 in 20 words affected by the textual debate! One would hope that the NKJV people are better linguists than they are mathematicians. The new bible bunch will answer that it is one word in a thousand of "significant" variation or that "affects doctrine". They feel free to judge which Words of God are significant although God Himself has given more honor to His Words than to His name (Ps.138:2). Some of these people "despise" God's Word (despise God Himself?). Dr. D.A, Waite collated the entire KJ/TR Greek New Testament with both the Westcott and Hort Greek text, and the Nestle-Aland/United Bible Society UGT text, and found not .1% (1/4 page of variation), but 7% (he ended up with 46 pages of different words). (See D.A. Waite, THE FOUR-FOLD SUPERIORITY OF THE KING JAMES BIBLE, Ref.5.)

Note: we are considering NKJV textual variant footnotes the same as translating from the Critical Text, because the NKJV translators obviously did, judging from the often verbatim collusion found over 80% of the time when NKJV differs from the KJ, as shown in Part I, The Fruit Inspection. Also, we suggest that textually variant footnotes could be as bad or worse than omitting texts from Scripture as most other modern versions do, because the footnotes possibly cause more doubt to the reader about the reliability of the Bible than missing texts which he might not even be aware are missing. (Dr. DiVietro, WHY NOT THE KING JAMES BIBLE!, p.22, found almost 800 of these textual variant footnotes. This book is available from Ref. 5.)

4.) One **NKJV Preface** says, "very few scholars still favor [the Textus Receptus] as such, and then often for its historical prestige as the text of Luther, Calvin, Tyndale and the King James Version." Actually here are four strong votes <u>for</u> the Textus Receptus: as there have not been found any <u>significant</u> new textual readings since the time of the KJ (and the TR isn't missing the thousands of words that the Critical Text is.)

5.) A **NKJV Preface** states: "Today scholars agree that the Science of textual criticism is in a state of flux." This statement needs some translation of its own: "Scholars agree" sounds impressive, but if what they agree to is "a state of flux", then they are agreeing to disagree! Floyd Jones, PhD, ThD, puts it, "The [Critical] text is in a state of continuous flux, vacillating between the opinions of enormous egos" (Ref.1b, p.125). Compare this Critical Text to the KJ TR, where every letter is defended—as the Lord Jesus promised! (Matt. 5:18; 24:35)

6.) Why did the **NKJV Preface** say that it was "decided to retain the Traditional Text" in producing "The latest edition of the best-selling translation" (quoted off the cover of a NKJV Bible)? One can only hope that publishing profits and royalties of the "best-selling translation" aren't the main reason. The NKJV "Traditional Text" is "the fifth revision" of the KJ TR (1990 **NKJV Preface**). Who did these revisions, and how extensive they were, sadly is not stated, but in any case the NKJV "Traditional Text" is not nearly identical to the TR used in 1611 although the **Preface** to the 1982 edition of the NKJV says that they are one and the same: "The Greek used for the New Testament is the one that was followed by the King James translators: the traditional text of the Greek-speaking churches, called the Received Text or Textus Receptus, first published in 1516." Many people have been misled to believe that the NKJV New Testament is based on the basically identical text as the KJ. However, Part I, Fruit Inspection, demonstrates that in over 80% of the differences noted, the NKJV verses quite apparently are translated from the Critical Text.

7.) Here is a fundamental flaw in the entire NKJV project. They cite a "Majority Text" as a basis of much of the NKJV translation. The majority text the NKJV **readers** think of is simply the majority of manuscripts with the same readings. What the NKJV calls their "Majority Text", is based on the Von Soden 20% of extant Papyri (Ref.4, p.74)—an insufficient and faulty foundation to represent a majority of manuscripts.

Majority Text Only people have a problem because there are several "Majority Texts" out there, and they differ from each other and the TR in thousands of places. God did a much better job of preserving His Word than just a majority text—see Psalm 12:6.

8.) In order to qualify for a copyright under the "Derivative Copyright Law", the new work must either add a substantial amount of new material—which a Bible version cannot easily do— or it must make enough substantial changes. Just modern spellings aren't enough; they must change the meanings in many verses. Key words must be changed or substituted. However, the KJ is a precise, literal translation. Virtually any substantial change from it makes the verse at best, less literal, often inaccurate, or sometimes even non-sense! This must explain the hundreds of maddeningly poor translation changes encountered in the course of this ENOUGH. (Do see Gal.5:4a, p.36, in the Fruit Inspection, Part I, for examples of how many of these changes not only confuse the message, but also, of necessity, use a _more_ difficult to read and understand vocabulary.) One aid to the NKJV in earning their copyright is that the NKJV translators apparently felt free to translate from the Critical Text where it differs from the KJ manuscripts to generate their changes. However, these changes aren't just poor translations; they are sometimes wrong—incorporating some of the Critical Text creatively subtle diabolical twists!

9) A **NKJV Preface says,** "It is most important to emphasize that fully 85% of the New Testament text is the same in the Textus Receptus, Critical Text, and the Majority Text." That is: Don't worry, we still have 85% of the New Testament we are sure of. Or, in the thinking of the NKJV, God gets an "A" for inspiration, but a "C" for preservation! Also, as we noted repeatedly in the "Fruit

Inspection", this 100%–85% =15% of text these people aren't sure about strategically warps many key, pivotal passages, definitely affecting doctrine!

Eighty-five per cent agreement? It would be wonderful to live a life or preach a sermon 85% in agreement with the total Word of God, but when it comes to what the Bible text itself actually is, even 5% of doubt prevents us from having 100% faith!   We are told, "*If ye have faith as a grain of mustard seed ... nothing shall be impossible unto you*" (Matt.17:20). That is, our faith may be small, but it must be 100% in what we know God has said. However, if we have any doubt in what the Scripture text itself actually is, then we <u>can't know</u> what God has said; we are cut loose and drifting in our faith. The Lord promises, "*ask of God, ... nothing wavering. For he that wavereth* [= to hesitate, to keep on forever analyzing the problem, rather than to trust God and act on what He's shown us] *is like a wave of the sea, driven with the wind and tossed. For let not that man think that he shall receive anything from the Lord*" (James 1:5-8). It is either "<u>*nothing*</u> *shall be impossible to you* " (Matt.17:20) OR you shall not "*receive* <u>*anything*</u> *from the Lord*"! (James 1:7) SELAH (= "stop", think about this.) (Underline added in verses above.)

10.) Many of these passages compared in the "Fruit Inspection" are seemingly crafted so they **can** be interpreted rightly from the NKJV **if** you already understand the contextually correct interpretation, but from which it is precariously difficult to grasp aright if you don't already have this understanding. This is like turning or removing the street signs to the emergency hospital. If you already know the way to the hospital from previous trips, you will probably not be misdirected; but if you are wholly dependent on the signs, you will be misled with possibly permanent consequences to your injured or ill passenger. (See Heb.12:13—in the KJ!) This is spiritually a matter of life and death!

11.) We will never **fully** understand a single verse of the Holy Bible; but what we do understand, we must (1.) trust and (2.) obey. However, what if footnotes in our Bible indicate something possibly should be changed in the passage we are studying, or possibly should be added to it? Or what if footnotes suggest that maybe the text we are working on shouldn't be in the Bible at all! To say, as the **NKJV Preface** states, that variations in the Bible text itself aren't significant, doesn't make sense, does it? Again we ask, what is the Holy Bible to these people?

12.) A **NKJV Preface** goes on, "no established doctrine is called into question by any doubts about the correct reading of this text or that"—but, see Acts 3:13, Ps.50:1; Prov.16:10 in the Fruit Inspection, Part I, of this **ENOUGH**, where the very doctrine of the Deity of the God of the Bible is diminished in the NKJV. Please don't attempt to justify these omissions by saying that the faithful saints of His-story disobeyed their God (Rev.22:18,19, etc.) by making these thousands of "Expansions of piety" additions to Scripture when God has repeatedly forbidden this. Many of those who made the copies of the NT gave up their very lives, and sometimes their whole families—being crucified, fed to the lions, and more. For modern scholars, who sit comfortably in air conditioned or centrally heated offices, to accuse the Martyrs of deliberately altering the Scriptures is an accusation of the brethren worthy of the "*accuser of our brethren*" (Rev.12:10). To add to, take from or change God's Word is the most "reckless" (="Lightness", Jer.23:32) thing you could ever do!

Really, is not the doctrine of the Inspiration and Preservation of the Word of God, from which all other doctrines come, "affected"? All "established doctrine" is defined by the Bible and is certainly "called into question" by over six times as many "footdoubts" in the NKJV than in the NIV, stating doubts about the reliability of the actual texts translated from. In these verses the NKJV says "NU Text says ...; M Text says ..." and NKJV doesn't even vote which they prefer. What is the reader to do? Try switching to a Bible based on the promised preserved Original—which makes every variant wrong. Does such a Bible exist today? Jesus said He would preserve His Words, so believe Him, or believe the bible sellers.

Is doctrine affected by the textual differences between the TR and the Vaticanus? The Lord Jesus said *"When the Son of man cometh, shall He find faith on the earth?"* (Luke 18:8) The Word "faith" used here is articular, "he pistos", "the faith", the whole body of doctrine—from Christ's promised coming, to His resurrection and Second Coming; God's revelation defines doctrines, contracts, and plans. These are "blown up" (John 10:35) by any changes in contract "language" in all the new versions. So, Bible doctrine is not just "called into question", sometimes it is "blown up"!

13.) The Critical Text omits hundreds of statements found in the Textus Receptus. (See Appendix K. p. 191 for 200 omissions/ changes.) The NKJV is not missing any of these 200, yet **135 of them are questioned in their footnotes**—which is the same thing as omitting them, or worse because it's easy to read over a deletion, not even noticing that it's not all there (certainly truth is missing but your confidence isn't shaken); but don't footdoubts gender doubts in the reliability of God's Word? The omissions are the acid test for finding out which text a Bible is based on—for instance, does that Bible omit those texts the Critical Text omits? A farm boy can check out a new Bible during his lunch break by use of a list of omitted texts to see if certain texts are there or not. However, since the NKJV has not actually omitted the texts which the Critical Text does (just questions their reliability in footdoubts in their Study Bibles), our farm boy brother would incorrectly conclude that the NKJV is not influenced by the Critical Text. Brothers don't do Brothers that way.

14.) Note that the NIV has 120 textual variant footnotes, the NASV has 133, and **the NKJV has 772**. The NIV is out front about using the Critical Text. However, the "Fruit Inspection" proves that, over 80% of the time, where the NKJV differs from the KJ, the NKJV has the same translations as versions that follow the Critical Text. Yet the NKJV Prefaces pledge to follow the TR Text, and they do seem to in regard to deletions—but it's those "footdoubts"! Over six times as many as the NIV. Couldn't all this be pled as Fraud:

(a.) in attempting to pass off the NKJV as a new KJ with just spelling and a few word updates, and

(b.) being done in a manner as to be very difficult to discern from which Text NKJV was being translated?

15.) Why do many seemingly stalwart conservative Christians use and even promote the NKJV? <u>Maybe they were ambushed!</u>

When "called to preach", they entrusted their souls to a seminary (cemetery) that didn't have a preserved Bible—that says they believe in it but don't use it. This is walking *"in the counsel of the ungodly"*(Ps.1:1a). For those who don't flee from there, it leads to standing *"in the way of sinners"* (Ps.1:1b)—not making waves about the loss of the Bible, and taking courses in how to lie to Pulpit Committees that ask them if they believe in the inerrant Word of God. Yes, you believe in the Verbal Plenary Inspired Word of God, "as originally written" (but not the bible that you will preach from). Only if you have a wolf's heart (and stomach) can you hold all this down without upchucking, and soon you will be sitting *"in the seat of the scornful"* (Ps.1:1c), endorsing books like THE KING JAMES ONLY CONTROVERSY and "counseling" others with *"the counsel of the ungodly"* (back to Ps.1:1a, an endless loop) as you ridicule anyone who stands (on God's promises) for a Preserved Verbal Plenary Inspired Bible.

Why do the sheep put up with this?

(a.) Because few are aware of the facts (not even as aware as you are now, having read this ENOUGH).

(b.) Because of the twilight of Beam Splitter overlays (Hollywood special-effects technique) coming from those "disguised" (as "to change external appearances") as *"angels of light"* (II Cor.11:13-15) who blind the eyes (or pad the wallet—I Tim.6:10) of many of God's servants.

(c.) Because the NKJV Preface (and NKJV OT Senior Editor Dr. James Price) state that they translated from the TR so the NKJV would be just a New KJ without the old words. However, review Witnesses 1,2,4,7,15 in this list who testify that the NKJV did not use only the TR and did Dynamic Equivalently translate in some two thousand places.

(d.) And, certainly because some Christians aren't.

16.) Consider carefully Dr. D.A. Waite's documented conclusion: " ... if the translators use this DYNAMIC EQUIVALENCE [see Appendix F, p. 179] technique of translation, they can ... **add, subtract** or **change** the Words of God like the Devil did in the Garden of Eden ... at will. The Bible is not just another book. If they want to do that with their comic books or fiction books [or even their Bible commentaries], that is one thing ... But don't do it to God's Book! This is serious. This is diabolical. This is deadly .... <u>I believe the NEW KING JAMES version is probably the most dangerous of the new versions</u> ... because it is the foot in the door ... to lead eventually to ever more Dynamic Equivalency .... Don't let anyone say the NEW KING JAMES is an accurate, faithful, verbal equivalent [to the KING JAMES]." (Dr. Waite is qualified to make this preceding statement, having more hours of formal Greek instruction than this author of the ENOUGH spent to earn his degree in Engineering from UCLA. He continues,) "The deceptive use of 'KING JAMES VERSION' in the title would lead many to think that there are only a few small incidental changes in their New KJV but it is basically just the KING JAMES VERSION with a few minor changes in it to bring it up to date .... [There are over <u>100,000 changes!</u>]

"Another assumption by the use of the words 'King James Version' in the title is that they make use of THE SAME TRANSLATION PRINCIPLES as were used in the King James Version of 1611 .... The editors go on to say how they have used 'COMPLETE EQUIVALENCE' and have shunned 'DYNAMIC EQUIVALENCE'. " (Ref. 18, Dr. D.A. Waite, pp.122-124) This really seems to be a lie! As we have shown repeatedly in the evidence herein reproduced, the NEW KJV is replete with the DIABOLICAL "DYNAMIC EQUIVALENCE"! This is seen in the over 2000 actual documented examples given in the book being quoted here: # 1442, available from Ref.5. The writers of this ENOUGH say, in the good company of the Apostle Paul: "What if some did not believe [in God's promise of a preserved Bible]? shall their unbelief make the faith of God without effect? God forbid! Yea, let God be true and every man a liar" (Rom.3:3,4a).

IN CONCLUSION—"CLOSING ARGUMENTS"

Why? What is the purpose of all this obviously intentional meddling with God's Word? There has been a "Counter-Reformation"

(Appendix J)—the main focus of which is to get rid of the Book of the "Great Reformation", the KJ Bible, and then the meddlers can supplant God's Plans from *"the beginning"* (Gen.1:1) with their own. Lucifer ("Light bearer") became Satan (The "Adversary") when his *"heart was lifted up"*. Heaven's Worship Leader became the father of lies (John 8:44). He is your father if you knowingly follow his lies.

The lie that there is anything wrong with the Bible, anything that needs man's Reasoned Eclectic Method (REM) or other man's words to fix, is PERHAPS THE DEVIL'S DEEPEST WILE. (He is the trans-millennial Head Scrolldugger himself.)   Consider the true men of God who have been taken in by this wile and the consequences to ministries of trying to serve God while not being sure He cared to (or could?) keep His Word intact. They become bereft of God's true counsel and Authority (read, "Power") for ministry because of confidence in bogus bibles. We are meant to be throwing trees around (Luke 17:6)—it is our "duty" as His servants (Luke 17:7-10). We should be moving mountains, (very carefully so as not to squash any innocents) Matt.17:20; but, how can anyone *"not doubt in his heart"* (Mark 11:23) if he has a holey bible?!

The "Scrollduggery" investigation done here has presented much Scriptural, historical, and linguistic evidence supporting the claim that the KJ is literally ("every-word-accounted-for", not "dynamically" = paraphrased) and formally (grammatically identical whenever possible) translated from the preserved TR. We have also viewed considerable evidence that the NKJV is not. Please listen to these concluding voices:

1.) Dr. Walter S. Beebe tells us that in the late 1970's "The original [NKJV] committee was told only a few 'archaic words' were to be updated and the Original Text preserved. However, it is very apparent that it became an entirely new version." ("Which Version?", p. 13, Beebe Publications, 166 Swan Lake Dr, Stockbridge, GA. 30281). Something went very wrong with the good intentions of most of the men that did the NKJV. If circumstances and/or bad judgment make a landing approach unsafe, the professional pilot reckons his pride dead and goes around again—rather than risk littering the landscape with bloody sheet metal. Isn't the NKJV Bible, as it ended up, a crash landing for the Body of Christ? If this question seems contentious, it is prayerfully Scripturally so—"... *earnestly contend for the faith* [that comes by hearing the preserved Word, Rom.10:17] *which was once delivered unto the Saints*" Jude 3.

2.) "In a day when Bible publishers proclaim that we now have God's word in an English form that anyone can read and understand, it is amazing how little impact these Bibles seem to have on the lives of their readers .... Just as Job's plight is known to be attacks by the enemy of the Faith to discredit God's servant, so many today see the attacks on the Authorised Version as ... not mere arguments from scholarly men, but attacks ... from the enemy himself .... This is not to say that ... the Greek and Hebrew can be corrected to what is found in the English ...." (THE AUTHORISED VERSION, G.W. and D.E. Anderson, Trinitarian Bible Society, London, England.)

3.) "No one can recognize the inspired, preserved Word of God apart from faith .... This is the root error of those who defend the modern critical texts and versions. They ... approach it by human reason and scholarship [alone]. The Bible says that *'without faith it is impossible to please him'* (Heb.11:6)." (David Cloud, Ref.4, p.6) Both academic integrity and spiritual discernment are required.

4.) Dr. James Price (see Appendix H, p. 182) goes into perhaps the most detailed modern defense (Ref.13, especially Chap. 12) of what this ENOUGH calls, "The Logic of Unbelief"—that the bible text **must** have textual variant footnotes. Dr. Price says, "textual footnotes provide the supporting evidence .... {T[]the words, phrases or verses that are lacking or added in the main body of the critical text are contained in the textual footnotes along with the supporting textual evidence .... This declaration cannot be made for the ... Textus Receptus. [The TR] provides no textual evidence at all. Instead, the text implies all its words, phrases, verses, and sections are equally certain with no alternatives." BEAUTIFUL. There it is. Those who call it intellectual suicide to receive "the Received Text" (the TR) would have to admit that if you had the Autograph of John's Gospel, **any** textual variant to it would be an error. If the TR is the refined 99.9999% preserved text, then it would have virtually no alternative readings. The issue is "<u>Preserved</u> Verbal, Plenary Inspiration".

5.) Dr. Edward Hills says,

"... if the providential preservation of the Scriptures is not important, why is the doctrine of the infallible inspiration of the original Scriptures important? If God has not preserved the Scriptures by His special providence, why would He have infallibly inspired them in the first place? And if it is not important that the Scriptures be regarded as infallibly inspired, why is it important to insist that the Gospel is completely true? And if this is not important, why is it important to believe that Jesus is the divine Son of God? In short, unless we follow <u>the logic of faith</u>, we can be certain of nothing concerning the Bible ...." (Ref.14, p.225, underline added)

6.) THE SCRIPTURALLY AUTHORIZED <u>SEPARATION</u> PROCESS: *"Be not unequally yoked with unbelievers ... be ye separate, saith the Lord, and touch not the unclean thing ... and I will receive you, and will be a Father unto you, and ye shall be my sons and daughters, saith the Lord Almighty"* (II Cor. 6:14-18). If you are His son or daughter, *"Separate ... touch not"* Vaticanus which was resurrected by German Rationalists, propagated by Westcott & Hort. Perhaps use them as (man's words) Bible commentaries, but guard the flock; the Lambs tend to pick them up as Bibles. Please listen! Absolute separation is the <u>only</u> defense against leaven. Charles Spurgeon said, "Nothing maintains the true like separation from the false."

7.) *"All scripture is given by inspiration of God"* (II Tim.3:16), and *"Man shall not live by bread alone, but by every word that proceedeth out of the mouth of God"* (Matt.4:4). Not "85%" of them as the **NKJV Preface** tolerates. Add to, change, or take anything away, since *"the scripture cannot be broken"* (John 10:35), <u>and you have a broken bible</u>. This is absolutely a matter of God's honor *"... for thou hast magnified thy word above all thy name"* (Ps.138:2)! Note well, that it is written *"to the angel* (a high ranking officer on Jesus' own staff, Rev.1:16-20) *of the Church in Philadelphia"* as well as to us who are members of the last days remnant church, *"I know thy works: behold*

I [Jesus!] *have set before thee an open door, and no man can shut it: for thou hast a little strength, and hast kept my word, and hast not denied my name"* (Rev.3:7,8). To not keep (= guard against man's words bibles) His Word is to deny His name! To keep His Word is to *"hold that fast which thou hast, that no man take thy crown"* (Rev.3:11) and to be *"... perfect, throughly furnished unto all good works"* (II Tim.3:17), *"and having done all, to stand"* (Eph.6:11,13)! Thank you God for the Bible!

THE PROSECUTION RESTS.

"Compromise of any sort between the" preserved/inerrant TR Words of God, and the hopelessly edited words of man bibles "is impossible ... there cannot exist any middle view ... for the issue concerns the inner life of the whole community—touches men's heart of hearts ... GOD'S TRUTH will be ... the one object of all our striving" (Ref.17, pp.365,366).

NOW WE ASK YOU, THE READER/JURY/JUDGE, **WHICH BIBLE ?**   No hung jury is allowed.

I HAVE BEEN VERY JEALOUS FOR THE LORD GOD OF HOSTS! **ENOUGH**

APPENDIX A-L

APPENDIX A

All verses quoted in this Book are italicized. <u>Underlined words in those verses represent those supplied by the translator.</u>

The following abbreviations are used:

SC = Strong's Exhaustive Concordance
Lex = Analytical Lexicon,1969 Greek, 1970 Hebrew, by Davidson,
    published by Zondervan
Thayer's Lex. = Thayer's Analytic Lexicon (used with care due to
    Thayer's Unitarian bias)
Dict = Merriam Webster Dictionary (various)
KJ = King James Bible
NKJV = New King James Version
NASV = New American Standard Version
RSV = Revised Standard Version
NRSV = New Revised Standard Version
ESV = English Standard Version (basically a new NRSV)
NIV = New International Version
HCSV = Holman Christian Standard Version
ERV = English Revised Version
B = Codex B (Vaticanus)
BHS = Biblica Hebraica Stuttgartencia
DE = Dynamic Equivalency
LXX Vorlage = Septuagint (ENOUGH, p. 158)
MS = manuscript
MSS = manuscripts
NU Text = Nestle/UGT
REM = Reasoned Eclectic Method
TR = Textus Receptus
TT = Traditional Text
UBS United Bible Society
UGT = United Bible Society Greek Text
W&H = Westcott and Hort

Jesus swore on oath *"Verily I say unto you, Till heaven and earth pass, one jot or one tittle shall in no wise pass from the law, till all be fulfilled"*(Matt.5:18), *"It is easier for heaven and earth to pass, than one tittle of the law to fail"* (Luke 16:17), and *"Heaven and earth shall pass away, but my words shall not pass away."* (Matt.24:35; Mark13:31)

The Lord Jesus Christ here has <u>given His Word</u> that the Word of God will "no wise" be changed, down to the smallest written characters—"jot"=iota, the smallest letter in the Greek alphabet. Here, it is the Greek translation for "jodh", the smallest letter in the Hebrew. Could words be more clear that this is His promise that His God-breathed Words will be preserved? Giving His Word "confirms" a legal contract (covenant) and <u>makes His honor</u> "security" for this contract that His Words will be preserved! NOW TO QUESTION WHETHER OR NOT WE HAVE A PRESERVED BIBLE WOULD BE PERHAPS **THE GREATEST DISRESPECT FOR THE LORD IMAGINABLE!** *"Brethren ... Though it be but a man's covenant, yet if it be confirmed, no man disannulleth,* [takes from] *or addeth thereto"* (Gal.3:15). If the Scriptures have not been preserved, the "language" of God's Bible contracts has been changed; this would be <u>fraud by God—or He lied!</u> (I John 5:9,10)

Confidence in the Words of God is a life or death matter, for only in the Bible do we find God's offer of pardon and a secret, personal, eternal relationship with Himself. This relationship is entered when one believes the Imperial Edict of God's Word that *"all have sinned and come short of the glory of God"* (have you ever told a lie or lusted ...?) and that *"The wages of sin is death; but the gift of God is eternal life through Jesus Christ our Lord"* (Rom.3:23,6:23).

Have you accepted Jesus Christ (= "Messiah") as your God and Savior (Rom.10:9)?

P.S. If you do not use the NEW KING JAMES VERSION, please compare your Bible to the KING JAMES in the verse comparisons—you will make some surprising and needful discoveries. We are not saying that the Lord Jesus has not used these new bible (lowercase "b" for errant bibles) versions in your life; we are seeking the *"more excellent way"*, which is the completed **and preserved** Canon of Scripture (I Cor.12:31-13:13, the last verse of chapter 12 and all of chapter 13).

APPENDIX B

THE GOODS ON THE (BC/AD ?) SEPTUAGINT

Virtually the only historical evidence for a BC Greek Old Testament called the "Septuagint" (= seventy man or seventy day translation, depending on which legend followed) is "The letter of Aristeas" found in a highly spurious, non-canonical collection of writings called "The Forgotten Books of Eden". The Zondervan Preface to their Septuagint calls Aristeas a "fable". The Encyclopedia of Religion and Ethics (p.308) calls it a "manifest forgery". Notable Old Testament scholar Paul Kahle calls Aristeas "propaganda". Internally there are many factual errors in "Aristeas", such as: "Demetrious was never the royal librarian, and he died long before Alexandria's naval Victory ...." (Thackeray, THE LETTER OF ARISTEAS). "The letter tells of a conversation between Demetrius and Theodektes, but Theodektes died before Demetrius was born, and the letter itself is [tentatively] dated some 200 years later than the supposed 300 BC translation of the Old Testament into Greek." (THE INTERNATIONAL STANDARD BIBLE ENCYCLOPEDIA, p. 2724)

There is no proof demonstrating that Josephus ever saw a Septuagint, statements to the contrary notwithstanding—ask to see the evidence—though Joe does quote Aristeas; and he, along with one place in the Talmud, does mention a BC Greek PENTATEUCH (the first five books of the Bible). This is a far cry from a BC Greek Old Testament. The only "extant" BC Greek Old Testament scripture, the Ryland Papyrus, consists of just several chapters from Deuteronomy, which only demonstrates that part of the Pentateuch was translated BC.

Please consider: If the Septuagint was the Jewish Scriptures of the ten thousands of Hellenized (and literate) Jews since 300 BC, as is claimed by the Septuagint fan club, it seems that there would be some manuscript evidence of this before the oldest extant copy of the Septuagint, the "Old Testament" of the 350 AD Vaticanus manuscript.

KEY COMPARISON COMMENT: Many are aware that the "New Greek"—the "Critical Text" of the New Testament—is the Vaticanus New Testament, reconstituted when Westcott and Hort arbitrarily changed the Textus Receptus (KING JAMES) Greek text by some 40,000 words from 1870 to 1881. However, it is not such common knowledge that the Septuagint, or "Critical" Old Testament text, is the Vaticanus Old Testament. "**The text of the current edition of the Septuagint is mainly derived from this [Vaticanus] manuscript**" (OUR BIBLE AND THE ANCIENT MANUSCRIPTS, Dr. Frederick Kenyon, p.121); Westcott, Hort, Tischendorf, Swete, A.T. Robinson ... concurring. So, **the Vaticanus Old Testament is the Septuagint**! Perhaps some conservative scholars who do not accept the Nestle-Aland Critical New Testament as reliable, have been sold a bill of goods regarding the Septuagint Greek Old Testament, not realizing that it is the Old Testament of the same Roman Catholic Vaticanus manuscript which is the basis for the Nestle-Aland/UGT Greek New Testament!

The following are six indictments of the Septuagint:

1.) THE APOCRYPHA FIRST FOUND IN THE SEPTUAGINT
The Vaticanus OT/Septuagint has the Apocrypha interspersed throughout it, (as if it were part of the inspired Canon)—which would mean that the seventy Jewish wise men would have had to have translated the Apocrypha **before most of it was written** if they made their translation any time around 300 B.C!   Also, this means that the Septuagint, whenever it was written, is the culprit which first polluted the Old Testament Canon with the Apocrypha, for there is no evidence found that the Apocrypha was a part of any Bible prior to Origen's Hexapla. The publisher of the 1611 KJ had the Apocrypha inserted <u>between</u> the two Testaments, but it was never included <u>within</u> the Old Testament, and it was dropped in the second printing in 1613. (The first edition stated that the Apocrypha was not part of the Canon of Scripture.)

2.) THE SEPTUAGINT A VERY POOR TRANSLATION OR IS FROM A VERY POOR MANUSCRIPT
The Septuagint, apart from the Pentateuch, generally is a very poor translation, with whole books paraphrased, many documented errors, incompetence in translation, many edits by scribes, and

sometimes even with substitutions of Greek words for Hebrew because they sounded the same! Dr. Floyd Jones sums up: "to attempt to reconstruct the Hebrew text, as many connected with the modern versions are trying to do, from such a loose, deficient and unacceptable translation, would be analogous to trying to reconstruct the Greek New Testament text from the English LIVING NEW TESTAMENT." (Ref.4, pp.8-15—seven pages, quite an exhaustive and scholarly treatment of the Greek here.)

3.) THE COVENANT OF LEVI CORRUPTED

"For the priest's lips should keep knowledge, and they should seek the law at his mouth: .... But ... ye have corrupted the covenant of Levi...." Mal.2:7,8. Also see Deuteronomy 17:18; 31:9,25,26; *"And Moses wrote this law, and delivered it unto the priests the sons of Levi ...."* "Aristeas" spoke of six men from each of the 12 tribes translating the Tanakh into Greek. If this had actually happened, it would certainly have been a corruption of *"the covenant of Levi"*— God's appointed guardians of the sacred text! Look at what those Levites did in virtually perfectly preserving the Hebrew text—one demonstration of this is the 95% support of the Dead Sea Scrolls for the Masoretic Text in the thousands of differences between the Masoretic Text and the Septuagint. Note that the Dead Sea Scrolls are not necessarily all authorized manuscripts, since the Dead Sea "Essenes" were not specifically Levites. With over 1000 years between the Dead Sea Scrolls and the earliest Masoretic Hebrew text, these are by far the oldest extant copies of the Old Testament— stunning historical documentation of the preserved Hebrew Bible.

4.) MOST O.T. QUOTES SAME IN LXX AND MASORETIC

Most of the 85 direct quotations from the Old Testament in the New Testament found in the Septuagint are texts where the Septuagint agrees with the Masoretic Hebrew; therefore these quotations in no way support the contention that some of the N.T. writers quoted from the Septuagint and not the Masoretic Hebrew. (Ref.4, pp.27-34—again, five pages of proof.)

Ronald Youngblood, of the NIV Translation committee, thinks that "Most of the New Testament citations of the Old Testament are from the Septuagint ... they made primary use of the LXX [the

Septuagint] even when it disagreed with the Hebrew". (Ref.8, p.140) If the writers of the New Testament did make "primary use of the LXX", rather than the Masoretic Hebrew text, when quoting from the Old Testament, then we do not have a preserved Bible today, because, based just on the problems with the Septuagint summarized here, that would mean that the (inspired!) writers of the New Testament didn't have a preserved Old Testament, and that they incorporated that imperfect Old Testament into the New Testament. NOTE: If you believe that the Septuagint dictated any part of the Bible text, you have lost any confidence in, or argument for, a preserved Bible! Could it be that some people push for the Septuagint (the Vaticanus O.T.), for the purpose of destroying confidence in the KJ "preserved texts"? Have these Septuagint fans actually "collated" (= word by word comparison with relevant texts) the Septuagint and seen what a poor translation it is? Do they know how weak the textual evidence is for the Septuagint compared to the Masoretic Text?   This whole Septuagint issue really seems:
a.) ignorance,
b.) self deception (*"yea, they are prophets of the deceit of their own hearts"* (Jer. 23:26) or
c.) a malicious, not scholarly attack against the preservation of God's Word. If the writers of the New Testament did not make <u>any</u> use of the Septuagint, then we have poor NKJV/NIV Old and New Testaments, because the NKJV/NIV did!

    5.) REVERSE EDITING DONE

Texts of the <u>few</u> Old Testament quotes in the New Testament which are found in the Septuagint but not in the Masoretic text are claimed to be proof texts that the Septuagint was used by the writers of the New Testament, instead of the Masoretic Hebrew. However, these verses are demonstrated, in Ref.4, pp.39-46, to be translator editing of the Masoretic Old Testament text to agree with the New Testament. This would be "reverse editing", where the translator(s) of the Septuagint apparently took an Old Testament passage <u>wrongly</u> assumed to be the source of a New Testament quote, and then conformed their translation of the Hebrew Old Testament into Greek to agree with the Greek New Testament passage. If this is so, and the exhaustive evidence given in Reference 4 is compelling, it could obviously only be done if the Septuagint translator(s) had a copy of the Greek New Testament—and therefore was translating the Septuagint after the New Testament was written, not BC.   In other words, in these few texts the Septuagint really seems to be quoting from the New Testament, and not vice versa!

Another explanation for New Testament quotes being different from the Old Testament is: There are a few places where the Divine Author of the New Testament quoted Old Testament prophecies as they had been fulfilled in the ministry of the Lord Jesus. Then these texts were quoted in the Septuagint from the New Testament. Compare Hosea 11:1 with Matthew 2:15 and Hebrews 10:5 as quoted from Psalm 40:6 where the writer of the Septuagint is quoting from the New Testament when he translates Psalm 40:6. (Ref.4, p.45)

6.) THE LEGEND OF THE VORLAGE

The Septuagint, which differs from the Masoretic Text in thousands of places, is supposed to be translated from a Hebrew manuscript called the "LXX Vorlage", that is supposed to be superior to the Masoretic Text, and which would be quite different from the Masoretic Text because the Septuagint is.   However, there is absolutely no extant manuscript evidence for this Hebrew manuscript to support this therefore baseless fiction.

Now, the older a manuscript is, generally the better (closer to the Originals) it is. Some of the Dead Sea Scrolls, which we can actually handle (very carefully), are easily as old as this supposed "LXX Vorlage"; they agree overwhelmingly with the Masoretic Text and are way over 1000 years closer to the Originals than is the Masoretic Text. This is perhaps the most convincing, stunning, historical confirmation of the reliability of the Masoretic Text ever found in His-Story!

The Pentateuch represents the best translation in the Septuagint, "still it ... disregards consistency in religious technical terms, and shows impatience with the repetitive technical descriptions in Exodus, by mistakes, abbreviations, and wholesale omissions. Yet comparatively few books in the LXX attain even to the standard of the Pentateuch.... The book of Isaiah in the Septuagint shows obvious signs of incompetence. As a translation it is not only bad, it is the most inferior book within the LXX. [This is significant because the book of Isaiah is so important, sometimes called "the fifth Gospel", and because the Dead Sea Scrolls of Isaiah are virtually verbatim copies of the Masoretic of Isaiah.]   H.B. Swete concludes that the Psalms are but little better. Esther, Job, and Proverbs are not faithful translations but merely free paraphrases. The original LXX version of Job was much shorter than the Hebrew; it was subsequently filled in with interpretations from Theodotian ... Hebrew sentiments are freely altered to suit the Greek outlook. The rendering of Daniel was so much of a paraphrase that it was replaced ... one of the translators of the book of Jeremiah sometimes rendered Hebrew words by Greek words that conveyed similar sound but utterly dissimilar meaning ..." (Ref.1a, p.9)!

RIP enigmatic Septuagint!

APPENDIX C

CRITIQUE OF JAMES WHITE'S
The King James Only Controversy (Ref.10)

James White seems to have "stolen" (Jer.23:30) the New Evangelical viewpoint of Grand Canyon University and the new Fuller Seminary with little or no first-hand research into the abundant manuscript evidence which documents our position here in this ENOUGH. Many (most) people "steal" their words from someone else without verifying the facts when possible—it's always inconvenient—and without occasionally calibrating the quote source by first-hand research to be sure he is doing his own verification. White broad-brushes KJ supporters by focusing on several extreme views of Dr. Peter Ruckman and Gail Riplinger which are not held by the majority of TR supporters. Therefore, it "is a dangerous book" says David Cloud in his book, EXAMINING "THE KING JAMES ONLY CONTROVERSY" (Ref.4, p.6, available from Ref.5, which discusses White's book virtually point for point). Please do not decide for White's New Evangelical bias, with his seemingly sound treatment (so many undocumented and unproven statements!), without checking out Cloud's documented arguments. If you must deal with "dangerous" things (such as articulate biased salesmen), do so with great care!

White humbly says "Misrepresenting others—even those we *strongly* feel are in error—is not an option for one who follows Jesus" (Ref.10, p.95). However, here are four examples of what this ENOUGH feels are misrepresentations and misleading statements:

(**1**.) "Erasmus sometimes used textual criticism in arriving at the forerunner of the Textus Receptus" (Ref.10, pp.57,58).

(**2**.) "One of the marvels of Erasmus' work is that he was able to produce such a fine text with so few resources" (Ref.10, p.54).

(**3**.) "The Textus Receptus does call for revision", (quoting Dean John Burgon, Ref.10, p.91).

(**4**.) "[between the TR and the Critical Text] There are some readings ...on which the manuscripts are almost equally divided" (quoting Dr. Edward Hills, Ref.10, p.93).

These statements seem to support White's conviction that the modern Bible texts are better than the King James texts (the TR); but let's look at these four statements again, in context:

(1.) Erasmus did use "Biblical" textual criticism, which is a scientific technique of collating (comparing) manuscripts word by word, but he quite apparently did so to verify that his manuscripts were majority texts. **White is not giving us a true picture of Erasmus' Greek text.** He is implying it is a subjective critical text when actually it is the first refinement of the majority text.

In fairness, White's description of "higher" (subjective) textual criticism (Ref.10, pp.27,28) is excellent, and he clearly describes its pitfalls; but then he jumps into the pit without so much as warning his readers that he is a proponent of Higher Textual Criticism, and uses it, in most of his textual analysis: "Conflation" (pp. 43,168), "Expansions of piety" (pp. 43,46,153), "Harmonization" (pp. 37, 156, 163), "Full" text (pp. 43,45), "Parallel influence" (pp.156,162), "Scribal errors" (pp. 36,37,57), "Tenacity" (pp. 47,48,62,124), etc. These are the subjective tools of the "ten higher critics in a room" (Ref.10, p.28) Translator's Union who will produce ten (or more) different translations.

James White is incorrectly implying here that those who held the KJ manuscripts to be preserved by God, did not use textual criticism in arriving at the TR and, therefore, were hypocritical to use the text of Erasmus, who did. The facts are that the KJ scholars did have and did compare all <u>the significant</u> readings we have today, which is "**Biblical** Textual Criticism" (Ref.6, p.110; Ref.5, BFT#83, pages 48-55). The very Title Page of KJ Bibles says, "...with the former translations diligently compared and revised". However, these were all Majority Text translations, and they did not employ <u>higher</u> (hunch, by gosh) textual criticism, and they, along with Erasmus, rejected the "refuse copy" documents such as Vaticanus.

(2.) Why wouldn't Erasmus have produced a "fine text"? He rejected the "short" text (Vaticanus) as internally mangled and simply compared the "fuller" text represented by the vast majority of the manuscripts. **White fails to tell his readers that Erasmus had <u>previously consulted</u> a full representative sample of manuscripts.** In his second and third revisions, he consulted and divided these manuscripts into "majority text" and "edited text" lists in his "Annotations", not just the relative few he had on hand when he hurriedly printed his first edition of the Greek New Testament. Erasmus rejected the unsupported Vaticanus readings and omissions, and he specifically gave his reasons for doing so. (Ref.4, pp.78,79). Also, since 98% of the 6000 NT manuscripts are "pre-TR" and similar, almost any one of them would do to form a Greek N.T.

(**3.**) Dean Burgon implicitly applies the Scriptural doctrine that it is a repetitive "refining" process to zero in on the true text. (Analyze Psalm 12, especially vs. 6 & 7, for Scriptural authority for finding the "preserved" text through a repetitive refining process.) This refining process has obviously been lost on the "ten higher critics in a room" Translator's Union who keep on asking, "which TR is the best?". Obviously the best was Beza's as refined by the KJ translators in 190 places.

So to say that "the Textus Receptus does call for revision" (as in "refining")—that is, the TR isn't totally there yet—is the careful statement of a statesman and believing scholar; but the TR is 99.9999% the "Original Text". **White seems ignorant, and therefore his readers are ignorant, of the contrast between the TR and the Nestle-Aland** "New Greek" (UGT) text which has 36,000+ variant readings (an average of five doubts about what the "Original" Text is <u>in every verse of the New Testament!</u>). The entire KJ Bible had some 15 (fifteen) variant reading footnotes—which were all settled hundreds of years ago by comparing hundreds of majority manuscripts. Again, please note that in the Nestle-Aland "Critical" Text, every textual finding, sound or speculative, only adds another variant—and that text gets *more* unsettled **not** further refined!

(**4.**) As with Burgon, Dr. Hills deals fairly with the evidence in acknowledging that there are a few TR texts without overwhelming textual support. These relatively few texts with equal textual support do not detract from the vast majority of the NT with overwhelming textual support for the TR. After examining the few texts with equal textual support, some of the admittedly greatest textual scholars of His-story, who have actually word by word collated tens of thousands of verses, have concluded that the TR readings in these not overwhelmingly supported texts are better than the CT.

James White seldom if ever appears sufficiently informed to discuss many of these matters as a first-hand authority, especially along with Hort, in having done little or no textual collation—in stark contrast with such scholars as Burgon, Hills, and Waite whom he repeatedly criticizes. An interesting case in point is White's comments that Hebrew is "an ancient tongue"(Ref.10, p.21) and therefore, by an apparent evolutionary perspective, primitive. Ancient, yes—probably the God-given language to Adam! White says that Hebrew "does not contain nearly the same ability to express subtle nuances and shades of meaning as either English or Greek"; this is simple ignorance of the Hebrew language.

These four subtle misrepresentations by White just discussed must cause you to exercise caution with his book. Without God's promised preserved Bible, even Origen can't be called a heretic (Ref.10, pp.44,50,51). Origen was the origin of the Critical Text since Vaticanus is demonstratively his edited bible. He believed in soul sleep, universal salvation (that even Satan will be saved), purgatory, reincarnation, transubstantiation (that the communion wafer at the Catholic Mass actually becomes Jesus' body—so Christ dies again at every Mass!), that the Bible was not inspired by God, that there was no actual Adam, and that salvation was not a gift but must be worked for. These beliefs—and unbeliefs—as revealed in his own writings, indicate that he was a lost Greek philosopher who called himself a Christian because he was baptized (he believed in "baptismal regeneration") (Ref.4 pp. 90-92). Yet reading Ref.10, you get the gist that calling Origen a heretic is just another KJ Only hangup. This is significant because it demonstrates that to those with an edited bible, none dare call anything heresy! For that which the preserved Bible calls "leaven", **separation** is the only defense, enabling us to *"Prove all things; hold fast to that which is good. Abstain from all appearance of evil"* (I Thess.5:21,22). White's New Evangelicalism repudiates separation (Ref.4, p.43). (The magazine, "Christianity Today" now has several Roman Catholic editors, and Thomas Nelson, owner of the NKJV copyright, has an entire Roman Catholic publishing division!) Top front cover endorser of White's book, Norman Geisler, graduate of a Jesuit university, says of Catholics and Evangelicals that they, "have so many convictions and commitments in common that it would be foolish as well as wrong...to wrangle with each other" though he does state that the Roman Catholic Church historically has been "decidedly uncharitable" toward Bible-believing Christians. David Cloud says, "To describe Rome's fearful, bloody, centuries-old persecution of Bible-believing Christians as 'decidedly uncharitable' is insanity" (Ref.4,p.50,52).

THREE MORE OF WHITE'S "PROOFS" GO POOF!

1.) White says, "Every one of the papyrus manuscripts we have discovered has been a representative of the Alexandrian [B] not the Byzantine [TR] text type" (Ref.10, pp.43,152). The Papyri discoveries are the oldest extant New Testament witnesses by far— 100 to 300 years older than B, and Doctors Wilbur Pickering and H.A. Sturz absolutely disagree with James White. They "surveyed all the available Papyri ... each new manuscript discovered, vindicated added King James readings ..." (Ref.8, pp.480,481), and they further "concluded that the KJV readings [TR] dominated the early Papyri to a greater percentage than the readings of ... B [Vaticanus]seen in the new versions" (Ref.8, pp.481,482). Certainly there are also Alexandrian readings in the Papyri (after all they were best preserved in dry Alexandria, Egypt), but "There is more attestation for the TR than for Vaticanus ... evidently the TR reflects an earlier text than [Vaticanus]" (Ref.8, p.483). Note that White refers to "Text Types", whereas Pickering and Sturz refer to "readings". Unfortunately for White, modern textual scholars go by "readings" and very little by "text types" these days (Ref. 12, p.30; Ref. 1b, p.83). Dr. Kurt Aland made almost 500 changes to the Nestle-Aland Critical Greek text, back to KJ/TR readings, in the 27th edition, due to these Papyri readings (see Vaticanus argument "F", p.132). We would like to ask Dr. White if he, or any of his cover endorsers, has actually collated (m)any of these Papyri? We are not calling Dr. White a liar, but neither are Drs. Pickering or Sturz, who represent a cutting edge of Papyri research, lying! The reader has reason to be confused here; let's get to the truth. White's mentor, Hort, doesn't see a "Byzantine [TR] Text Type" before 400 AD, and so of course, the preponderance of pre-B TR readings aren't a "Text Type". This is another sleight of hand gimmick to attempt to trick the jury—but again we note that the whole artificial "Text Type" idea has been virtually dropped in modern scholarship—the manuscripts defy "Type" grouping.

2.) White says "the early translations of the New Testament reveals [sic.] that they were done on the basis of Alexandrian type manuscripts" (Ref.10, p.153). However, Bishop Ellicott, head of the Westcott and Hort 1881 project, stated that the Peschito (Aramaic translation of the Greek N.T.) was so old that it was conceivably handled by the Apostle John himself! (Ref.17, pp.9,275)—that is, 300 years older than B. Dr. Bruce Metzger stated that the Peschito represents TR readings, (See Ref.15, p.136). Both Ellicott and Metzger were genuine textual scholars who, for whatever reason, were also absolute supporters of the Critical Text over the TR and so are impeccable witnesses regarding the Peschito! These oldest translations were very conveniently dated by Hort to be younger (more recent) than B, by what now is seen to have been fabricated history. That is, Hort's theory incorrectly, and apparently without any historical support, placed these TR-supporting early versions later than B because if they were earlier, Dr. Frederick Kenyon himself says Hort's theory would collapse (Ref.8, p.34). They are now accepted to be much older than Vaticanus— "the Peschito or ancient Syriac Version; which like the old Latin is (by consent of the Critics) generally assigned to the second Century of our era" (Ref.17, p.275); and the Peschito with most other older translations came from the pre-TR text. Isn't this a "strike two" for James White?

3.) White says, "The early church fathers who wrote during the early centuries gave no evidence in their citations of a familiarity with the Byzantine [TR] text type" (Ref.10, p.153). (Note White's obsolete Text Type analysis again.) REALLY? Dean John Burgon word by word collated over 1,000,000 (one million) Scripture texts from some 87,000 (eighty-seven thousand) extant writings of the early church Fathers, in the Greek (and without a computer). Burgon said, "The Traditional Text [basically the TR] receives more support from the early Church Fathers than does the Critical Text

[B]" (Ref.17, p.245) "At a ratio of 2:1 before 350 AD, and 3:1 for important passages" (Ref.8 p.488). Do note that all these Scripture quotes are hundreds of years <u>older</u> than B ; B is supposed to be so reliable because it is so old. Dr. James Price (Ref. 13, p.227) says Burgon's conclusions are "hasty and unwarranted"! There is no "hasty" way to compare (collate) 50,000,000 (fifty million) extant ancient words from   87,000 MSS. "(U)nwarranted"? Burgon simply tallied the score of what text the Fathers were quoting from —objective, not subjective findings. (Burgon's sixteen volume work is preserved in the British Museum.)

The chart on the top of Ref.10, p.153 is misleading, if not actually inaccurate, because it doesn't deal with much older Papyri, first and second century versions (especially the Peschito), or any Church Fathers, <u>which we have documented are all older and predominantly TR</u>. (James Price has the same misleading chart in Ref.13, p.244.) We must keep in mind that White views everything through the filter of <u>subjective</u> ("internal criteria", Ref.10, p.153) textual criticism which he considers to be "sound methods"...harmonization, parallel influences and the 'expansiosn of piety' " additions, etc. He quotes Gordon Fee's use of "a good critical edition of a father's text" (Ref.10,p.188), whereas Burgon's 87,000 Church Father documents were unedited, actual extant MSS! Is someone trying to sell us something that actually is not for sale—like truth?

SO CALLED "STICKY PROBLEMS" for KJ

Either White is ignorant of the scholarly answers already given to his "problems" in the literature, much of it before he was born, or he is broad-brushing these issues by just talking about the minority of KJ people for whom the KJ translation has authority over the KJ Hebrew and Greek (Ref.4, pp.72-84). A quick read of Ref.10, pp.39-46 reveals that White (and apparently all of his list of endorsers on the cover of Ref.10) are still unabridged believers in Westcott and Hort's <u>now generally "debunked" textual theory</u>—and White accuses KJ people of anachronism! Indeed, it seems as if all today's "new" evangelicals are addicted to Westcott and Hort; isn't this **truth abuse**?

If you found "The Naked Truth", in this ENOUGH pp.114-130, is at least significant, then isn't White in trouble? He states agreement with all of W&H's debunked theory (Ref.4, p.6) as follows:

(1.) The Bible should be treated as every other "ancient book" (Ref.10, p.54 top and throughout chapter 4).

(2.) B the oldest manuscript (Ref.10, p.43 bottom)

(3.) TR late and secondary (Ref.10, pp.43, 44)

(4.) No malicious modification of the Bible, and no devil (Ref.10, pp. 176, 178, 186, 187)

(5.) Shorter text better (Ref. 10, p.185 top)

James White (Ref.10,p.99) says, "Modern Greek texts [Nestle-Aland, UGT] are not identical to that created by Westcott and Hort [W&H]". Well, let's see: W&H delete (from the Word of God!) 48 whole verses, while the Nestle-Aland/UGT only 45; W&H delete 193 significant portions of verses, and Nestle-Aland/UGT only 185; W&H delete 221 names and titles of the Lord, while Nestle et al only 212. (From EVALUATING VERSIONS OF THE NEW TESTAMENT by Everett Fowler, available from Ref.5.) True, these texts are not "identical"— but they are damnably close! Is White ignorant of how close these texts are, having never collated them in Greek? Dr. Waite has collated the entire TR New Testament with both the Nestle-Aland and the UGT, in the Greek, (D.A. Waite, THE FOUR-FOLD SUPERIORITY OF THE KING JAMES BIBLE, Ref. 8), yet Dr. Waite is quoted almost with scorn ten times in Ref. 10. Haven't White's readers been misled into thinking that the "Modern Greek" is not basically the same old Westcott and Hort re-creation of the Roman Catholic Vaticanus text? Heavy-duty textual scholar Dr. Ernest Cowell says,"THE DEAD HAND OF ... HORT LIES HEAVY UPON US.... David Cloud adds, "Any man who discounts the continuing significance of Westcott-Hort in the field of Bible texts and versions is probably trying to throw up a smoke screen to hide something." (Ref.4, p.88.90)

This ENOUGH is written on the premise, the benchmark, that God has inspired and preserved His Word, as He promised, so shouldn't we choose those holy men who have that confidence in God? James White accuses those people who have that confidence, as Dr. Hills, of beginning "with the conclusion of his argument ['the TR is the God-preserved text']" which, indeed, would be "circular reasoning" (Ref.10, p.92). However, Dr. Hills did not assume the TR is the God-preserved text. He assumed a preserved Bible existed based on God's promises to preserve His Word and spent much of his life at the highest University level as a published textual scholar, proving (not assuming) by the finest scholarly reasoning and research, but not subjective "higher" textual criticism, that the TR is that "preserved text".   White seems to feel it a shame that poor Dr. Hills had more confidence in God's promises to preserve His Word than in his own otherwise bright mind (Ref.10, p.93). Please consider the following options: (1) White is ignorant of Hill's research and that of many other great textual scholars; (2) he is confused by this depth of objective first-hand manuscript   research; (3) he is just regurgitating the New Evangelical line of Grand Canyon University and the modern Fuller Theological Seminary or, (4) could there actually be a real Devil who wiles men (Eph.6:10-12)?!

How few modern "scholars" do original document research—as did Dr. Waite, who actually compared every word in the Greek New Testaments, in contrast with the editors of the NKJV who just echoed the error about the textual differences being only "one in a thousand" or .1% (which would amount to approximately 1/4 page of text; Dr. Waite's calculated 46 pages of differences = 7%). What is going on here? Surely Dr. A.T. Robertson knew that there were actually some 46 pages of variation. James White addresses this in Ref.10, pp.38-40, where he agrees with Dr. Robertson, the **NKJV Preface,** and Westcott and Hort in their assessment that 90% of the variants are "trivialities" (Ref.10, p.39).   WHOA!   "*Who hath known the mind of the Lord? or who hath been his counselor?*" (Rom.11:34), and more Scriptural authority, "*a little leaven leaveneth the whole lump*" (I Cor.5:6). To make judgments about which verses are significant to God's Word and which are not is to get on Satan's shoulders (who only said, "*I will be like the most High*" Isa.14:14) and to try to stand <u>higher</u> than God, editing His Word to which He has given more honor than to His name (Ps.138:2). We are dealing with "*All Scripture ... God-breathed ... profitable*" (II Tim.3:16). We must choose our holy men carefully; these issues are the watershed to choose them. A.T. Robertson is a notable Greek scholar; but if he disagrees with the Lord Jesus Christ—Almighty God, Who said, *"Till heaven and earth pass, one* [written] *jot or one tittle shall in no wise pass from the law, till all be fulfilled"* (Matt.5:18), a truly wise man goes with the Lord!

White's claim that KJ supporters are anti-scholarship and anti-inquiry, anti-freedom, anti-intellectual (Ref.10,p.151, Ref.4:22) because they don't utilize the subjective tools of "higher" criticism is answered as follows: If you had the Autograph of John's Gospel, then any variant to it would be in error--WOULDN'T IT? (See Ref.4,p.22.) If God wanted to communicate with mankind in every generation, could He inerrantly inspire that communication, and wouldn't He, couldn't He preserve it? James White and friends say that Nestle-Aland's five questions about what the original Greek text is in every verse of the New Testament (36,000 textual doubts ÷ 7000 verses in the NT) is the way God chose to preserve His Word. Do they really believe that is "preservation"? Evidently they do not have a Holy Bible. Do you? *"Man shall not live by bread alone, but by every word* (lit. "each and every word") *that proceedeth out of the mouth of God"* (Matt.4:4). God offers "life"—but only by each and every word of His preserved Holy Bible. These are life and death issues.

Here's the danger: If Anton Lavey, who wrote the SATANIC BIBLE, said we do not have a true copy of the Original Bible, God's people just consider the source and ignore him.   But if someone like Josh McDowell says (as he does) that the original Bible readings are out there somewhere in the variant manuscripts of the Critical (eclectic) texts, and by "higher" textual criticism the scholars are putting it back together pretty well, most Christians say, "That's wonderful". James White says: "... the tenacity of the New Testament text, while forcing us to deal with textual variants, also provides us with the assurance that our work is not in vain. One of those variant readings is indeed the original. We are called to invest our energies in discovering which one it is." (Ref.10, p.48) White's "we", and "our" in the preceding sentence might be a Greek or Hebrew frog in his pocket; it certainly isn't referring to him and Joe Christian because Joe simply isn't able to compare any ancient Greek or Hebrew documents—which the NKJV requires him to do in choosing between NU, M, and the NKJV text in almost 800 verses footdoubted in the NKJV. White calls this "deficient preservation" and is an impossible position to try to stand on. See Ref.19, p.61.

Does Joe Christian need to hire some scholar to do this for him (at least hire him by buying a bible full of these subjective critical speculations)? God has preserved the "Original" for him in the TR, overwhelmingly supported by the vast majority of manuscripts, and so majestically and literally translated for him into English in 1611. (Again, note carefully that the 1611 translation is the last time the KING JAMES TR manuscripts were translated into English—and no significant better textual readings have been found since then!) The KING JAMES manuscripts are the ones we have been comparing to Mr. White's "one of those variant readings" which has the pea —as in the "Shell Game". However, the pea isn't under any of those three walnut shells, it's up the guy's sleeve, and he slips it back where he wants—under Vaticanus, or under his favorite eclectic "I prefer", "I guess" text!   Sure it isn't fair; so don't gamble; don't trade trust in God's promises of a preserved trustworthy Bible for dependence upon subjective critical textual scholars.

THE KING JAMES ONLY CONTROVERSY enters finally with another clear example of misinformation: it presents "the logic of faith" totally out of context. Dr. Hills has just concluded a massive treatise with "the logic of faith" as a fitting and superbly reasonable conclusion. This concept of "the logic of faith" is not some context-less, unreasonable mental hangup of an otherwise brilliant textual scholar. Please observe carefully just how White presents this "logic of faith" to his trusting reader: "We will take the opportunity to review the argument as presented in its best form by Dr. Hills" (Ref.10, p.93). Dr. Hills has given his explanation of the "logic of faith". (See ENOUGH, p.111-112. Do stop here and read Hills' definition.) Yet amazingly, White bypasses Dr. Hills' definition by starting with Dr. Hills' ending statement and only naming the concept ("In short, unless we follow the logic of faith, we can be certain of nothing concerning the Bible ...."). This does not help White's readers to grasp the concept. Could it be that White is afraid his readers will appreciate "the logic of faith" rather than ridicule it as he proceeds to do? White declined to review

Hills' own definition, after saying that he was going to, but then he has a conclusion for us anyway: "It is argued that unless we embrace the KJV as our 'final authority', we have no final authority at all, and hence all is subjectivity and uncertainty." The quality of the arguments found in White's book, and the "scholarship" of subjective textual criticism in general, certainly are "subjectivity and uncertainty". Hopefully, these repeated problems with THE KING JAMES ONLY CONTROVERSY will at least flag this book for caution; there are documentable but often subtle what we must call ignorance or error on virtually every page. The writer of this **ENOUGH** would gladly discuss this with anyone who honestly disagrees or has been confused.

IN CONCLUSION

It does seem as if James White believes what he has shared with us in his book, even in John 1:18 (which is quite possibly the source of the Arian Heresy that believes that Jesus is a lesser, created god ("*The only begotten God who is in the bosom of the Father*")—count them, two Gods in the Critical Text of John 1:18). White sides with (NIV editor) Palmer in translating this passage from Vaticanus but interprets it to weakly **attest** to Christ's deity. However, doesn't "begotten god" imply, if not outright claim, that Jesus is not eternal God but had an "origin" (NIV Micah 5:2 and first edition NKJV Phil. 2:6)? The "*only begotten*" refers back to John 1:1 and 1:14 — the only begotten Son is the Word, who is absolute Deity!

White's argument for "only begotten god" just seems oblivious to the bloody drama going on. White says "Men and women had fine Christian lives for fifteen hundred years before the KJV came on the scene" (Ref.10, p."v"). White seems totally ignorant of the pre-TR textual tradition in the 1) Old Latin, 2) Waldensian, 3) the pre-TR text quoted 3:1 by the early Church Fathers, 4) the pre-TR text foreign translations (such as the possibly first century Syrian Peschito), 5) first to third century Papyri as well as 6) the Byzantine majority manuscripts—the true Words of God made available to every generation (Ref.4 p.26) as God promised. Isa.59:21 "*This is my covenant with them, saith the Lord;...my words which I have put in thy mouth, shall not depart out of thy mouth, nor out of the mouth of thy seed, nor out of the mouth of thy seed's seed, saith the LORD, from henceforth and for ever."* So every generation has had God's precious preserved Word—not 1000 years without it until 1880 when Westcott and Hort gave us the Critical Text. White dismisses these preservation promises in passing, (mockingly?). He calls "preservation" an average of five doubts per verse, in the Nestle-Aland Greek NT as to what the "original" Bible said — that's a joke, he can't be serious!

In addition, in reality, it is estimated that there were millions of "fine Christian lives" martyred during this time (many killed by Arians for believing in Christ's deity)—killed for copying and sharing His Bible, the pre-TR manuscripts—a period so appropriately called "The Dark Ages"; a number of historians put the body count at over 70,000,000! That the Roman Catholic Church used wholesale and systematic torture before killing to intimidate and reduce all opposition, deprive mankind of the true words of God (and to confiscate great riches) is a fact.

Let's look one last time at White's subjective critical methodology for finding the Word of God: 'God' (B reading in John 1:18) was changed to 'son' because " 'only begotten Son' is Johannine in character, and hence would cause a scribe to write 'son' upon writing 'begotten' rather than 'God'. " (Ref.10, pp.259,260) There is a surface logic to "Higher Textual Criticism", but people who are prepared to die to maintain and share the true Bible don't make many stupid mistakes!

Dear Reader: you will choose to love and follow the awesome God Who uses precise words for His precise thoughts, and actually does keep His promises to preserve His book of promises, or you can live in White's dismal world with a god who stutters and doesn't care to (or is it is unable to) preserve His Words and finish what He began (Gen.1:1, Rev.1:8). In White's world, there is no apparent Devil to corrupt everything and who must therefore be resisted earnestly (Jude 3) by God's faith which comes from hearing (Rom.10:17) a preserved Bible we can hold in our hands.

Dr. White, God's preservation promises are a two-edged sword—in blessing, **and in cursing** if we deny them. Don't resist the Devil, and you will be devoured, I Peter 5:8,9!

APPENDIX D
PATTERNS IN THE BIBLE CHANGES

BEWARE THE GAINSAYING OF KORAH! Jude 11
Korah died for contra-dicting (="*gainsaying*"=antilogos) God's
Word through Moses. Likewise, virtually all Bibles since 1611 are
paraphrased (man's words) translations of messed-with manuscripts—
"gainsaying" God's preserved Original Words. Aren't these *"Tares"*
(Matt.13:24-30) look-a-like wheat that causes sleepiness, dizziness, and
even death—unhealthy grain for *"the Bread of Life"*? Jesus hates this!
(Rev. 2:6,15)

"Korahites" today usually do say they believe the Bible was
perfectly inspired by God, BUT ONLY "as originally written",
NOT PRESERVED TO OUR DAY. Aren't they <u>contradicting God</u>?
(1) In not trusting His promises to preserve His Word (Ps.12:6,7;
138:2; Matt.5:18 *"every jot"*; 24:35 *"my words, ..."*) and (2) in the
substitution of the one Roman Catholic "Vaticanus" manuscript for
the 6000+ KING JAMES manuscripts (1: 6000).

This Vaticanus MS (=Manuscript, also labeled "B") is a
"fabricated" MS—that is, it was fashioned from the original
(especially by deleting thousands of words). See "The Naked
Truth", pp 114-130 discussion of the Critical Text for <u>proof</u>. This
fabrication was done by "Nicolaitan" scholar/priests (whose deeds
and doctrine Jesus said twice, "I hate". (Rev.2:6,15). The Lord of the
Remnant could not be more extreme here regarding His attitude
toward those who would attempt to usurp the position of His "Kings
and Priests" (Rev.1:6) as keepers of the Words of God who are to
"earnestly contend for the faith which was once delivered unto the
saints" (Jude 3). We suggest that it is those "that are sanctified by
God the Father, and preserved in Jesus Christ, and called" (Jude 1)
who are to "agonize" (Greek word for "contend" in Jude 3) for the
Autographs!

Korahites have been seen grinding their private theological axes
in the holy place; for instance, F.J. Hort said, "Mary worship and
Jesus worship have very much in common in cause and in their
results" (LIFE OF HORT, Vol.2, p.50—this feminine co-redemptor
heresy began at the Tower of Babel!) Do keep Hort's theological

convictions in mind as we look at changes he and Westcott made in the Bible (the 9,000 words changed in the Greek New Testament), basically turning the KJ into Vaticanus to form a Greek text which is **unquestionably the main basis of virtually all modern bible versions**. "Contradicting" the Divinely strategic preserved Word is serious to God—screaming children swallowed up by the earth, and 15,000 people dead, in judgment for Korah's Satanically strategic power grab (Numbers 16).

This Appendix (1) shows some dark secrets about bible versions, (2) reveals attempts to lead us (astray) by **the patterns in the Bible changes, a "bend sinister":**

Pattern # 1

TRYING TO DEMOTE THE LORD JESUS CHRIST— THE ARIAN HERESY AGAIN:

Matt.26:45 *"Sleep on now, and take your rest"* KJ, the Shepherd's tender care, becomes *"Are you still sleeping and resting?"* NKJV, NIV, NASV, RSV, ESV, HCSV.

Hundreds of verses where names of Deity are deleted: "Christ Jesus" becomes "Jesus" or "He", separating "Christ" from "Jesus"; the Vaticanus/New Greek tends to resurrect the Gnostic heresy which denied the Lord's humanity and the Arian heresy which denied Him being Christ—His Deity. See I John 4:2,3.

Luke 12:49 *" what will I, if it be already kindled?"* KJ, (Subjunctive mood: if/when) becomes*"how I wish it were already kindled!"* NKJV, NIV, NASV, RSV, ESV, HCSV.

What? The Almighty, The Lord Jesus Christ, "wishes" to burn mankind, but is unable to do so? (Do see Ps.2:6-9—the Son need only to ask for the entire world!)

Matt.20:20 *"... the mother ... with her sons, worshipping him"* KJ, becomes*"... the mother ... with her sons, kneeling down"* NKJV, NASV, HCSV, ESV. It's called "genuflection"—a religious act. This translation weakens the proof here that, as God, Christ accepted worship. The Greek doesn't say "kneel".

(Also see in this ENOUGH Acts 9:1,2; 17:22; Gal.2:20; +Phil. 2:6 NKJV first edition;...)

Pattern # 2

MIXING HUMAN WORKS WITH GRACE, AND FALLING FROM GRACE:

II Cor.2:15 *"Are saved"* (I Cor.1:18, too) KJ, somehow becomes *"are being saved"* NKJV, NIV, NASV, ESV, as in purgatory and other works-based religions.

Rom.11; Heb.3 *"belief"* KJ, becomes *"obedience"* NKJV, NIV, NASV, RSV, ESV, HCSV, which is Grace converted to works so *"grace is no more grace"* (Rom.11:6).

Gal.5:22 *"Faith"* KJ, becomes *"faithfulness"* NKJV, NIV, NASV, RSV, ESV—a work.

(Also see in this ENOUGH Eph. 4:22; I Thess. 4:11; II Thess. 3:5; Rev. 19:8 ....)

Pattern # 3

CHALLENGING PAUL'S APOSTLESHIP WEAKENS HIS EPISTLES, ALLOWING HERESY INTO THE CHURCH:

Col.4:10 *"Commandments"* KJ, becomes *"instructions"* NKJV, NASV, HCSV, ESV. This was, in effect, a "command" to receive the Gospel of Mark which was inspired through Mark!

Acts 26:16 *"I will appear unto thee"* KJ, becomes *"I will yet reveal to you"* NKJV, NIV. The Lord Jesus Christ personally "appeared" to the Apostles. (*"Am I not an apostle? ... have I not seen Jesus Christ our Lord?* I Cor.9:1.)

II Cor.10:13 *"rule"* KJ, becomes *"sphere"* NKJV, ESV. The context (chapters 12-12) is perhaps the prime Scriptural treatise dealing with Apostleship. (Also see in this ENOUGH Acts 15:37-39; I Cor. 6:4; II Cor.11:12; Gal. 2:6;...)

Pattern # 4

REDUCING OUR CONFIDENCE IN THE WORD OF GOD BY CONTRADICTIONS:

Matt.9:18 *"my daughter has just died"* NKJV, NIV, ESV but, Luke 8:42 (Mk.5:23) *"she was dying"* NKJV, NIV, ESV; they contradict themselves!

Matt.26:15 *"And they counted out to him thirty pieces of silver"* NKJV, NIV, HCSV, ESV, but in Mark 14:11 *"promised to give him money"* NKJV, NIV, HCSV, ESV; they contradict within themselves again!

Rom.3:25 Saved *"through faith in his blood"* KJ, the true Gospel—not faith in faith as in: Saved *"by His blood, through faith"* NKJV, NASV, RSV, ESV.

I Tim.6:10 *"love of money is the root of all evil"* KJ, becomes *"love of money is a root of all kinds of evil"* NKJV, NRSV, ESV, NIV, HCSV. "Fondness for silver" drives some to make bad bibles if there's good profit!

For exclusive sales right, The Derivative Copyright Law states that the NKJV had to be sufficiently changed from the KJ. Many of the required changes were generated by translating a highly edited TR text using Dynamic Equivalency, wherein they added, subtracted, and changed what the Hebrew and Greek says in 2000+ places. Knowingly change *"one jot or one tittle"* of God's Word, and it is no longer God's Words, but man's words. NKJV replaced the KJ Hebrew with R. Kittel's "The New Kittel" BHS Hebrew (which has more doubts what the Hebrew text is than there are verses in the Old Testament) and with the Septuagint (the 350 <u>A.D.</u> Greek Old Testament of Vaticanus is the Septuagint!) NKJV replaces 1000's of TR texts with Vaticanus N.T. texts.

Should we buy such "salvage-yard" bibles, provoking the Lord by "contradicting" His preserved Word? In our controlling "Korah" parallel passage, Moses said *"Depart, I pray you, from ... these wicked men, and touch nothing of theirs"* (Num.16:26). This is a hard saying, but doesn't this say *"touch nothing of"* the modern versions; call them commentaries! But if the Original Bible is preserved to our day, where is it? For English speakers, the KJ is the Original Bible (the 10-15 legitimate textual questions about the KJ Hebrew and Greek TR have all been answered, the text refined and preserved, as promised in Psalm 12:6,7 hundreds of years ago).

Please consider the following when a PhD protests that there are variant readings in different manuscripts, and that you aren't "scientific" if you don't consider them: If you had a preserved "Original" Bible text (which Jesus promises) wouldn't this make every textual variant an error? Then please consider Appendix E to find that preserved Original.

APPENDIX E

THERE ARE NO SCIENTIFICALLY SUPPORTABLE REASONS NOT TO ACCEPT THE TEXTUS RECEPTUS (TR) AS THE PRESERVED WORDS OF GOD.

You certainly may have confidence that the KJ texts are absolutely the best available and that the KJ translation is the only every-word-accounted-for, formal English translation of those texts available.

Now note that in 1881 Westcott and Hort changed this TR New Testament in some 10,000 words by means of what they called "The Scientific Theory of Textual Criticism". Dressing up a theory as "scientific" does not make it so. The janitor putting on the scientist's white lab coat does not teach him Chemistry, Physics, or higher Mathematics .... Please read Scrollduggery "The Naked Truth" (pp.114-130) where Dean John Burgon in his book, THE REVISION REVISED (Ref. 17) "falsified" (= "to show not to be supported by the evidence") Westcott and Hort's "Scientific Theory" **point by point**. Burgon's arguments were never answered by Hort or anyone else; they were just ignored long enough for the public to forget them or to become so post-literate that some people could get away with pushing these non-Bibles to make a profit, and enough individuals would buy them. (Think about it—the modern bible business is a confidence game. Don't get conned!)

In stating that "there are no scientifically supportable reasons" not to accept the KJ texts, we are not talking about "Science falsely so called" ("scientism"—please see I Tim.6:20, in the Fruit Inspection, Part I, of this ENOUGH). What really appears to be an example of Scientism is Westcott and Hort's now debunked "Scientific Theory of textual criticism". Some in this textual debate define "science" as "nothing supernatural" and would therefore try to treat the Bible as any other ancient book (one of the fallen pillars in Westcott and Hort's textual theory, as we saw previously). They refuse even to discuss the relevance of God and His promises to preserve His Word (or inspire it in the first place). However, "scientific" does not = "pagan". The origin of the Universe, whether by blind chance, as held by the consistent evolutionist, or by the Person of Almighty God, is not in the realm of "scientific" theorizing. It is a matter of (religious) belief. "This is because the very essence of the scientific method is based on observation and experimentation, and it is impossible to make observations or conduct experiments on the origin of the Universe" (THE COLLAPSE OF EVOLUTION, p.17, Scott M. Huse, Baker Books)—likewise on how the Bible was originally written or was supernaturally canonized into the 66-book Bible. Most evolutionists, and "higher critics" of the reliability of the Bible, refuse to acknowledge this basic canon of science: there are matters with which the Scientific Method can not deal and which therefore are taken or rejected by <u>faith</u>. (The evolutionist needs more faith than does the creationist, because, candidly, the laws of thermodynamics say that evolution cannot happen, and the fossil and geologic records say that it did not happen, Ref.1b, p.110.)   See Dr. Henry Morris' climaxing work: THE LONG WAR AGAINST GOD, (Ref.9) where Satan's "cunningly devised fable" (II Peter 2:16) of Evolution is seen as the unifying theme throughout "time" under all the world's superficially different religions. "In fact, evolution *is* the world's religion!" (Ref.9, p.232), the faith of atheists. Evolution/Humanism (like a fungus) cannot grow in the light of God-inspired/preserved Revelation, and that has been the reason behind the battle for the Bible throughout history. The Bible must be discredited, made to appear untrustworthy, in the minds of most people in order for evolution/humanism to grow.

However, regarding Scripturally promised PRESERVATION, the seven principles listed in the first paragraph of this Part II, "Scrollduggery" (p.101) <u>are</u> quite susceptible to scientific analysis. This has been analyzed in the books of such qualified individuals as Dean John Burgon, Sir Hoskier, Cloud, and Dr.'s Hills, Pickering, Ruckman, Floyd Jones, Waite, and many others, (most of whose books are available from Ref.5) **making this issue of faith in our God's 100% inspired and promised preserved Word a watershed to divide the true shepherds** (Jer.23:3-5) **from the false** (Jer.23:1,2a; Jude 11-12).

APPENDIX F

DYNAMIC EQUIVALENCY,
PRESUMED LIBERTY TO EDIT GOD'S WORDS

Dynamic Equivalency (hereinafter DE; also called "Functional Equivalence" and "common language") = paraphrased translation of God's Word,[1] is a root problem. In the long war against God (Ref.9), Satan has a **strategy** ("wiles")—basically his age-long evilutionary challenge to Intelligent Design/Creation. "Just imagine," over 90% of the mass necessary to hold the Universe together is missing—so evolutionary science creates "dark matter" which hasn't yet been found anywhere to examine in a laboratory. The Bible says that by Jesus *"were all things created...by him all things consist* (hold together)" Col.1:16,17. It takes more faith to believe in "dark matter" than in Intelligent Creation! Many scientists and higher critical Bible translators must consider themselves to be God's counselors. (Read Isa.40:13 and Rom.11:33-36.) Satan's first **tactic** to implement his strategy is to create doubt in God's Words, which is doubt in God Himself, for the two are inseparable—Heb.4:12, the written Word blends seamlessly into the Living Word, Heb.4:13 (Ref.19, p.39). For Bible translators who hold unorthodox views, it is guaranteed that key truths will be obscured or exchanged after DE—which is why God forbids any knowing additions, subtractions or changes from His Scripture.

Actually, if the translator begins with a text like Vaticanus, which was already DE edited by Origen/(Constantine)Eusebius, he can produce a perverted perverted (= perverted[2]) bible. For example, Bible For Today ran the NIV on their computer and found over 6000 DE "additions, subtractions, or changes" from the TR whereas the NKJV, being based on a (heavily revised) TR had **only** 2000+ edits. (The KING JAMES BIBLE, using the same software, had none. This may look like "circular testing", but if the TR is the preserved text, a literal translation of it would net nothing amiss.)

---

1   (in contrast to LF (literal/formal: literal = every word account-ed for; formal = the identical grammar whenever possible)

The highly subjective methods and attitudes of higher criticism, as applied in DE translation, are simply the current formulation of an ancient craft, which was first so effectively used against the Words of God in the Garden of Eden to Eve. DE is an open can of live worms which, if permitted, will perforate the Bible, turning it into a holey bible. All of us, but for His elevating grace, are worms before God. However, here are worms that are eating holes in God's Words. There! Do you see Theodoten's gnostic version of the OT crawling into Origen's Hexapla, along with Origen's team of Alexandrian worms composing the Vaticanus bible? (In Origen's own words, he believed a whole snake's den of heresies. See p. 163.) There are worms Graf-Wellhausen with their Documentary Hypothesis; worms Westcott and Hort—maggots moving as if there were still life in Origen's grave; modern formulators of DE worms Eugene Nida, succeeded by Bratcher at United Bible Society (Bratcher, who denied the deity of Jesus and the efficacy of His blood), Worm Bruce Metzger, who swallowing the Documentary Hypothesis, thought of the Old Testament as a "matrix of myth, legend, and history" and did not believe in a worldwide flood. He said that "the Pentateuch took shape over a long period of time" (not written by Moses, as Jesus said), and he did not believe that Paul wrote the Pastoral Epistles. In contrast, God-glorifying faith knows *"that no prophecy is of any private interpretation"* II Peter 1:20. *"Private Interpretation"* = "Dynamic Equivalency" paraphrase translation! This has been a desperately brief treatment of DE. Please see Refs. 18 & 19 for much more.

Those who practice DE **would seduce the Church to invite Satan to be the visiting speaker (or pastor)** by using his bibles.

APPENDIX G

THE COURTROOM SCENE

This **ENOUGH** is a trial:

JUDGE: God; at least in this trial the Due Process of God's law will be protected.

JURY: the Remnant must give a verdict on whether or not we have a preserved Bible. **Their vote is cast by what Bible they use.**

LAWYERS: for both sides, advocates for the KJ manuscripts or for the Critical Text. (An unethical lawyer only thinks about winning his case, not about justice.)

EXPERT WITNESSES: textual scholars (choose your holy men carefully—an impeached scholar is not to be feared).

THE PEOPLE: the world, "society", those harmed by attacks on the Bible, and who will be deprived of the Gospel if the verdict is unjust (if the "Bible" becomes a "bible") so that the church is too crippled to fulfill its Great Commission.

THE CRIME: "Blowing up" the Bible (John 10:35b). Fraud is a willful misrepresentation or concealment of the truth to induce another to act to his own injury.

APPENDIX H

CRITIQUE OF JAMES PRICE'S KING JAMES ONLYISM:
A NEW SECT (mainly of chapter 12)

The "bible bible, who's got the Bible?" game is usually spoiled from any positive usefulness because the players start calling each other liars and deceivers. We are confident Dr. James Price considers himself a Christian believer, but we sincerely ask him what he bases this security upon since he believes that the Word of God is only 85% preserved. Dr. Edward Hills wrote BELIEVING BIBLE STUDY. In chapter 3, entitled "Bible Versions and the Logic of faith", he connects the Bible version we use to whether or not we have Biblical Faith or are trusting in some mystical (Emerging Church) experiences and possibly even a works-based gospel. Dr. Hills Scripturally discusses doctrinal basics, beginning with Divine Election all the way to the current ministry of God the Holy Spirit in enabling saving faith through the verbal, plenary inspired and preserved "Scriptures". The question is asked: Can we have saving faith without a preserved Bible? This is an intriguing, if not fateful question.

Dr. Price (NKJV OT Sr. editor) has chapter conclusions which often seem pre-written, not arrived at. We will now discuss Chapter 12 which concludes, "The Textus Receptus **Is Not to Be Preferred** ... over the Majority Text or the text derived by the Reasoned Eclectic Method." (REM Text) (Ref.13, p.276, bold added.)

1.) Dr. Price's basic argument leans heavily on "Text Traditions" (also called "Text Families", or "Text Types")—Byzantine, Western, Caesarean, and Alexandrian. "Text Traditions" was an argument essential to Westcott and Hort's textual theory because it was the "Great Leveler"; it enabled them to compare readings between the TR and Alexandrian as 1:1, not as it actually is—like 6000 TR manuscripts to 1 Vaticanus (6000:1). Westcott and Hort had to do this because 92% of the 10,000 word changes they made in the TR were based strictly on Vaticanus, just one out of over 6000+ manuscripts!

However, "Today it is admitted that because of their lack of uniformity, the Western and Caesarean can no longer be regarded as text types. This leaves the Received and Alexandrian, and the Alexandrian is very small ...." (Ref.12A, p. 30) Dr. Price's quote of

Dr. Kurt Aland, "No early trace of the Byzantine 'text' exists" (Ref.13, p.241) is misleading to Price's readers because actually the Byzantine readings **predominate** in the earlier century Papyri, Church Fathers, early Versions (and even the other Uncials, which are as old or older than B). Aland must be giving a technical definition of "text" (notice that it is in quotes) referring to "Text Tradition", but this is not explained to Price's readers. This whole Text Type concept has been seriously challenged (see next paragraph and Ref.12A, p.30), and arguments based on it are definitely weakened.

2.) Dr. Price says that the REM text is better than the TR, having "improved [Westcott and Hort's] theory and methodology. Their method now attempts to assess more completely the consensus of the evidence from all text traditions." (Ref.13, p. 251) Whoa, they mean both of the Text Traditions remaining since the Western and Caesarean are now seriously questioned. There has been an unanswered, perhaps because unanswerable, challenge to this "text type" argument since it was raised by Westcott and Hort in 1881. Now the validity of text type analysis is under question all together. PLEASE NOTE: The Nestle-Aland REM Text has moved backward, closer to the Westcott and Hort Text (Evaluating Versions of the New Testament, Ref.5), and the Westcott and Hort Text itself was generated by their pseudo-scientific theory ("debunked" in the "Naked Truth", ENOUGH, p. 114) so the REM Text certainly hasn't made much difference.

3.) Dr. Price said nothing about the many Divinely given promises for preservation of God's Words, (especially how our God intended to do this preserving work, via repeated refinings of the Traditional Text, Ps.12:6). These Scriptural refinings are nothing like the Nestle-Aland eclectic textually unsupported insertion of variant readings. He also, with James White, underestimated the following: a) the large number of Greek manuscripts Erasmus had initially read before his first edition of the NT Greek text,   b) the many additional manuscripts he accessed by his 2nd and 3rd editions even making them into two groups—"preserved" and "edited" and, c) the fact that Erasmus had all the significant "readings" we have today, even before the first printed edition. THIS IS KEY: Erasmus categorically rejected Vaticanus as a witness to the Original NT. (Do review this ENOUGH's pp. 132-138, A-P reasons for not relying on B, as well as Appendix C, p.160.)

4.) Dr. Price seems justified in correcting Dr. Hills for loose use of the "Traditional, Byzantine, TR" names, but his NKJV seems to do worse with these same names in the NKJV Prefaces!

5.) Dr. Price asks how the KJ justifies using the Latin Vulgate over the Greek text (Ref.13, p.254, 261). The answer is that the Old Latin (very old, like first and second century) apparently had <u>three</u> original readings preserved within Jerome's Vulgate which aren't in extant Greek texts.

6.) Dr. Price faults Dr. Hills for sometimes denying "every canon and procedure in New Testament textual criticism" (Ref.13, p.262); BUT, if you had the Autographs, wouldn't that make every textual variant to it an error? The evidence is beyond reasonable doubt that TR is the promised 99.9999% preserved Autographs as prophesied in Psalm 12:6,7 and as Jesus promised. Therefore, the critical canons can scarcely be applied.

7.) Dr. Price calls the TR, "a late offshoot of only one of the four ancient traditions" (Ref.13, p.264). He must surely know that the TR **predominates** the early witnesses (i.e., the Papyri, Patristic quotes and early translations). Dr. H.A. Sturz "... surveyed <u>all</u> the available Papyri...each new MS (manuscript) discovered vindicated added Byzantine [TR] readings .... **Henceforth no one may reasonably or responsibly characterize the Byzantine text-type as being ... late."** Pickering (ThD, PhD) concludes, "(T)he TR has more early attestation than B (Vaticanus) and twice as much as Aleph (Sinaiticus)—evidently the TR reflects an earlier text than either B or Aleph" (Ref.8. pp.481-483). See Appendix L.

8.) Dr. Price treats the tens of problem texts in the TR in the same way as the 35,000 word differences between Vaticanus and the TR. This keeps coming up and is confusing, as here: i.e. saying 35 = 35,000. Does it seem accurate to call the TR "eclectic" because it relied on the Latin Vulgate three times (due to its old Latin) while Westcott and Hort eclectically used Vaticanus to change the TR in some 35,000 words? It helps to consider the numbers of times in knowing how much weight to give to some conclusions.

9.) Dr. Price (Ref.13, p.271) seems to be a believer in the historically invisible "Lucian Recension" of the TR (Ref.13, pp.241-243). People who believe in the Westcott and Hort theory must support the Lucian

Recension (=heavy revision), whether they believe it or not, because the theory is untenable without it. Do consider the following:

a.) Due to unique minor differences between virtually each TR manuscript, they couldn't be "father-son, sister, etc. genealogical descendants of one 300-400 AD Exemplar supposedly revised by Bishop Lucian.

b.) The TR predominates in all the early extant textual witnesses. (The possibly 1st Century "TR" Peschito certainly predated Lucian!)

c.) Actual history (in contrast to fabricated history) records that Bishop Lucian was an outspoken Arian who would never have allowed the Traditional/TR text since it denies the Arian Heresy.

10.) Dr. Price seems to this ENOUGH to finish unfairly with Dr. Hills by saying "If the **Textus Receptus** is the True Text, Hills failed to convincingly demonstrate it... Hills' faith is in his presumed acts of God's providence, acts not supported or validated by Scripture" (Ref.13, p.273). Dr. Price is correct in seeking Scriptural Authority for our faith, and Dr. Hills did not explicitly explain his treatment of the development of the TR as a Scriptural refining process, though he did implicitly by observing how the TR was progressively improved. We would encourage the reader to reread Hills' presentation with the need for Scriptural Authority in mind for what actually happened; Dr. Hills really communicates quite well. (ENOUGH pp.111, 148-49 & Ref.14) Also, note that Dr. Hill's faith is properly presumed because God did repeatedly promise to preserve every letter of Scripture.

For Dr. Price to conclude that Hills is an undercover member of a KJ Only Sect (Ref.13. pp.273,274) seems a reprehensible statement between two high level professional scholars. This ad hominem assault will, without adequate proof for such a serious accusation, tend to mislead his readers to ignore Dr. Hill's warnings against the very real dangers of accepting for their bible the Vatican's Vaticanus text which tends to return them towards the tyranny of the Roman Catholic Church that **murdered,** usually brutally, **some sources say 70 million** through the different inquisitions. Also, see FOXES BOOK OF MARTYRS to read about the many who were martyred for the crime of standing for the Word(s) of God (the pre-TR Bible)—believing it, copying it, and taking the true Gospel message around the world. Dr. Hills' warning is against incredibly bloody, dangerous religion at its worst.

11.) He gives a very misleading chart. See Appendix C, p.166.

CONCLUSION: The TR is to be preferred.

Dr. Price gallantly quoted from the "Translators to the Reader" of the KJ 1611, which said that honest readers "grant and embrace ... as much as a man proves, not as much as he claims." But then he only "claims" that "Doctrinal differences do not hinge on variant readings" (Ref.13, pp.413,14). This ENOUGH could not disagree more. God's precise thoughts were presented in Scripture in infinitely precise words, but if they weren't also virtually perfectly preserved, then even godly and honest men will inevitably and often irreconcilably have differences of interpretation, not having exactly God's words on the matters. Praise God He did keep His promises, and we can resolve any interpretation between those who accept God's Words as absolutely inerrant as verbally Divinely inspired and 99.999999% preserved (vs the textual critics' 85%).

Dr. Price's book, seems often wearisome because throughout it really seems to be a recitation of the REM party line, with little or no original research. We contrast it to the works of Dean John Burgon and D.A. Waite, whose reasoned arguments are supported by volumes of personally calculated research data when necessary. For example, the Philippians study (especially in Price's Appendix D, "An evaluation of Burgon's Test of Antiquity") is not convincing in what it says. Furthermore, the study was done by the United Bible Society (UBS), which, under the guidance of Nida/Bratcher, and Cardinal Carlo Martini, has become a biased foe of a preserved Bible—by no means impartial scholarship. (For an eye-opening look at the compromised nature of the UBS, do see David Cloud's excellent article "The United Bible Societies and Rome", February 2006, which can be read online at greatpreachers.org/ubs-rome. html.) Again, Dr. Price has not done original work even in scrutinizing the UBS "Philippians" data with suspicious care. Why bother to write if no new knowledge is produced, just a fat trial brief produced to support your client—irrespective of innocence or guilt?

APPENDIX I

CRITIQUE OF The English Standard Version (ESV)
(Try this Critique model on other modern bibles also.)

The 1950s RSV (Revised Standard Version) was revised again to form the New RSV or NRSV. Basically, the ESV is a New NRSV; the ESV Preface states that the "RSV text provided the starting point for our work". Both the ESV and RSV have approximately the same number of "footdoubts" (= textual questioning footnotes, over 500 Hebrew and about 200 Greek). This indicates they are based on the same texts, for better or worse.

Please take note in this ENOUGH Part 1, "Fruit Inspection", that this "new" ESV is almost inseparable from the RSV/NRSV in making the same errors in the same verses in almost every one of the hundreds of verses compared—no significant difference.

The ESV Preface states that they used the BHS (Biblia Hebraica Stuttgarttencia) which had the Kittels as editors—and more footdoubts than verses in the entire O.T. (The Kittels did not believe in the infallible inspiration of Scripture but did believe in evolution). Then the ESV people used the Nestle-Aland 27th edition Greek New Testament (which has on an average five doubts of what the Original was in every verse of the New Testament). This is the "Critical Text" upon which every major English bible is based since the KJ; and the ESV is simply a late English version of this Critical Text, which doesn't even make a pretense of acknowledging any inerrantly preserved text.

After talking about the ESV in general terms, now let's look at some samples of what you will find if you try to use it; or rather, let's start with what you won't find: Matt:17:21; 18:11; 23:14; Mark 7:16; 9:44; 9:46; 11:26; 15:28; Luke 17:36; 23:17; John 5:4; Acts 8:37; 15:34; 24:7; 28:29; Romans 16:24; I John 5:7 are simply omitted! For example, if you look in the ESV in Matthew 17, you will find the verses go from v.20 to v.22, with a footdoubt saying "Some manuscripts insert verse 21 ...." Truly the ESV is a holey bible.

The Vaticanus manuscript (a single manuscript, out of over 6000 extant manuscripts of the New Testament) accounts for over 90 percent of the differences between the Critical Text, and the KJ

TR. The ESV has thousands of "Gnostic"-supporting perversions of God's Word. Gnostics don't believe that the Lord Jesus Christ is Lord (God), and !Bingo! Acts 9:6 is changed from *"And he trembling and astonished said: Lord, what wilt thou have me to do? And the Lord said unto him, Arise ...."* (KJ) becomes *"But rise ...."*(ESV). Saul/Paul doesn't acknowledge Jesus as Lord in the ESV; apparently the Apostle Paul didn't get saved in the Critical Text since he doesn't acknowledge Jesus' Deity! For a sampling of many more places where the Lordship of Jesus is diminished, compare the ESV to the KJ in Luke 22:31; 23:42; Acts 9:5; 22:16; Romans 1:3; 6:11; 16:24; II Cor.4:10; Eph.3:14; I Tim.1:1; Titus 1:4... . Docetic Gnosticism (as today's Jehovah Witnesses) deny that their God was a flesh and blood man, but the Apostle John warned *"For many deceivers are entered into the world, who confess not that Jesus Christ is come in the flesh. This is a deceiver and an antichrist."* (II John 7).

Now, regarding the Lord Jesus' Messiahship (Christ = Messiah), note: Acts 19:4 *"Jesus Christ"*(KJ) becomes *"Jesus"*(ESV). Compare also: John 4:42; 6:69; Acts 2:30; 8:37; 19:4; Rom.1:3; 16:24; I Cor.15:4; Gal.6:15; Eph.3:9; 3:14; Col.1:2; II Tim.4:22; Heb.3:5; I John 1:7... .

We find an overall pattern of diminishing the person of our Lord: Luke 2:33 *"And Joseph and his mother marvelled"* (KJ) becomes *"And his father and his mother marveled ..."* (ESV). Was Joseph the father of Jesus? I Tim.3:16 *"God was manifested in the flesh"*(KJ) becomes *"he was manifested in the flesh"*(ESV) with no clear antecedent for the pronoun "he"; this change in Scripture simply removes this very clear attestation to Jesus' Deity. Also see Luke 6:48; John 1:18; 3:13; Eph.3:9; Rev.1:11; 11:17... .

There is also a diminishing of Jesus as the Son of God. Compare: John 6:69 *"thou art that Christ, the Son of the living God."*(KJ), becomes *"you are the holy One of God"*(ESV). See also John 9:35; Acts 8:37; John 8:28; 10:32; 14:28; 16:11; Eph.3:14... .

Aren't just these observations sufficient to reject the RSV/ESV even from being used as a commentary reference?

(Dr. Sorenson, GOD'S PERFECT BOOK (Ref. 19), Chapter 8, is the source of most of this exposé of changes to Scripture in the Critical Text as found in the ESV.)

APPENDIX J
THE *COUNTER*-REFORMATION

Crucifixion is probably the most painful, humiliating way mankind has devised to kill his fellow man—then Burning at the Stake would be the second. (With 1st degree burns over most of their bodies, martrys would sometimes agonize for days!) The Stake was the method of preference chosen by the Dark Ages Church to kill those "criminals" who would dare to translate and teach the Bible in the common language to their countrymen. Many **thousands**, including William Tyndale ("one of the finest men that ever lived"), gave their lives this way to give us THE KING JAMES BIBLE.
To explain:

In the first century, the New Testament was spoken by God through Apostles in Greek, the main language of the Roman Empire. Other languages needed God's Words. The Syrian Peschito translation was the first, possibly handled by the Apostle John himself. The Old Latin, the Coptic, and many other translations soon followed, and the world was turned upside down (Acts 17:6). These early versions were translated from the Original Manuscripts, or copies directly from them, and they (along with the majority of the earliest Papyri, and the 1,000,000+ Scripture quotes by the early Church Fathers) are from the Pre-Textus Receptus Greek text—stunning proof that the King James Textus Receptus Hebrew and Greek preserves the Original "Autographs".

However, we are missing the drama and heroism here.
Through the first centuries after Christ, there were <u>ten empire-wide</u> attempts by the Roman Caesars to wipe out Christianity. Thousands (Millions?) died, but the Church grew! Failing by force, Constantine legalized Christianity and, in effect, became the first Pope. (Constantine called himself, "Pontifex Maximus" as does the Pope today.) He ordered the Bible to be edited to agree with his Arian, Gnostic (Babylonian, evolutionary) beliefs. This bible is extant today in the "Vaticanus" (= "the Vatican book") manuscript from which came Jerome's "Latin Vulgate". Simultaneously (and we suggest causally), the Dark Ages began. During this time, the Roman Catholic Church brutally murdered literally millions trying

to stamp out those who loved, copied and taught the true Words of God—which was the Pre-Textus Receptus text. Then in 1516, Erasmus printed the first copy of the Textus Receptus Greek and then a translation from the Greek into Latin on one page with the Latin Vulgate on the page facing, and everyone could see Constantine's deadly changes to the Bible. Then Luther translated this Greek into German, Tyndale into English, and many other languages followed. These translations were printed in so many copies on the newly invented printing presses that the Dark Ages church could not burn them fast enough to keep them from the common people. Again, as in the first centuries, THE SUN CAME OUT—for the first time in 1200 years. This started the Protestant Reformation (which then caused the Renaissance and the Industrial Revolution).

However, there has been an all but accomplished *Counter-Reformation*, and *every* bible since 1611 has been translated from the Constantine/Vaticanus/Vulgate/ bible! We have been conned! For English speakers, the KING JAMES BIBLE is so much more than just a beautiful historic treasure. It is "the Forbidden Book" (do see A LAMP IN THE DARK DVD, Ref.20). It is the crowning product of the Protestant Reformation, for which literally millions have been brutally murdered in preserving it to us and with which we can overcome by the Blood of the Lamb and by the word of our testimony if we love not our lives unto the death (Rev.12:11) as they did—otherwise their sacrifice is becoming wasted. Without Bibles literally based on the Textus Receptus Text, the human race is falling back into a Last Days Dark Ages! Look at the immininent total chaos around you in the whole world today. The preserving "salt of the earth" isn't there — it's either lost its savor in the petrified traditional churches or heaped up in piles in the megachurches. Too much salt in one place kills everything— the Church is supposed to go into all the world.

APPENDIX K

200+ VERSES OMITTED OR CHANGED from the TEXTUS RECEPTUS
in the modern New Testaments, some compared in the ENOUGH
("FOOTDOUBTED" in the New King James Version Study Bibles)

MATTHEW
1:25 FIRSTBORN (Speaking of the Lord Jesus)
5:44 BLESS THEM THAT CURSE YOU
6:13 KINGDOM, POWER, GLORY
8:29 JESUS (As Son of God)
9:13 TO REPENTANCE   (calling sinners...)
12:35 OF THE HEART   (good treasure...)
12:47 Whole verse   about Christ's mother
13:51 JESUS SAITH UNTO THEM and LORD
15:8 DRAWETH UNTO ME WITH THEIR MOUTH
16:3 O YE HYPOCRITES
16:20 JESUS
17:21 Whole verse   about prayer and fasting
18:11 Whole verse   tells Jesus came to save
19:9 Last 11 Words   about adultery
19:17 GOD   (none good but...)
20:7 WHATSOEVER IS RIGHT... RECEIVE
20:16 MANY BE CALLED BUT FEW CHOSEN
20:22 BAPTIZED WITH CHRIST'S BAPTISM
21:44 Whole verse   about Christ the stone
23:14 Whole verse (Woe scribes and... hypocrites)
25:13 WHEREIN THE SON OF MAN COMETH
27:35 FULFILLED SPOKEN BY THE PROPHET
28:2 FROM THE DOOR
28:9 THEY WENT TO TELL HIS DISCIPLES
MARK
1:14 OF THE KINGDOM (preaching the gospel...)
1:31 IMMEDIATELY (the fever left)
2:17 TO REPENTANCE   (call sinners...)
6:11 MORE TOLERABLE FOR SODOM
     & GOMORRHAH
6:16 FROM THE DEAD   (John is risen...)
6:33 HIM changed to "them"
7:8 WASHING OF POTS AND CUPS
7:16 Whole verse   about having an ear to hear
9:24 LORD (—; I believe, help...)
9:44 Whole verse about fire not quenched
9:46 Whole verse (Where the worm dieth not)
9:49 EVERY SACRIFICE SHALL BE SALTED
10:21 TAKE UP THE CROSS (Jesus said,...)
10:24 FOR THEM THAT TRUST IN RICHES
11:10 IN THE NAME OF THE LORD
11:26 Whole verse (If ye do not forgive...)
13:14 SPOKEN BY DANIEL THE PROPHET
13:33 AND PRAY or in italics
14:68 AND THE COCK CREW
15:28 Whole verse (Scripture was fulfilled...)
15:39 THE SON OF GOD is "a son of God"
16:9-20   12 verses   from some versions
LUKE
1:28 BLESSED ART THOU AMONG WOMEN
2:33 JOSEPH changed to "his father".
2:43 JOSEPH AND HIS MOTHER changed to
     "parents"
4:4 BUT BY EVERY WORD OF GOD

4:8 GET THEE BEHIND ME SATAN
4:41 CHRIST (...the Son of God)
6:48 FOUNDED UPON A ROCK changed to
     "well built"
7:31 AND THE LORD SAID
9:54 EVEN AS ELIAS DID
9:55 YE KNOW NOT WHAT MANNER OF SPIRIT
9:56 SON OF MAN IS COME TO SAVE LIVES
11:2-4 Much of the Lord's Prayer
11:29 THE PROPHET   about Jonah
17:36 Whole verse (One taken, another left.)
21:4 CAST IN UNTO THE OFFERINGS OF GOD
22:20 Whole verse from some versions
22:31 AND THE LORD SAID
22:64 THEY STRUCK HIM ON THE FACE
23:17 Whole verse from many versions
23:38 LETTERS OF GREEK, LATIN, HEBREW
23:42 LORD,   ...(remember me when ...)
24:6 HE IS NOT HERE, BUT IS RISEN
24:12 Whole verse   of Peter's testimony
24:40 Whole verse   regardingChrist showed
     them hands, feet
24:49 OF JERUSALEM
24:51 CARRIED UP INTO HEAVEN
JOHN
1:14 BEGOTTEN from 1:18, 3:16, 3:18
1:27 PREFERRED BEFORE ME   (Jesus is)
3:13 WHICH IS IN HEAVEN
3:15 SHOULD NOT PERISH
4:42 THE CHRIST
5:3 WAITING FOR MOVING OF THE WATER
5:4 Whole verse regarding the Pool of Bethesda
6:47 ON ME   (he that believes)
6:69 THAT CHRIST THE SON
7:53 to 8:11 omitted or in brackets or italics
9:35 SON OF GOD or changed to "Son of man"
11:41 WHERE THE DEAD WAS LAID
16:16 BECAUSE I GO TO THE FATHER
17:12 IN THE WORLD
20:29 THOMAS
ACTS
2:30 ACCORDING TO THE FLESH, HE
     WOULD RAISE UP CHRIST or changed.
7:30 OF THE LORD (an angel)
7:37 HIM SHALL, YE HEAR (speaking of Christ)
8:37 Whole verse or in brackets, or italics.
9:5-6 Much of verse concerning God's will
10:6 WHAT THOU OUGHTEST TO DO ...
15:18 KNOWN UNTO GOD... HIS WORKS ...
16:31 CHRIST
17:26 BLOOD
20:25 OF GOD (The Kingdom)
20:32 BRETHREN
23:9 LET US NOT FIGHT AGAINST GOD
24:6-8 Much of verse, in brackets or italics

24:15 OF THE DEAD   (Resurrection...)
28:16 Half of verse, in italics or brackets.
28:29 Whole verse, in italics or brackets
ROMANS
1:16 OF CHRIST or in italics, brackets
1:29 FORNICATION
5:2 BY FAITH from some versions.
8:1 Last 10 words   or in italics
9:28 IN RIGHTEOUSNESS
10:15 OF PEACE   (Gospel...)
10:17 OF GOD   Christ is substituted
11:6 Last 18 words
13:9 SHALL NOT BEAR FALSE WITNESS
14:6 15 words   regarding the day
14:21 OFFENDED, MADE WEAK
15:29 OF THE GOSPEL
16:24 Whole verse, in italics or brackets
1 CORINTHIANS
5:7 FOR US   (Christ sacrificed...)
6:20 Last 7 words   (your spirit...)
7:5 FASTING (joined with prayer...)
7:39 BY THE LAW   (the wife is bound...)
10:28 THE EARTH IS THE LORD'S and more
11:24 TAKE EAT   (this is my body...)
11:29 LORD'S   referring to the body
15:47 THE LORD (...from heaven)
16:22 JESUS CHRIST
16:23 CHRIST
2 CORINTHIANS
4:10 THE LORD
5:18 JESUS or in italics
11:31 CHRIST or in italics
GALATIANS
3:1 THAT YE SHOULD NOT OBEY TRUTH
3:17 IN CHRIST
4:7 THROUGH CHRIST
6:15 IN CHRIST JESUS
6:17 THE LORD
EPHESIANS
3:9 BY JESUS CHRIST   (God created...)
3:14 OF OUR LORD JESUS CHRIST
5:30 OF HIS FLESH AND OF HIS BONES
6:10 MY BRETHREN
PHILIPPIANS
3:16 LET US MIND THE SAME THING
COLOSSIANS
1:2 THE LORD JESUS CHRIST
1:14 THROUGH HIS BLOOD or in italics
1:28 JESUS
2:11 OF THE SINS OF
3:6 CHILDREN OF DISOBEDIENCE
1 THESSALONIANS
1:1 FROM GOD OUR FATHER AND LORD JESUS
2:19 CHRIST
3:11 CHRIST or in italics
3:13 CHRIST or in italics
2 THESSALONIANS
1:8 CHRIST or in italics

1 TIMOTHY
1:17 WISE   (from the only **wise** God)
2:7 IN CHRIST or in italics
3:16 GOD   (...manifest in the flesh)
4:12 IN SPIRIT
6:5 FROM SUCH WITHDRAW THYSELF
2 TIMOTHY
1:11 OF THE GENTILES
4:1 LORD
4:22 JESUS CHRIST   or in italics
TITUS
1:4 THE LORD or in italics
PHILEMON
1:6 JESUS
1:12 RECEIVE HIM
HEBREWS
1:3 BY HIMSELF   (...purged our sins)
2:7 SET HIM OVER THE WORKS OF THY
    HANDS
3:1 CHRIST
7:21 AFTER THE ORDER OF MELCHIZEDEK
10:30 SAITH THE LORD
10:34 IN HEAVEN
11:11 WAS DELIVERED OF A CHILD (Sarah...)
1 PETER
1:22 THROUGH THE SPIRIT
4:1 FOR US   (Christ suffered...)
4:14 LAST 15 WORDS or in italics
5:11 GLORY AND DOMINION from some
     versions
2 PETER
2:17 FOR EVER or in italics
3:9 US changed to "you"   (Destroys meaning)
1 JOHN
1:7 CHRIST
4:3 CHRIST IS COME IN THE FLESH
4:9 BEGOTTEN from some versions
4:19 HIM or in italics (we love...)
5:7-8 Many words out or changed
5:13 LAST 13 WORDS
JUDE
1:25 WISE (referring to God)
REVELATION
1:8 THE BEGINNING AND THE END
1:11 TEN WORDS (Alpha and Omega...)
2:13 THY WORKS
5:14 HIM THAT LIVETH FOREVER AND EVER
6:1,3,5,7 AND SEE
8:13 ANGEL changed to "eagle" (Gr. text says
     angel)
11:17 AND ART TO COME
12:12 INHABITERS OF (...the earth)
12:17 CHRIST
14:5 BEFORE THE THRONE OF GOD
16:17 OF HEAVEN
20:9 GOD OUT OF   (fire came from...)
20:12 GOD changed to "throne"
21:24 OF THEM WHICH ARE SAVED (nations)

Here is how the versions cited in **ENOUGH** do in these 200+ references. (Words omitted, questioned in footnotes, placed in brackets or parentheses are considered as not authentic in these bibles.)

NRSV 191

HCSB 189

NIV   180

ESV   180

RSV   174

NASV 168

NKJV 137

KJV   0

It looks at first glance that the NKJV is better than the other six versions compared in "The Fruit Inspection". However, actual statements in "footdoubts" that a text shouldn't be in the Bible could be more damaging to one's faith than just omissions which many readers might not notice (but there is damage done to God's message by their omissions). Therefore, perhaps the NKJV is the worst because it has <u>so many more</u> of these footnotes?

APPENDIX L

SINAITICUS—The oldest MS or written in 1840?

This Sinaiticus (aleph) Manuscript has fallen on hard times of late as its antiquity has been strongly challenged (even from its appearance in mid 1880's). (See Ref.24 WAS CODEX SINAITICUS WRITTEN IN 1840? by accomplished textual critic Dr. Jack A. Moorman.) Since Vaticanus (B) accounts for 35,000 of the 40,000 words different between the Traditional Text (TR) and the Critical Text, we have chosen to just focus on Vaticanus in challenging the historicity of the Critical Text. It is extremely interesting that a scientific comparison (collation and physical study of the vellums these two MSS were written on) shows that Vaticanus and Sinaiticus were both produced (wherever they came from), affected by Roman Catholic influence, and form almost the total textual suppport for the Critical Text. Sinaiticus, Vaticanus, and the Critical Text all stand **or fall** together..

Alphabetical index

Dynamic Equivalence(y), Equivalent(ly) (DE) 11, 13, 14, 44, 69, 73, 74, 83, 93,
      102, 104, 105, 108, 134, 135, 145, 146, 176, 179, 180
early, earlier, earliest 122, 128, 131, 135, 156, 164, 165, 183-185, 189.
      See also older(est)
eclectic text 132, 138, 169
Ellicott (Bishop) 122, 165
Elzevir 107,129
Erasmus, Desiderius 103, 117, 160-162, 183, 190
Eusebius 131, 139, 179
evidence 101, 106, 116, 119, 120, 123-128, 132, 136, 146-148, 154-162, 165,
      177, 183
evolution(ary)(ism)(ist) 105, 122, 137, 163, 177, 178, 189
Expansions of piety 8, 131, 143, 161
extant 103, 107, 132, 135, 136, 141, 154, 156, 158, 164-166, 185, 187, 189
falsification (falsified) 126, 127, 177
footdoubt(ed)(ing)(s) 8, 105, 116, 143, 144, 170, 187, 191, 193
footnotes 101, 105, 107, 116, 139, 140, 142, 144, 148, 162, 187, 193
Foxes Book of Martyrs 136, 185
fraud 101, 110, 144, 153, 181
Fuller, David (Ref.16) 102, 127, 135, 205
Garden of Eden 102, 145, 180
genealogical (method) 121, 122, 185
Gipp, Samuel (Ref.6) 107, 161, 204
Gnostic(ism), gnostically 18, 41, 102, 133, 174, 188, 189
God-spoken 27, 104, 114
Greek manuscripts 133, 135, 183
Greek New Testament (N.T.) 3, 25, 107, 116, 119, 132, 134, 139, 155-162, 165,
      174, 183, 187
Greek Old Testament 154, 155, 176
Greek text(s) 106-109, 115, 116, 120, 139, 167, 184
      See also Critical Text, Critical Greek Texts
Williams, H.D. (Ref.23) 121, 125, 128, 205
HANDBOOK OF BIBLICAL HEBREW 105, 205
Hebrew 163, 176
Hebrew manuscript 158
Hebrew Old Testament 104-106, 157
Hebrew text 57, 80, 97, 104, 105, 108, 109, 156, 157, 176
heresy, heretic, heretical 34, 115, 133, 163, 171, 173, 174, 185
Hexapla (Origen's) 155, 180
Higher Critical (Critics) 9, 25, 105, 178, 179
Higher (textual) Criticism 105, 128, 131, 132, 161, 162, 168, 169, 172, 180
Hills, Edward F. 111, 112, 119, 149, 160, 162, 167, 168, 170, 171, 178, 182,
      184–186, 205
holy men 25, 59, 61, 167, 168, 181

INDEX OF SCRIPTURE REFERENCES

INDEX OF REFERENCES

1a. A CRITICAL ANALYSIS OF THE SEPTUAGINT. Floyd Nolen Jones, Th.D., Ph.D, 6th edition, Floyd Jones Ministries, Inc., Box 130220, Woodlands, Texas 77393. Available from Ref.5

1b. WHICH VERSION IS THE BIBLE? Floyd Nolen Jones, 1998, 16th ed.; Floyd Jones Ministries, Inc., Box 130220, Woodlands, Texas 77393. Available from Ref.5

2. REMARKS ON THE NEW KING JAMES VERSION .... D.K. Madden, Pilgrim Brethren Press, 1991. Available from JR Book Distributors, 1909 Thomas Rd., Fort Worth, TX 76117; (817)838-7184

3. "The New Eyeopener". JJ Ray, 1980; The Eye Opener Publishers, P.O. Box 7944, Eugene, Oregon 97401. (200 Scriptures)

4. EXAMINING 'THE KING JAMES ONLY CONTROVERSY'. David W. Cloud, 1998; Way of Life literature, PO Box 610368, Port Huron, MI 48061-0368

5. Bible For Today (BFT). D.A. Waite, 900 Park Ave, Collingswood, N.J. 08108; (800)John 10:9; www.biblefortoday.org

6. THE ANSWER BOOK. Dr. Samuel Gipp, Daystar Publishing

7. PROBLEM TEXTS. Dr. Peter S. Ruckman, Pensacola Bible Institute Press,1980; 511 pages. Available from Amazon.com

8. NEW AGE BIBLE VERSIONS. G.A. Riplinger, eleventh printing; A.V. Publications, P.O. Box 280, Ararat, VA 24053

9. THE LONG WAR AGAINST GOD. Dr. Henry Morris, Master Books, 2005. www.icr.org

10. THE KING JAMES ONLY CONTROVERSY. James R. White, Bethany House Publishers, 1995

11. THE IDENTITY OF THE NEW TESTAMENT TEXT, Dr. Wilbur Pickering. Available from Ref.5. (BFT#556)

12A. MODERN BIBLES – THE DARK SECRET. Dr. Jack Moorman, Jan. 2004. Available from Ref.5, (BFT #2623)

12B. EARLY MANUSCRIPTS, CHURCH FATHERS, AND THE AUTHORIZED VERSION. Dr. Jack Moorman, Jan. 2004. (BFT #3230)

13. KING JAMES ONLYISM: A NEW SECT. Dr. James D. Price, 2006 Published by James D. Price

14. THE KING JAMES VERSION DEFENDED. Dr. Edward F. Hills, 2000; The Christian Research Press, available from Ref.5

15. THE TEXT OF THE NEW TESTAMENT. Dr. Bruce Metzger, Oxford Press, 3rd Edition, 1992

16. WHICH BIBLE? Dr. David Fuller, Institute For Biblical Textual Studies, 16th printing, 2004; Available from Ref.5

17. THE REVISION REVISED. Dean John William Burgon, 2nd printing, 2000; The Dean Burgon Society Press. From Ref.5

18. DEFENDING THE KING JAMES BIBLE. Dr. D.A. Waite, Available from Ref.5

19. GOD'S PERFECT BOOK. Dr. David Sorenson, Northstar Ministries, 1870 W. Morgan St., Duluth, MN 55811; www.northstarminstries.com

20. "A LAMP IN THE DARK" DVD, Abdullam Films Production, www.ADULLAMFILMS.COM; 1(888)780-5049

21. HANDBOOK OF BIBLICAL HEBREW. Dr. William S. LaSor, Erdman's Publ. Co., Vol. 1 & 2.

22. THE NEW KING JAMES BIBLE. Thomas Nelson, Inc, Nashville, TN.

23. THE LIE THAT CHANGED THE MODERN WORLD. H.D. Williams, PhD, MD. Available from Ref.5, (BFT #3125)

24. WAS CODEX SINAITICUS WRITTEN IN 1840? Dr. Jack A. Moorman, The Old Paths Publications, 2018

ABOUT THE AUTHOR

Chris Sherburne is a Vietnam veteran with a B.A. in Systems Engineering from U.C.L.A. who worked for years in computer numerical control manufacturing. Chris accepted the Lord Jesus Christ in 1960 and grew in Christ under the "precept-upon-precept; line-upon-line" discipleship of Dr. Milo F. Jamison. While pursuing his passion of defending the Word of God, he has attained a Master of Theology degree and been awarded a Litt.D. "honoris causa". Many assert that the modern bible versions don't affect any doctrine of the Christian faith. Chris has come to believe that any omissions or changes to the Bible **would** affect doctrine since all Biblical doctrine is defined by Scripture. Certainly the doctrine of inerrancy is affected by omissions or changes. Dr. Chris says, "Our Lord Jesus Christ was not confused or lying when He promised that every 'jot and tittle' of the Bible would be preserved.ENOUGH of making excuses for alleged errors in the Bible."

Chris is also Dean of the Institute for the Preservation of God's Word, part of Triune Biblical University, www.tbuworldwide.com. He has created two courses for credit which are available through TBU.

- Syllabus for an undergraduate level study of the ENOUGH
- Syllabus for a graduate level study of Dean John Burgon's book, REVISION REVISED

Chris is married to his wife Trudy who was a full time missionary with the American Board of Missions to the Jews. She now supports him in this critical outreach of defending the preservation of God's Word. Chris and Trudy live in Arizona and have six adult children.

Other strategically related publications by Dr. Chris include:

- Micro Strong's Exhaustive Concordance—6" x 9" x ½"
- KJ2011—King James Bible with comprehensive spelling, but no textual, changes.
- "Tour Guide to the Tribulation"—another End times Timeline but soundly and literally based on the book of Revelation Jewish roots.
- La Gran Aventura: A Spanish translation of Milo F. Jamison's daily devotionals of the Gospel of John.

IT'S ABOUT TIME!

Thousands of spelling changes have **already** been made in the AV King James Bible since 1611 (but spelling changes are not **textual** "revisions"). Now, here is the AV King James Bible with **21ˢᵗ Century spelling**, normal book format, and **no other changes** – look at the difference:

King James 1611	King James 1611/2011 ("KJ2011")
Ruth 2:11 And Boaz answered and said unto her, It hath fully been shewed me, all that thou hast done unto thy mother in law since the death of thine husband: and how thou hast left thy father and thy mother, and the land of thy nativity, and art come unto a people which thou knewest not heretofore.	Ruth 2:11 And Boaz answered and said unto her, It has fully been showed me, all that youˢ have done unto yourˢ mother in law since the death of yourˢ husband: and *how* youˢ have left yourˢ father and yourˢ mother, and the land of yourˢ nativityᵈ, and are come unto a people which youˢ knew not heretofore.
John 3:7 Marvel not that I said unto thee, Ye must be born again. 3:8 The wind bloweth where it listeth, and thou hearest the sound thereof, but canst not tell whence it cometh, and whither it goeth: so is every one that is born of the Spirit.	John 3:7 Marvel not that I said unto youˢ, You must be born again. The wind blows where it listsᵈ, and youˢ hear the sound thereof, but can not tell whenceᵈ it comes, and whitherᵈ it goes: so is every one that is born of the Spirit.

The superscript " ˢ " in the "KJ2011" tells the reader that the "you" is singular. In the King James Bible, "thee" and "thou" is always singular; "you" and "ye" is always plural. To translate "ye", "you", "thee", and "thou", all as "you", without conveying whether the Hebrew or Greek is singular or plural, is to **mistranslate one-half of the verses in the Bible**, as is done in virtually all modern English versions. This is more serious in some verses than others when it makes it impossible or guess work to tell who is being spoken to. For example, in John 3:7 (above), since "you" *without* a superscript " ˢ " in the "KJ2011" is always plural, the Lord Jesus said to Nicodemus *"You must be born again"*, that is, "you all" (all mankind). And most of us thought He was **just** talking to Nick!

The superscript " ᵈ " tells the reader that this word is in the dictionary in the back of the "KJ2011" Bible; most in-Bible dictionaries don't get used much because most words you look for are not there. With the superscript " ᵈ ", every word you look up is there, and it covers virtually all words not in common use.

The "KJ2011" is not a "new" King James Bible. Historically, the 1611 King James Bible is the last (and best, especially because it corrected earlier versions) English translation ever made from the **not critically edited** Masoretic Hebrew and the the the Greek text of 98% of the 6000+ Greek manuscripts of the New Testament, including the oldest. Please entertain the following question: Doesn't this make the King James the only English translation **that can even claim** to be from the inspired and preserved Bible? (This question is well answered in ENOUGH OF THIS BIBLE CONFIDENCE GAME.) This is not a subtle "King James Only" statement, wherein these dear people claim that the Hebrew and Greek can be corrected from the King James English; however, there **are many promises** in which **God guarantees** to every generation the true 100% inspired and 100% preserved "Original" Scriptures: Ps. 12:6,7; Isa. 40:8; II Tim. 3:16,17; II Peter 1:19-21; John 10:35b.... It's about getting our Bible back, not "King James Only" **nor** "scholar/priest preserved" dogma. We are contending *"for the faith which was once delivered unto the saints"* (Jude 3b)!

The Authorized King James 1611/2011 Bible (KJ2011):
  available from: chris.sherburne@tbuworldwide.com
  or download for free from www.armoredsheep.com

Also available, Micro Strong's Exhaustive Concordance —compact 6" x 9" x 1/2"

CONCERNING WHICH BIBLE IS WORTHY OF YOUR TRUST,

would you like to be able to change

FAT (Frequently Assumed Teachings) into FACTS?

FAT #1: The modern Bible versions are based on older, better texts, many of which have been uncovered *since* 1611.

FACT: This *was* the theory which has now been "debunked" because other equally "old" manuscripts, the even older Papyri, the oldest translation versions, most of the over 1,000,000 Scripture quotes of the early Church Fathers, and the Dead Sea Scrolls, all 3:1 support the King James over the New King James and even more over other modern versions. The King James translators had all the significant textual readings we have now.

FAT #2: Supporters of the King James Bible are sort of backwoodsy "snake handlers" who don't (or can't) deal with the real scholarly issues concerning the reliability of the Bible.

FACT: It is reprehensible ignorance or outright misinformation to not consider the brilliant, often unanswerable arguments authenticating the King James Bible as the most accurate English translation of the only Bible text that can even claim to be the Divinely promised "Preserved Text".

FAT #3: The Critical Greek text (basis of all modern English Bible versions) is a scholarly attempt to get closer to the original Bible.

FACT: Westcott and Hort said that the Critical Greek text (now growing to over 60,000 alternative readings of what the Original was) would need "perpetual correction and recorrection". This is in the opposite direction from getting closer to the original Word of God.

FAT #4: The Bible should be treated like other great ancient Classics; a few (thousand) copying errors or edits don't matter, it's the thoughts that count.

FACT: God's precise thoughts *require* precise words. Those who do not find a 100% inspired and 100% preserved Bible are logically left with religion without Revelation—Humanism, which believes that Jesus was just a good man, that there is no Almighty Creator God Who so loved you that He gave His only begotten Son to die in payment for your sins. Though humanism doesn't believe in the devil, the humanist still has to deal with him who is behind all the hurts and horrors in what would appear an ultimately purposeless life—and beyond.

If all this FAT is not acceptable to you,

YOU MAY WANT TO READ THIS BOOK!

www.ingramcontent.com/pod-product-compliance
Lightning Source LLC
Chambersburg PA
CBHW080515090426
42734CB00015B/3061